WORLD WOODS
IN
COLOUR

WILLIAM A. LINCOLN

STOBART DAVIES

Published 1986, reprinted 1991, 1993

British Library Cataloguing in Publication Data
Lincoln, W. A.
 World woods in colour
 1. Wood—Dictionaries
 I. Title
620.1'2'0321   TA419
ISBN 0–85442–028–2

Stobart Davies Ltd., Priory House, Priory Street, Hertford SG14 1RN

Printed in Singapore

Acknowledgements

During forty-odd years' in the timber and veneer trade I have had the good fortune to meet people from all parts of the world, who studied, worked or created with woods, many of whom became personal friends. My thanks are due to them all – far too numerous to mention individually by name – who have contributed information, research material or actual wood specimens from their collections for this book.

Special thanks in particular are due to those friends who sent me their complete range of wood specimens: to Mr L. Reed, my successor at the Art Veneers Co Ltd of Mildenhall, Suffolk; Glenn R. Docherty of Albert Constantine & Sons Inc., of New York; Curt C. Meddaugh of The Woodshed, Buffalo, NY; Gary L. Rockler of the Woodworker's Store, Rogers, Minnesota; D.G. Brims & Sons Pty Ltd of Queensland, who sent me their range of Brimsboard veneer panelling woods; Mr C.H.M. Dunn of Finewood Veneers, Cape Town.

As past-President of the Marquetry Society, I naturally turned to members and groups around the world for their assistance, which was freely given. John K. Brown of St Albans, put me in touch with overseas friends with whom I had lost touch. John Sedgwick of the Marquetry Society of Ontario was extremely helpful and also sent a range of Canadian hardwoods and softwoods. Lionel Pavey of the Marquetry Society of Victoria, and members of the South Australia Society responded with local wood specimens; Mr E. Robins of Cape Town, for his efforts in obtaining African woods for me; Larry R. Frye, President of the Fine Hardwoods and American Walnut Association of Indianapolis, very kindly shipped a complete range of American hardwoods for which I am especially grateful.

Thanks are also due to E.B. (Gene) Himelick, of Urbana, Illinois, editor of *World of Wood*, bulletin of the International Wood Collectors Society, for his kindness in introducing me to their archivist, Arthur N. Green of Bastrop, Louisiana, who selected and shipped specimens from his extensive collection, and to other members of the IWCS, such as K. Iwasaki of the World Arts Co Ltd of Kobe City, who sent me a collection of Japanese woods, and Makoto Nishio of Enagun Gifken, Japan, for his help.

Also, many thanks to Florentino O. Tesoro, Director of the Forest Products Research and Development Institute of Laguna, Philippines; M.R. Blakeney of the New Zealand Forest Service; W. Gabb, Director of the New South Wales Forestry Commission, Wood Technology and Forest Research Division, each of whom sent specimens for inclusion. And to the many Timber Research and Development Associations and Forest Research Institutes and Laboratories in the major timber producing countries who made some contribution to the book by sending research material and technical information.

The Timber Research and Development Association, Hughendon Valley, High Wycombe, Bucks., of which I am a professional member, were a mine of information. Special thanks are due to Mrs Anne E. Peters, their librarian, who was extremely helpful; and to the Forest Products Research Laboratory at Princes Risborough, for their valuable assistance.

Also thanks to Paul Simmon of Simmon Sound and Vision of Bradford for photographic work.

Finally, I must express my gratitude to my wife, Kathy, who undertook the task of collating the mass of research material, and who cross-checked the often contradictory facts on properties, characteristics, densities and uses; and to Brian Davies of Stobart Davies Ltd for his constructive criticism and advice; for editing the manuscript and for providing the opportunity to have published the results of a lifetime in the timber business, and a book which I hope will fill a longfelt need.

Contents

Introduction

Of the 70,000 different woods known to man, fewer than 400 are commercially available. Many of these are consumed in their country of origin and not exported to other parts of the world. The aim of this book is to provide a representative colour illustration of the most important and useful timbers generally available.

THE ILLUSTRATIONS

The sapwood of most, but not all, trees is usually of little commercial value, and most of the illustrations here feature the heartwood. In species where the sapwood forms the bulk of useful timber or in others where there may be an intermediate zone of a different colour, the illustration will depict the colour of the most valuable part of the tree.

The colour of wood is mainly caused by infiltrates into the cell walls and may vary even in the same species growing near to each other, depending on the location of the site, type of soil and soil content; also the colour may vary in the same board or leaf of veneer. Many timbers fade upon exposure to light, others darken, and most will deepen in colour when polished.

The illustrations are reproduced *actual size* from polished specimens of veneer and solid timber and as such have the distinct advantage of displaying the full-size surface structure as well as the actual colour.

THE FIGURE

The surface pattern on a piece of timber, known as the figure, results from the interactions of several natural features. They include the difference in density between earlywood and latewood cells; the quantity of growth rings; the natural pigments and markings in the structure; the reaction of the tree to the effects of tension or compression due to external forces during its life; contortions around knots, swollen butts or limbs, and the stunted growth of burrs or burls. These natural features, combined with a variety of grain types, and the method of cut, produce the figure.

THE GRAIN

The word "grain" is often misapplied and misunderstood. Such terms as "coarse grained" or "fine grained" actually refer to the texture of the surface and not to the grain. "Silver grain" is used to describe the prominent ray figure on quartered oak.

The descriptions "end grain", "side grain" and "flat grain" are commonly used when referring to the transverse cross cut surface, the tangential cut parallel with the growth rings; or the radial cut at right angles to the growth rings.

The grain is the natural formation of the wood fibres relative to the main axis of the tree. There are eight types:
(a) **Straight grain**: The fibres run parallel to the main axis of the tree.
(b) **Cross grain**: The fibres do *not* run parallel to the main axis.
(c) **Interlocked grain**: The fibres form first a left- and then a right-handed spiral, and then alternate the spiral direction every few years.
(d) **Spiral grain**: The fibres spiral in a regular direction giving the tree a twisted appearance.

(e) **Wavy grain**: The fibres form short undulating waves in a regular sequence.

(f) **Curly grain**: The fibres undulate in an irregular sequence.

(g) **Irregular grain**: The fibres contort and twist around knots, etc.

(h) **Diagonal grain**: Either a flat cut board of spiral grain or a milling defect in straight grained timber.

TYPES OF FIGURE

Wavy and curly grains produce "fiddleback" or "beeswing" figure; wavy grain combined with spiral grain causes "block mottled" figure, roe figure is caused by a combination of wavy and interlocked grains; interlocked grain will provide ribbon striped figure.

The variations in density between earlywood and latewood zones show a pronounced growth ring figure on flat sawn boards, and many softwoods reveal their resin ducts in the form of fine brown lines on longitudinal surfaces. Natural pigmentation from infiltrates can cause variegated streaks, patches or stripes; irregular grain results in "blistered" or "quilted" figure, while other permutations reveal freak figured wood such as pommelle, plum pudding, snail, finger-roll, moiré, and many more.

Curl or crotch figure, also known as fan, fork, and crutch, is a cut through the junction of a branch with the main stem of the tree, or between two branches, which produces a "double-heart" feature.

Burrs (or burls) are the wart-like growths which appear on trees, sometimes below ground, caused by an injury to the tree at an early stage of its growth. These have the appearance of tightly clustered dormant buds, with a darker pith, forming tiny knot formations like a mass of small eyes, with swirling, contorted veins and lines surrounding them.

Butts, or stumpwood, is the junction of the trunk with the roots, where the fibres are distorted by the changes of direction and the effects of compression caused by the weight of the living tree.

CONVERSION OF THE LOG

Flat sawn: The cut is made *tangentially* to the direction of the growth rings, which should meet the line of cut at an angle of less than 45 degrees. This produces an attractive figure of arched loops, caused by the growth rings, on longitudinal surfaces. Walnut, Brazilian rosewood, and teak are examples of timber where this cut is used.

Quarter sawn or rift sawn: The line of cut is made at 90 degrees to the growth rings and parallel to the rays. To achieve this the log is first sawn into sections, roughly a quarter of a log – or more, depending on the log diameter – in order that the radial cutting is approximately parallel to the rays, which radiate from the the heart like the spokes of a wheel. This produces striped figure and the pronounced "silver", "raindrop" or "splash" figure in oak, and the "lace" figure in planetree.

Veneer cutting methods

There are four methods of slicing decorative veneers: (a) flat sliced crown (b) true quartered, radial (c) flat quartered, tangential (d) faux quartered, diagonal (at 45 degrees to both growth rings and rays).

There are five methods of rotary peeling logs:

(1) Rotary cutting, in one continuous sheet, by revolving on a lathe.

(2) Eccentric rotary cutting. Off-centre rounding for extra wide veneers.

(3) Stay-log cutting. A complete log, fastened to a stay-log in the lathe, revolves and meets the knife once in each orbit.

(4) True half-rounding (stay-log), where cutting commences on the sapwood side of a half log.

(5) Half rounding back-cutting (stay log), where the cutting commences on the heart side of a half log; used for cutting fancy butts, stumpwood, curls and crotches.

All veneers are kept in consecutive leaves, in exactly the same sequence as cut from the log (except in the case of rotary cutting) so that that features on one leaf will correspond exactly to those on adjacent leaves, which is essential for veneer matching purposes. For a full description of the veneer cutting methods and processes, refer to *The Complete Manual of Wood Veneering*, by W.A. Lincoln, Stobart Davies Ltd., Hertford, and Charles Scribner's Sons Inc., New York.

TEXTURE

The texture or *feel* of the wood surface is the result of the difference between the dimensions of the pores, and the width and quantity of rays. Timbers which have wide vessels or broad rays are **coarse textured**, and those with narrow vessels and with thin rays are **fine textured**.

Softwoods vary from fine to moderately coarse textured as their cells are of small diameter, and the texture resulting from the difference between early and latewood zones. When these zones are strongly marked as in Douglas fir or larch, the texture is **uneven**, and where there is little contrast between the zones as in spruce, the wood is **even textured**.

Sometimes, this terminology is applied to hardwoods, when diffuse porous woods are described as even textured, and ring porous woods as uneven textured.

LUSTRE

The ability of the wood cells to reflect light gives the surface lustre. Compact, smooth textured woods such as sycamore, are more lustrous than coarse textured woods such as oak. Quartered surfaces are usually more lustrous than flat sawn. The ability of wood to provide an excellent polish does not equate to its degree of lustre.

ODOUR

Most woods lose their natural odour during the phases of conversion. A few retain their odour and may be put to good use: for example, camphor or cedar are used to line the interiors of clothes chests, and on the other hand the choice of wood for use as food containers is restricted to those without either odour or taste.

MINERAL STAINS

Many timbers coming into contact with iron compounds, either in the soil or in damp conditions of use, are subject to severe black or blue-black mineral stains. This is caused by the chemical reaction between iron, and the tannin or related compounds such as polyphenols which are present in wood. The main timbers affected are oak, chestnut, afrormosia, idigbo, makoré, kapur, obeche, "Rhodesian teak" and walnut. Softwoods contain little tannin, but some have tannin-like substances and are affected, such as Douglas fir, and sequoia. Reaction between iron compounds and other chemicals of a class known as *tropolones* cause red stains in western red cedar, and brown stains in yellow cedar.

CORROSION

The presence of acetic acid in oak and sweet chestnut can actually cause the corrosion of metals under damp conditions although the two phenomena are not connected.

STANDARD NAMES: These are names recommended in the *Nomenclature of Commercial Timbers* (BS 881 and BS 589; 1974) of the British Standards Institution.

COMMERCIAL NAMES: These are trade names based upon long established trade custom, and always include the standard name. For example, in the UK, the name "Scot's pine" is used for homegrown timber and "redwood" for the imported species.

Many trade names are invented by merchants seeking to glamorise an indifferent species with a more romantic name. These names, especially colour descriptions, can be very misleading. For example, "black Italian poplar" is white in colour and grows in the UK. There are more than 80 different species called "ironwood".

Some commercial names have become standard names even though botanically unrelated. "Queensland walnut" is from the *Lauraceae* family, "African walnut" from the *Meliaceae* family, neither of which are true walnuts from the *Juglandaceae* family.

Therefore, in this book, where this occurs, the standard name has been distinguished by quotation marks to indicate that there is no botanical relationship, between, for example, "Tasmanian oak" and the true oaks such as European or American oak, and will not be listed alphabetically with the true oaks.

The importance of standard names is underlined by the wide divergence of commercial names in the English speaking world. For example – "Australian silky oak" (*Cardwellia sublimis*) in the UK, is known as lacewood in America. Lacewood (*Platanus acerifolia*) of the UK is known as sycamore in America, while sycamore (*Acer pseudoplatanus*) in the UK, is known as maple in America.

OTHER NAMES: The local, vernacular names that appear in shipping documents, and are generally accepted throughout the timber trade, are listed as "other names". This is especially important when the name is in a foreign language and only known by that name in the country of origin. Apart from the country of origin, the name of the locality of growth, or even the port of shipment may also be critically important.

Timbers of the same species will vary in quality depending upon local conditions, rate of growth, soil, climate, methods of felling, speed of conversion, degree of selection, and the grading expertise of the exporter.

This is aggravated by the fact that many countries combine closely related species, and sell them all under a "group" name, such as white lauan, for example.

In view of the many problems associated with standard, commercial and other names, specialists in the timber trade around the world have come to rely upon the botanical names for specific identification.

BOTANICAL CLASSIFICATION

Every tree has a botanical classification which enables anyone, whatever his native tongue, to identify species of wood accurately. The importance of this "scientific name" cannot be over-emphasized.

In the case of European walnut for example:

Kingdom	Vegetable
Division	Angiospermae
Class	Dicotyledoneae
Order	Juglandales
Family	Juglandaceae
Genus	Juglans
Species	Regia

It is the universal practise to use the last two names, and is known as the binomial system, where the first name is assigned to the genus and the second to a specific epithet to indicate a species of that genus. In the above example European walnut is *Juglans regia*. The family name is also given in this book for information and interest.

HARDWOOD OR SOFTWOOD are identified in the text by the initial (H) or (S).

DISTRIBUTION

This refers to the main source of supply of the species. Many species are cultivated in other countries: e.g., eucalyptus from Australia has been widely planted in South Africa, but is not indigenous to that continent. Wherever possible the native source is given.

DESCRIPTION

The range of colour tones of the species is given to amplify the coloured illustration, together with details of the type of grain, texture, peculiarities of markings; calcium, resin, tannin content, and liability to thunder shakes, etc.

The weight depends on the amount of water it contains. The figure given for the weight, or, more correctly, the density of the species is calculated at 12 per cent moisture content, or kiln dried. To calculate the weight of a species at any other moisture content percentage, add or subtract 0.5% of the stated weight for every one per cent moisture content above or below 12% (within the range from 5% to 25%).

The specific gravity is also given, which is the relative weight of a substance compared with that of an equal volume of water. The specific gravity of wood varies a great deal, even in the same species and depends upon the amount of wood substance per unit of volume, and the rate of growth of the tree.

The following table is a quick reference guide.

Density	Weight kg/m³ at 12% M.C.	Specific gravity at 12% M.C.
Exceptionally light	Under 300	.30 or less
Light	300–450	.30 – .45
Medium	450–650	.45 – .65
Heavy	650–800	.65 –.80
Very heavy	800–1,000	.80 – 1.0
Exceptionally heavy	1,000 or above	1.00 or more

MECHANICAL PROPERTIES

To determine the strength and suitability of a species for a particular use requires a knowledge of certain mechanical properties.

(a) Maximum bending strength of a timber required for transverse bending (b) the stiffness, or modulus of elasticity, which is critical in determining the strength of a strut or long column; (c) shock resistance to suddenly applied loads, or impact, and (d) the crushing strength, parallel to the grain, which determines the ability to withstand loads on the end grain and is important when the wood is to be used for short columns or props. The following table explains the classification used.

Classification at 12% M.C.	Bending Strength N/mm²	Stiffness kN/mm³	Maximum Crushing Strength N/mm²	Shock Resistance (Impact) m
Very low	Under 50	Under 10	Under 20	Under 0.6
Low	50–85	10–12	20–35	0.6 – 0.9
Medium	85–120	12–15	35–55	0.9 – 1.2
High	120–175	15–20	55–85	1.2 – 1.6
Very high	Over 175	Over 20	Over 85	Over 1.6

WOOD BENDING PROPERTIES

The minimum radius of curvature at which a reasonable percentage of faultless bends can be made in clear specimens 1″ thick (25 mm) after being subjected to saturated steam at atmospheric pressure for not less than 45 minutes before bending. This radius will vary if the piece was bent with or without a supporting strap, or by varying the end pressures. Alternatively, assessment may be made by cold bending of laminates at 12% moisture content.

Radius of curvature at which breakages during bending should not exceed 5%		Classification of bending properties (material supported by a strap) and 25mm thick
mm	inches	
Less than 150	Less than 6	Very good
150–250	6 – 10	Good
260 – 500	11 – 20	Moderate
510 – 750	21 – 30	Poor
Exceeding 750	Exceeding 30	Very poor

SEASONING

The drying rate for each species is given, based on the time required to dry 1" (25 mm) thick boards in a kiln from green down to 12% moisture content.

Rapid	up to 1½ weeks	Slow	3½ to 4 weeks
Fairly rapid	1½ to 2½ weeks	Very slow	Over 4 weeks
Rather slow	1½ to 3½ weeks		

Movement in Service:

This is based on the sum of radial and tangential movements resulting from a change in humidity from 90 to 60 per cent relative humidity, at 25°C in both cases, and corresponds to the movement or dimensional changes in seasoned timber subjected to atmospheric changes in service.

Small movement	Under 3 per cent
Medium movement	3.0 – 4.5 per cent
Large movement	Over 4.5 per cent

Note that shrinkage in seasoning and movement in service are not directly related and a timber which may show large shrinkage in drying, may only have small movement in service.

Working Properties

The classifications applied to resistance in cutting and blunting effect on tools are based on kiln dried material of 12% moisture content.

Where space has permitted, details are given in the text regarding sawing, planing, moulding, boring, mortising operations, and in particular recommendations when to employ a reduced cutting angle for planing and moulding.

It is not always possible to do this, because most commercial planing machines have pre-set cutter positions and cutter speeds, supplied by the manufacturer. Most machines have cutting angles between 30–35 degrees, which is suitable for most softwoods except the very dense or wavy grained type like yewtree.

If special blocks cannot be obtained for the planing machine, the reduction in cutting angle can be made by grinding and honing a bevel on the leading face of the cutter, for the 20 and 15 degree angles recommended for certain woods, when planing interlocked grain.

The nailing and screw holding potential of most woods is given and gluing characteristics are shown as good, variable or difficult.

DURABILITY AND PERSERVATION

This refers to the natural ability of the timber to resist fungal decay when in contact with the ground, or, in indoor situations of high condensation, where moisture penetration can exceed 20 per cent moisture content.

Natural durability (heartwood)	Approximate life in contact with the ground
Very durable	More than 25 years
Durable	15–25
Moderately durable	10–15
Non-durable	5–10
Persishable	Less than 5 years

Timber used externally, not in ground contact, will have a greater life expectancy.

Insect attack: Most timbers are susceptible to attack by wood boring insects, and these are the principal species:

Ambrosia beetles (*Platypodidae* and *Scolytidae*): These attack the standing tree and leave pinhole borer damage with dark discolouration around the holes. The attacks cease when the wood is seasoned.

Longhorn beetle (*Cerambycidae*) and the **Jewel beetles** (*Buprestidae*): Their dust-filled tunnels are usually eliminated in conversion, but the house longhorn beetle can seriously damage softwoods.

Powder Post beetles (*Bostrychidae* and *Lyctidae*): These attack sapwood for the starch content, usually at the sawmill or factory. The former type can reduce seasoned softwoods to powder, and attacks hardwoods in the topics; the latter type attacks in the temperate zones.

Furniture Beetles (*Anobiidae*): Attacks the seasoned sapwood of softwoods and old woodwork, furniture, panelling, and structural timbers. *Ptilinus pectinicornis* cause similar damage in fine grained temperate hardwoods. *Ernobius mollis* attacks the bark and outer sapwood of softwoods.

Wood Wasps (*Siricidae*): These attack coniferous trees, and the damage is similar to the larvae boreholes caused by the beetle *Serropalpus barbatus* (*Melandryidae*).

Termites or White Ants (*Isoptera*): Subterranean termites nest in the ground; dry-wood termites attack timber direct and have no ground contact.

Marine Borers – *Teredo spp.* (shipworm) and *Limnoria spp.* (gribble), etc: Timber used in the sea or in brackish waters is liable to attack by marine boring animals – particularly in tropical waters.

Timber should be impregnated under pressure with preservatives such as coal tar creosote, creosote-coal tar solutions, or copper/chrome/arsenic water borne mixtures, or organic solvent types.

Amenability to Preservative Treatment

Preservative treatment, correctly carried out, will usually outlast the most durable natural wood. Timber in the round containing an outer band of permeable sapwood is preferable to durable hardwoods which are resistant to preservative treatment. The classification used is:

Permeable: Can be penetrated completely by the hot and cold open tank process.

Moderately resistant: Fairly easy to obtain a lateral penetration up to 18mm (3/4″) in about three hours.

Resistant: Difficult to penetrate more than 6mm (1/4″) even after a long period of treatment.

Extremely resistant: These cannot be penetrated to any appreciable depth even after a prolonged period of pressurisation.

USES OF TIMBERS

The text gives a summary of typical uses for each timber, which is intended as a guide and not a definitive list.

A guide-chart for easy reference and comparison with other timbers with similar uses, is provided at the back of the book.

Alphabetical List
of World Woods

ABURA (H)

Mitragyna ciliata, (Aubrev & Pellgr)
Family: *Rubiaceae*

Commercial name: bahia.

Other names: subaha (Ghana); elolom (Gabon); elilom (Cameroon).

Distribution: Tropical West Africa.

General Description: The pale orange-brown to pink sapwood forms the bulk of the tree. The heartwood is reddish-brown, sometimes spongy, with darker streaks. Mostly straight grained, but interlocked and occasionally with spiral grain. The texture is fairly fine and very even. The weight varies from 460–690 kg/m³ (29–43 lb/ft³) but averages 560 kg/m³ (35 lb/ft³); specific gravity .56.

Mechanical properties: The wood is of medium density, low bending strength, very low stiffness, medium crushing strength and low shock resistance. Bending classification very poor.

Seasoning: Drying is rapid with only little degrade if shakes are cut out in conversion. It dries well and is very stable, with small movement during service.

Working properties: It works well, with medium resistance to cutters, but with moderate to severe blunting effect on tools. A sharp edge is maintained when carbide tipped tools are used. It stains easily and takes an excellent finish. Holds nails and screws tightly.

Durability: Liable to attack by both powder post beetle and common furniture beetle, and is not resistant to termites. The heartwood is perishable and not resistant to decay. Moderately resistant to preservative treatment, but the sapwood is permeable and often used for dyed black.

Uses: Interior joinery, furniture and cabinetwork, mouldings and lippings. Flooring, turnery, pattern making, vehicle bodywork, utility plywood. Being acid resistant, it is used for battery boxes, oil vats and laboratory fittings. Selected logs sliced for veneering.

Note: Other spp. include:

M. stipulosa (DC) O. Ktze, and *M. rubrostipulara* (K. Schum) Havil, and are sold as **nzingu**, chiefly from Uganda.

AFARA (LIMBA) (H)

Terminalia superba, Engl & Diels.
Family: *Combretaceae*

Commercial names: light afara, light limba, limba clair, limba blanc (plain, light wood); dark afara, dark limba, limba noir, limba bariolé (figured heartwood). **Other names:** korina (USA); ofram (Ghana); limba (Liberia); akom (Cameroon).

Distribution: West Africa.

General Description: The wood is pale yellow-brown to straw coloured; the heartwood may have grey-black streaks. It is a close, straight grained timber, sometimes with interlocked or wavy grain producing excellent figure, with a moderately coarse but even texture. The weight varies from 480–640 kg/m^3 (30–40 lb/ft^3), average 550 kg/m^3 (34 lb/ft^3); specific gravity .55.

Mechanical properties: The heartwood may be brittle, but light wood is resistant to shock loads, with low stiffness and medium crushing strength; bending class is very poor.

Seasoning: Dries rapidly with tendency to shake or split when air dried but kilning is easy with small movement.

Working properties: The timber is easy to work with hand and machine tools, with a slight blunting effect on cutters. Takes an excellent finish if filler is used. Pre-boring necessary in nailing and screwing.

Durability: It is non-durable and non-resistant to decay. Liable to attack by pinhole borers and graded in Nigeria accordingly. Sapwood liable to attack by powder post beetle. Moderate resistance to preservation treatment; liable to blue sap stain.

Uses: Interior joinery, shopfitting, furniture, desks, turnery, coffins and light construction. Greenish-grey plain wood used for corestock and utility plywood; black heartwood used for highly decorative veneers for furniture and panelling.

Note: See also **IDIGBO,** *Terminalia ivorensis*, sometimes called **black afara**.

'AFRICAN WALNUT' (H)

Lovoa trichilioides, Harms.
syn. *L. klaineana*, Pierre ex Sprague
Family: *Meliaceae*

Commercial names: Benin walnut, Nigerian walnut, Nigerian golden walnut, Ghana walnut (UK); alona wood, congowood, lovoa wood, tigerwood (USA).

Other names: eyan (Gabon); dibétou (Ivory Coast); apopo, sida (Nigeria); bibolo (Cameroon); bombolu (Zaire); eyan, dilolo (France); nvero (Sp. Guinea).

Distribution: Tropical West Africa.

General Description: The heartwood is bronze orange-brown, with gum lines causing black streaks or lines. The grain is interlocked, sometimes spiral, producing a striking ribbon striped figure on quartered surfaces. It has a moderately fine texture and is lustrous. The timber is of medium density weighing from 480–650 kg/m^3 (30–40 lb/ft^3), average 550 kg/m^3 (34 lb/ft^3); specific gravity .55.

Mechanical properties: The wood has medium crushing strength, low bending strength and resistance to shock loads, and very low stiffness. Bending classification is moderate.

Seasoning: The wood dries fairly rapidly but requires care in seasoning as existing shakes tend to extend, and some distortion may occur. There is small movement in service.

Working properties: Works well with both hand or machine tools with only a slight blunting of cutting edges. A reduced cutting angle of 15° is required to prevent the grain picking up during planing or moulding quarter sawn timber, which is fairly difficult to work. Cutting edges must be kept sharp to avoid tearing. Tends to split when nailed, and end grain tends to burn during boring or recessing. It glues, stains and polishes to an excellent finish.

Durability: Moderately durable; the heartwood is subject to insect attack and is extremely resistant to preservative treatment and the sapwood moderately resistant.

Uses: Extensively used for furniture and cabinetmaking, lipping and panelling, joinery, shopfitting, gun stocks and rifle butts, domestic flooring, billiard tables, etc. Slices into very attractive face veneers for plywood manufacture and decorative veneers for panelling, cabinets and marquetry. **Note:** Not a true walnut.

AFRORMOSIA (H)

Pericopsis elata, van Meewen,
syn. *Afrormosia elata*, Harms.
Family: *Leguminosae*

Commercial names: assamela (Ivory Coast and France); mohole (Holland).
Other names: kokrodua (Ghana); ayin, egbi (Nigeria); ejen (Cameroon).
Distribution: West Africa.
General description: The heartwood darkens upon exposure to deep orange-brown. The straight to interlocked grain produces a "rope" figure when radially cut. The texture is medium fine, (finer than teak without its oiliness). The weight varies from 620–780 kg/m^3 (39–49 lb/ft^3), average 690 kg/m^3 (43 lb/ft^3); specific gravity .69.
Mechanical properties: A heavy, dense wood, with high bending and crushing strength, medium stiffness and resistance to shock loads. The wood bending classification is moderate as it distorts during steaming and is intolerant of pin knots.
Seasoning: Dries rather slowly with little degrade and small movement.
Working properties: It works well, with medium resistance to tools, slight tendency to pick up the grain in planing, and a 20° cutting angle is necessary. Moderate blunting of cutting edges; requires tungsten carbide tipped saws. Pre-boring recommended for nailing or screwing; glues well and takes excellent finish.
Durability: A very durable wood, highly resistant to termites and extremely resistant to preservative treatment. It is very resistant to decay but must not be used in contact with ferrous metals in wet situations to avoid corrosion. Tannin in the wood can cause blue stains.
Uses: Suited for a wide range of exterior and interior applications such as boat building, sills, stairs, and flooring; shop fitting, high-class joinery, cabinetmaking, agricultural implements, and marine piling. Sliced veneers used for decorative veneering, flushdoors, and wall panelling.

AFZELIA (H)

Afzelia spp., including:
1. A. bipindenis, (Harms); *2. A. pachyloba*, (Harms);
3. A. africana, (Smith); *4. A. quanzensis*, (Welw).
Family: Leguminosae

Commercial names: (1 to 3) doussié (Cameroon); apa, aligna (Nigeria); lingué (Ivory Coast); papao (Ghana); bolengu (Zaire); mu mangala (Gabon); (4) chamfuta (Mozambique); mbembakofi, mkora (Tanzania).

Distribution: Tropical West Africa and East Africa.

General description: Pale straw sapwood sharply defined from reddish-brown heartwood. The grain is irregular, often interlocked, with a coarse but even texture. The weight ranges from 620–950 kg/m^3 (39–59 lb/ft^3), average 820 kg/m^3 (51 lb/ft^3); specific gravity .82.

Mechanical properties: It has high bending and crushing strength, medium stiffness and low resistance to shock loads, with a moderate bending classification due to distortion during steaming and exudation of resin.

Seasoning: Should be kiln dried slowly from green condition, slight distortion may arise with fine checking and extension of shakes but degrade is not severe. Small movement in service.

Working properties: High resistance to cutting makes it hard to work, with moderate blunting of cutting edges which should be reduced to 15° cutting angle. It is difficult to stain, but when the grain is filled, it polishes very well. Liable to chemical staining due to yellow dyestuff (*afzelin*) in the pores which may discolour textiles.

Durability: Although sapwood is liable to powder post beetle attack, the heartwood has outstanding durability and stability, with extreme resistance to impregnation and preservative treatment.

Uses: Heavy construction work, bridges, docks, garden furniture, high-class joinery, interior and exterior joinery, counter tops, office furniture. Also used for vats for acids and chemicals due to its acid resistance. Sliced veneers used for decorative veneering, flushdoors etc.

Note: Nos. 1 and 2 are the principal species producing afzelia from West Africa, with only a small quantity of No. 3. No. 4 grows in East Africa.

AGBA (H)

Gossweilerodendron balsamiferum, (Harms)
Family: *Leguminosae*

Commercial names: tola (Zaire); tola branca, white tola (Angola).
Other names: "Nigerian cedar" (UK); mutsekamambole (Nigeria); nitola (Congo).
Distribution: Tropical West Africa.
General description: The heartwood is pale pinkish-straw to tan coloured; grain straight to wavy or moderately interlocked, fine textured. Weight average 520 kg/m³ (32 lb/ft³); specific gravity .52.
Mechanical properties: Brittleheart is extensive in larger logs. Wood bending strength is low, resistance to shock loads is also low, with very low stiffness and medium crushing strength; bending classification is only moderate.
Seasoning: Dries fairly rapidly with little degrade and small movement in service, but exudes oleo resin or gum from pockets and high temperatures should be avoided.
Working properties: Works well with hand and machine tools with moderate resistance to cutting and slight blunting effect. Gum may cause saws to stick. Nails, screws and glues satisfactorily, stains well and when filled, takes a good finish.
Durability: This durable wood is very resistant to decay but the sapwood is liable to attack by common furniture beetle. It is resistant to preservative treatment, but the sapwood is permeable.
Uses: Interior and exterior joinery, boatbuilding, shopfitting, flooring, panelling, furniture, mouldings, coachwork, coffins, laminated frameworks, turnery. Resinous odour prevents use in contact with foodstuffs. Selected logs sliced for veneers.
Note: The name **tola** is also applied to *oxystigma oxyphyllum* (**tola mafuta**).

AKOSSIKA (H)

Scottellia chevalieri, Gilg.
Family: *Flacourtiaceae*

Other name: akossika a grande feuilles.
Distribution: Tropical West Africa.
General description: Pale yellow heartwood with darker streaks, mostly straight grained but occasionally interlocked, with a fine, even texture. Quarter cut wood produces a fine silver grain figure. Weighs between 580–640 kg/m^3 (36–40 lb/ft^3), average 620 kg/m^3 (38 lb/ft^3); specific gravity .62.
Mechanical properties: Despite its medium bending strength and stiffness and high crushing strength, the bending classification is poor.
Seasoning: Dries fairly rapidly with a tendency to split and check. Blue stain liable to occur during kiln drying. There is a medium amount of movement in service.
Working properties: The wood works well with hand tools and requires care in planing and moulding to avoid picking up interlocked grain. Edges should be kept sharp to overcome moderate blunting effect. Pre-boring necessary when nailing or screwing; takes glue well, stains and polishes to an excellent finish.
Durability: The wood is perishable, the heartwood having no resistance to termites, but permeable and able to be penetrated completely with preservative treatments under pressure.
Uses: Light construction, flooring, furniture, interior utility joinery, carving and turnery, and selected wood for cabinet work. Veneers are used for corestock and utility plywood, and, when staining is avoided, decorative faced plywood.
Note: Related spp. include *S. kamerunensis*, Gilg., producing **akossika a petites feuilles**.

ALBIZIA, WEST AFRICAN (H) *Albizia ferruginea*, (Guill & Perr) Benth.
sometimes also including
A. adianthifolia, (Schum) W. F. Wright,
A. zygia, (D.C.) McBride
Family: *Leguminosae*

Commercial names: sifou (Zaire); yatandza (Ivory Coast).

Other names: ayinre (Nigeria); okuro (Ghana); essac, ongo ayem (Cameroon).

Distribution: Tropical West Africa.

General description: Heartwood varies from deep red-brown to chocolate brown with a purplish tinge. The grain is irregular and often interlocked and the texture is coarse. The weight ranges from 580–720 kg/m^3 (36–45 lb/ft^3), average 640 kg/m^3 (40 lb/ft^3); specific gravity .64.

Mechanical properties: The wood is moderately hard, compact and very durable. Strength in bending is medium, with low stiffness but high crushing strength and very low ability to withstand shock loads. Bending classification is moderate.

Seasoning: Dries fairly rapidly, but kiln drying must be carried out very slowly to avoid risk of checking or twisting. There is small movement in service.

Working properties: Works very well and easily with medium resistance to cutting and with moderate blunting effect. The irregular or interlocked grain can cause tearing in planing; pre-bore for nailing. Stains and finishes well. Sanding dust can cause irritation.

Durability: Sapwood is liable to attack by powder post beetle. Heartwood is resistant to termites and very durable. It is extremely resistant to preservative treatment but the sapwood is permeable.

Uses: Heavy albizia is used for heavy construction and marine piling. Light albizia is used for light construction, utility and general joinery; carpentry and vehicle bodywork.

Note: *A. adianthifolia*, has a light golden-brown heartwood with a greenish tinge, while *A. zygia* has a pale brown heartwood with a pinkish tinge and is susceptible to staining. Both spp. are light albizia. *A. ferruginea* produces heavy albizia. *A. grandibracteata* (Taub) and *A. zygia* from East Africa are sold as red or white **nongo** according to its colour. Related spp. include *A. falcataria* (L) Fosb., producing **Moluccan sau**. See also Kokko.

ALDER, COMMON (H)

Alnus glutinosa, (L) Gaertn.,
including: *A. incana*, (Moench)
Family: *Betulaceae*

Commercial names: black alder (UK); grey alder (Europe); Japanese alder.

Other names: aune (France); eis (Netherlands); erle (Germany); hannoki (Japan).

Distribution: From North Russia to North Africa and West Asia, throughout Scandinavia and Japan, and throughout the United Kingdom.

General description: Dull, light reddish-brown with darker lines or streaks formed by broad rays. Straight grained, with fine texture but without lustre. Weighs an average 530 kg/m^3 (33 lb/ft^3); specific gravity .53.

Mechanical properties: Moderate bending classification with low bending strength and resistance to shock loads; very low stiffness but with medium crushing strength. There is a pronounced tendency for checks to occur on the ends of bends during setting.

Seasoning: The wood dries fairly rapidly with little degrade, and is stable in service.

Working properties: It has a low cutting resistance and is easy to work if cutting edges are kept thin and sharp as there is a slight blunting effect on tools. The wood nails and screws satisfactorily, glues well, stains and polishes to a good finish.

Durability: Alder is liable to attack by common furniture beetle; it is perishable, but permeable to preservative treatment.

Uses: A good turnery wood and used for broom and brush backs, hat blocks, rollers for textiles, toys, wooden clog soles, chip baskets, small laminated items, utility plywood, and for veneers. Gnarled pieces are used in Japan for decorative purposes.

ALDER, RED (H)

Alnus rubra, Bong.
Family: *Betulaceae*

Commercial names: Western alder, Oregon alder.

Distribution: Pacific coast of Canada and USA.

General description: Heartwood is pale yellow to reddish-brown in colour. Fairly straight grained and of uniform texture; it shows a pleasing but subdued figure. Weight about 530 kg/m³ (33 lb/ft³); specific gravity .53.

Mechanical properties: This is a soft, weak wood of medium density, low bending strength and shock resistance, medium crushing strength and very low stiffness.

Seasoning: It dries easily, fairly rapidly and well with negligible degrade and with little movement in service.

Working properties: The wood works well with both hand and machine tools, with only a slight tendency to pick up the grain in planing, overcome by a reduced cutting angle. There is a slight blunting effect on tools which should be kept sharp. It has good nailing and gluing properties and takes stain, paint or polish well.

Durability: The wood is perishable; liable to attack by common furniture beetle, but is permeable for preservation treatment.

Uses: Turnery and carving, plywood corestock, utility plywood, chip baskets and small laminated articles, woodenware, and veneers. In decorative veneer form, its natural defects are exploited, such as knots, burr (burl) clusters, minor stains and streaks, stumpwood etc., and for plywood panelling in contemporary style.

ALONE (H)

principally:
Bombax breviscuspe, Sprauge
Bombax chevalieri, Pellegr.
Family: *Bombacaceae*

Commercial names: kondroti, alone-bombax* **Other names:** ogumalonga (Cameroon, Gabon); akagaouan (Ivory Coast); kingue (Liberia); mungura (Mozambique).

Distribution: Tropical West Africa. Also in South America and S. Asia.

General description: The heartwood is pale reddish-brown and liable to fungal discolouration. The wood is straight grained, coarse textured, dull in appearance and very absorbent. Average weight is 550 kg/m^3 (34 lb/ft^3); specific gravity .55.

Mechanical properties: It has a moderate bending classification and is medium in strength, stiffness, crushing strength and resistance to shock loads.

Seasoning: The timber must be converted and dried rapidly to avoid degradation through splits, checks and fungal staining. When dry, there is only small movement in service.

Working properties: There is little resistance to cutting tools, and the timber works easily with both hand and machine tools. It nails, screws and glues easily and has good working potential. It stains well and can be brought to an excellent finish.

Durability: Although the wood is not durable and liable to both insect and fungal attack, its absorbency makes the wood completely permeable for preservative treatment.

Uses: It is extensively used for blockboard and laminated board corestock, and for plywood manufacture, interior joinery, cabinet fitments and furniture making.

***Note:** Not to be confused with **West African bombax** (*Bombax buonopozense*, P. Beauv.), which is lighter in weight (350 kg/m^3 – 22 lb/ft^3) and when shipped is often indistinguishable from **ceiba** (*Ceiba pentandra*, Gaertn.)

AMBOYNA (NARRA) (H)

Pterocarpus indicus, Willd.,
principally, and *P. vidalianus*
Family: *Leguminosae*

Commercial names: Phillippine or Solomons padauk, Papua New Guinea rosewood. The burr is marketed under the trade name of **AMBOYNA BURR.**

Other names: red narra, yellow narra, sena, angsena.

Distribution: East Indies.

General description: The heartwood varies from light yellow, through golden brown to brick red in colour. The timber from Cagayan is usually harder and heavier than from other areas and is blood red in colour. It has a characteristic odour. The grain is wavy, interlocked or crossed and these irregularities give rise to mottle, fiddleback, ripple and curly effects of figure. The texture is moderately fine. The more red the wood, the heavier it is, but on average it weighs 660 kg/m³ (41 lb/ft³); specific gravity .66.

Mechanical properties: Not normally used where strength properties are critical as it is a highly decorative wood. Medium strength in all categories. Steam bending only moderate.

Seasoning: Dries rather slowly but with little degrade. The red coloured wood requiring more care than the yellow variety. There is small movement in service.

Working properties: Straightforward to work with hand or machine tools with only a slight dulling effect on cutters on straight grained material. Can be nailed, screwed, glued and stained satisfactorily and takes an excellent polish.

Durability: It is very durable. The wood is extremely resistant to termites and insect attack, and is resistant to preservative treatment. (Shavings will turn water fluorescent blue).

Uses: High-class joinery and flooring, furniture and cabinets, panelling, carved feet and finials, cases for scientific instruments, musical instruments, interior trim for houses and boats, sports goods, turnery, fancy goods and novelties, caskets. Sliced into a wide range of highly decorative veneers in various figured effects. The burrs (burls) are the highly treasured Amboyna Burr.

ANDIROBA (H)

Carapa guianensis, Aubl.
Family: *Meliaceae*

Other names: crabwood (Guyana); krappa (Surinam); figueroa (Ecuador); carapote (Guadeloupe); carapa (Guiana); camacari (Brazil); masabalo (Columbia).

Distribution: Carribean, Central and South America.

General description: The wood is a light mahogany colour to red-brown, darkening when dry due to darker gum in the vessels. Mostly straight grained but occasionally interlocked with ripple marks in the denser tissue, producing fiddleback figure in larger logs. The texture varies from coarse to fine. The softer wood is coarse textured and woolly. Weight varies with growth conditions from 576–736 kg/m^3 (36–46 lb/ft^3), averaging 640 kg/m^3 (40 lb/ft^3); specific gravity .64.

Mechanical properties: The wood has medium bending and crushing strength and low stiffness.

Seasoning: Drying must be carried out slowly as there is a marked tendency to split, check, twist or collapse in early stages. A low temperature with high humidity schedule is best for kilning.

Working properties: It can be worked with moderate ease with both hand and machine tools, but a reduced cutting angle of 15° is recommended for planing quartered material; sanding is required for smooth finish. Pre-boring is necessary for nailing, but it glues well. When filled provides a good finish.

Durability: Moderately durable and resistant to preservation treatment.

Uses: Boat and ship decking and superstructures, light construction, flooring and rafters, high-class joinery and furniture, and turnery. Corestock for plywood, utility plywood, and decorative veneers for panelling.

ANINGERIA (H)

Aningeria spp. comprising:
(1) *A. robusta*, Aubrev & Pellgr.
(2) *A. altissima*, Aubrev & Pellgr.
(3) *A. adolfi-friederici*, Robyns
(4) *A. pseudo-racemosa*, A. Chev.
Family: *Sapotaceae*

Commercial name: anegré (UK and USA). **Other names**: aninguerie, aniègre (Ivory Coast); landosan (Nigeria); muna (Kenya); osan (Uganda); mukali, kali (Angola).

Distribution: (1) West Africa; (2) West & East Africa; (3) East Africa; (4) East Africa, principally Tanzania.

General description: Heartwood is cream to tan with a pinkish tinge. Generally with straight grain but sometimes wavy producing a mottled figure; quartered surfaces show a growth ring figure. The wood is lustrous, with a cedar-like scent, and is siliceous. Texture is medium to coarse in lighter grades but fine textured in heavier grades. Weight varies from 480–580 kg/m^3 (30–36 lb/ft^3), average 540 kg/m^3 (33 lb/ft^3); specific gravity .54.

Mechanical properties: Wood bending classification is medium and the bending strength and compression is medium.

Seasoning: Dries rapidly and well with no checking or twisting but liable to blue stain in early stages of air drying. Without degrade in either air or kiln drying. Little movement in service.

Working properties: Moderate to severe blunting effect on tools due to silica content and adequate support is necessary to prevent chipping out. Good nailing, screwing, gluing and staining properties. Takes a very good polish.

Durability: Non-resistant to termites. The heartwood is perishable but permeable for preservation treatment.

Uses: Furniture and cabinetwork, high-class joinery, light construction, general utility purposes and interiors. Used for plywood corestock, utility plywood, and also sliced for decorative veneering.

ANTIARIS (H)

Antiaris toxicaria, Lesch.
syn. *A. africana*, Engl.
A. welwitschii, Engl.
Family: *Moraceae*

Commercial names: bonkonko (Germany & Netherlands); kirundu (France). **Other names**: oro, ogiovu (Nigeria); chen-chen (Ghana); kirundu (Uganda); ako (Ivory Coast); andoum (Gabon); tsangu (Congo); akeche (Sierra Leone).

Distribution: West, Central and East Africa.

General description: Heartwood cream to yellow-grey. Straight to interlocked grain, medium to coarse texture. Weight range from 370–530 kg/m³ (23–33 lb/ft³), average 430 kg/m³ (27 lb/ft³); specific gravity .43.

Mechanical properties: The bending classification is very poor; with low bending strength, very low stiffness and resistance to shock loads, and with medium crushing strength.

Seasoning: Dries fairly rapidly, and has natural tendency to stain and distort, but kilning gives best results to avoid warping and splitting. When dry there is very small movement in service.

Working properties: The wood works easily with low resistance to cutters and only slight blunting effect on tools, which should be kept sharp to avoid the grain crumbling. Nailing, screwing, gluing and staining operations are satisfactory. Takes a good finish.

Durability: Logs are liable to pinhole borer and beetle attack in Africa. The heartwood is perishable, but permeable to preservation treatment.

Uses: Light construction, utility joinery, furniture interiors, carcassing and shelving, and plywood corestock. Slices into attractive quartered striped decorative veneer for furniture and panelling.

APPLE (H)

Malus sylvestris, Mill
syn. *M. pumila*, Mill and *Pyrus malus*, L.
Family: *Rosaceae*

Distribution: Throughout Europe and South West Asia; and as a minor spp. in USA.

General description: The heartwood is pinkish-buff, resembling peartree, and rather brittle. It is straight grained, with a fine even texture. The wood is heavy, weighing from 700–720 kg/m³ (43–45 lb/ft³); specific gravity .71.

Mechanical properties: This dense, heavy wood has moderate strength properties but a very low bending classification due to its brittleness.

Seasoning: The wood dries slowly with a marked tendency to distort in air drying, but may be kiln dried successfully with little degrade and small movement in service.

Working properties: It has a high resistance to cutting edges and a moderate blunting effect on tools, especially in sawing. It finishes cleanly in most cutting operations. Generally it is not difficult to work with either hand or machine tools. The wood stains easily can can be brought to an excellent finish.

Durability: It is non-durable, but easily permeable for preservative treatment.

Uses: Extensively used for fancy turnery, carving and inlay work. In USA for tool handles, pipes etc. Also slices well for decorative veneers.

ARARIBA (H)

Centrolobium ochroxylon, Rose
C. robustum, Mart
C. paraense, Tul
C. orinocense, Pitt
Family: *Leguminosae*

Commercial names: arariba amarillo (UK); balaustre (Columbia, Venezuela, USA).

Other names: arariba rosa, A. amarelo, A. carijo, A. rajado, A. vermelho (Brazil); amarillo logarto, amarillo de Guayaquil (Equador).

Distribution: Tropical South America, particularly in Brazil.

General description: The heartwood varies according to species from yellow (amarillo) through orange to red, but they are all variegated with dark red to purple-black streaks, especially in young trees. The grain varies from straight to irregular, and the wood is heavy and compact, with a medium texture. The weight varies considerably between 750 to 1,000 kg/m³ (46–62 lb/ft³), average about 850 kg/m³ (53 lb/ft³); specific gravity .85.

Mechanical properties: The brittle nature of the heartwood earns the wood a very low bending classification, but it is a tough, moderately strong timber in all strength categories.

Seasoning: Kilning must be carried out very slowly because of the wood's strong tendency to check and warp, but there is small movement in service.

Working properties: The wood works easily with both hand and machine tools, but special care is needed when working the black streaked zones which are hard and brittle and liable to break out in planing or moulding. Cutting edges need to be kept sharp. It nails, screws and glues well, and the surfaces provide a smooth, silken finish of excellent results.

Durability: Very durable with great resistance to preservative treatment.

Uses: Used locally for civil and naval construction, and generally for joinery, doors, flooring, tight cooperage, solid furniture making, fancy turnery, inlaid work. Sliced and peeled veneers are used for cabinetmaking, decorative veneering and wall panelling.

ASH, AMERICAN (H)

(1) *Fraxinus americana*, L.
(2) *F. pennsylvanica*, Marsh (3) *F. nigra*, Marsh
Family: *Oleaceae*

Commercial names: (1) white ash (2) green ash (USA), red ash (Canada); (3) black ash, brown ash (USA); (1) Canadian ash (UK). **Distribution:** USA and Canada.

General description: 1 & 2: heartwood is grey-brown, sometimes tinged with red. 3: Greyish-brown in colour and slightly darker than the other species. Generally straight grained and coarse but even textured. 1 & 2 weigh around 660 kg/m^3 (41 lb/ft^3) and No. 3 weighs 560 kg/m^3 (35 lb/ft^3); specific gravity of 1 & 2 is .66 and No. 3 .56.

Mechanical properties: Wood bending properties are variable, but generally very good, although not tolerant of pin knots in steam bending. The wood has good strength, elasticity, toughness, stiffness and hardness qualities allied to its relatively light weight. Excellent shock resistance (see footnote).

Seasoning: The timber dries fairly rapidly with little degrade, and small movement in service.

Working properties: There is a moderate blunting effect on tools, but can be worked satisfactorily with both hand and machine tools. Pre-boring necessary when nailing the harder species. It glues, stains and polishes well.

Durability: Ash is non-durable and perishable. The sapwood is liable to attack by powder post and the common furniture beetle; the heartwood is moderately resistant to preservative treatment; the sapwood is permeable.

Uses: (1) White ash is the famous sports' ash and used for all types of sports equipment, bats, cues, oars, handles for striking tools, spades, forks, hoes, etc; bent parts for boat building; vehicle bodies, church pews, shopfitting and high-class joinery. (2) Used for same purposes but for non-striking tool handles. (3) Cabinet work, interior joinery. All species used in plywood manufacture and also selected logs sliced into decorative veneers for furniture and panelling.

Note: These three species (and several more minor species) make up American ash. They are usually segregated into "tough" and "soft" grades. No. 1 and 2 provide the tough grades where strength and elasticity are required, and No. 3 a lighter and milder joinery wood.

ASH, EUROPEAN (H)

Fraxinus excelsior, I
Family: *Oleaceae*

Commercial names: English, French, Polish, Slavonian, etc. according to origin.

Distribution: Grows throughout Europe, North Africa and Western Asia.

General description: The heartwood is cream to pale tan coloured. In some logs, a dark brown to black heartwood is found which is strong and sound and sold as **olive ash**. The wood is tough, flexible and straight grained. The texture is coarse but even. The weight varies between 510–830 kg/m³ (32–51 lb/ft³), average 710 kg/m³ (44 lb/ft³); specific gravity .71.

Mechanical properties: This tough, heavy, dense timber is fairly split resistant and has excellent steam bending properties, and with low stiffness and medium resistance to crushing and shock loads.

Seasoning: It dries fairly rapidly and needs care to avoid surface checking and splitting, but this responds well to reconditioning kiln treatment; medium movement in service.

Working properties: Ash has a moderate blunting effect on tools and offers medium resistance to cutting edges, but it works well with all hand and machine tools. It is necessary to pre-bore for nailing. The wood stains easily and can be brought to an excellent, smooth finish.

Durability: The wood is non-durable and perishable. It is susceptible to insect attack by both powder post and common furniture beetle. The heartwood is moderately resistant to preservative treatment, but black heartwood is resistant.

Uses: Sports' ash is valued around the world for sports goods and striking-tool handles. Used for bats, racquets, hockey sticks, polo mallet heads, gymnasium equipment, cricket stumps and cues; bent parts for boat building, canoes, oars, tillers; deck beams and frames. Extensively used for cabinetmaking and furniture, chair making, agricultural implements, vehicle bodies, wheelwrighting, bentwork, fancy turnery and laminated articles. Corestock and plywood manufacture, and decorative veneers for furniture, panelling and marquetry. Ash also takes treatment as **harewood** (silver grey) and in veneer form, the olive ash figure is highly decorative, especially in stumpwood and burr form.

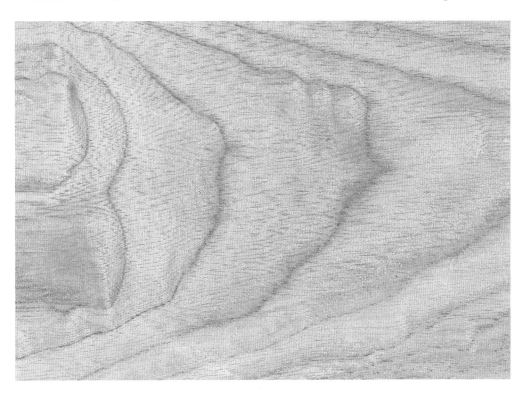

ASH, JAPANESE (H)   *Fraxinus mandschurica*, Rupr.
Family: *Oleaceae*

Other name: tamo (see footnote)

Distribution: S. E. Asia

General description: The heartwood is straw-biscuit coloured to light brown, slightly darker than European ash. Straight grained but sometimes wavy and curly, producing a bizarre "peanut" figured wood. Coarse textured. Weighs approximately 690 kg/m^3 (43 lb/ft^3); specific gravity .69.

Mechanical properties: The wood is strong in relation to its weight, but lacks the characteristic toughness of European ash. It has very good steam bending properties, low stiffness, and medium crushing strength and resistance to shock loads.

Seasoning: Dries fairly rapidly without much degrade, and there is medium movement in service.

Working properties: The wood works well with both hand and machine tools, but with a moderate dulling effect on cutting edges which much be kept sharp. It should be pre-bored for nailing, glues well and takes stain satisfactorily; can be brought to a good finish.

Durability: It is very susceptible to termite attack and is perishable. The heartwood is moderately resistant to preservative treatment but the sapwood is permeable.

Uses: Furniture and cabinetmaking, doors and flooring. Selected sports' ash widely used for racquets, bats, cues, skis, agricultural handles, etc. Extensively used in Japan and Manchuria for plywood manufacture. Selected veneer logs produce exceptional quality veneers with mottle, fiddleback, swirl, burrs, and the unique "peanut" figure, used for high quality cabinets and architectural panelling.

Note: Not to be confused with **sen**, *Acanthopanax ricinifolius*.

ASPEN, CANADIAN (H)

Populus tremuloides, Michx.
Family: *Salicaceae*

Commercial name: Canadian aspen.

Other names: trembling aspen (Canada); quaking aspen (Canada and the USA).

Distribution: USA and Canada.

General description: Heartwood is cream-grey to very pale biscuit, with a fine, even texture and straight grain which is inclined to be woolly. Weight 450 kg/m^3 (28 lb/ft^3); s.g. .45.

Mechanical properties: The timber is tough, but tension wood is inclined to be woolly with low bending strength and stiffness, and medium resistance to shock loads. It has a very low bending classification.

Seasoning: The wood seasons easily by kiln or air drying but is inclined to distort unless care is taken in piling to avoid warping and twisting. There is small movement in service.

Working properties: Works easily with both hand and machine tools but there is a tendency to bind on the saw or tear, so sharp, thin-edged tools are needed to avoid the surfaces crumbling across the end grain, or tearing in planing. The wood can be nailed, screwed, stained and polished well; on woolly surfaces, staining may be patchy although can be painted satisfactorily.

Durability: It is a non-durable wood, extremely resistant to preservative treatment, with the sapwood moderately resistant.

Uses: Light weight food containers such as cheese boxes, chip baskets and punnets; wood wool, pulp and paper making; brake blocks, vehicle bodies, furniture interiors and fitments; utility joinery, boxes and crates, utility plywood and chipboard manufacture. Selected, highly figured logs are sliced into decorative veneers for panelling and occasionally crotches (curls) are available. These decorative veneers often have a beautiful mottle and are streaked with pink, orange, and golden colours, ideal for marquetry work.

Note: Related spp. include: *P. trichocarpa*, Hook, produces **black cottonwood.**

P. deltoides, Bartr., produces **Eastern cottonwood.**

P. balsamifera, L., produces **Canadian poplar** (tacamahac poplar, USA; black poplar, Canada)

P. grandidentata, Michx., produces **Canadian poplar** (big tooth aspen, Canada)

'AUSTRALIAN WHITE ASH' (H) *Eucalyptus fraxinoides*, Dean & Maiden
Family: *Myrtaceae*

Commercial name: white ash.

Distribution: New South Wales, Australia.

General description: Heartwood is cream to pale fawn colour with a pinkish tinge, and with well-defined growth rings, similar in appearance to Tasmanian oak. The wood is straight grained, fissile, and the texture is open but even. Weighs 690 kg/m^3 (43 lb/ft^3); specific gravity .69.

Mechanical properties: It has excellent wood bending classification and is strong in bending and crushing strengths and in stiffness qualities, and resistant to shock loads.

Seasoning: The timber dries fairly easily with little degrade and small movement in service.

Working properties: This timber works well with both hand and machine tools, and takes glue, stain and polishes to a good finish.

Durability: It is a durable wood. The heartwood is fairly resistant to preservative treatment but the sapwood is permeable.

Uses: Widely used for every purpose where toughness and strength and bending qualities are essential such as cooperage, vehicle bodies, joinery and constructional work. Also used in aircraft construction. Selected logs sliced for veneers.

Note: Not a true ash of the *fraxinus* spp.

'AUSTRALIAN WHITE BIRCH' (H)

Schizomeria ovata,
D. Don & S. Whitei, J. Mattf.
Family: *Cunoniaceae*

Other names: crabapple, humbug, squeaker (Australia); schizomeria (Papua New Guinea); bea bea, malafelo, hambia (Solomon Islands).

Distribution: Australia, Papua New Guinea and Solomon Islands.

General description: This species has a very wide sapwood – up to 150mm wide – and not clearly defined from the heartwood which is creamy-brown in colour. The grain is fairly straight to interlocked, and the texture is fine and even. The weight varies from 560 kg/m³ to 670 kg/m³ (35–41 lb/ft³); specific gravity average .61.

Mechanical properties: The timber has medium strength properties and a moderate steam bending rating.

Seasoning: Dries readily with little degrade, and with medium movement in service.

Working properties: The wood works easily with hand or machine tools, and provides a good smooth finish in planing and moulding, except where interlocked grain is present when a reduction of 20° is advised in the cutting angle. It may be glued, stained and polished to a good finish.

Durability: The material is non-durable and permeable for preservation treatment.

Uses: Coffin boards, turnery, shelving and interior joinery, plywood manufacture, match splints. Also for furniture framing, furniture and cabinetmaking. Selected logs are sliced for decorative veneers.

Note 1: This species is not a true birch of the *Betula* spp.

Note 2: A closely related species is *S. serrata*; occurs in Papua New Guinea and the Solomon Islands.

'AUSTRALIAN CEDAR' (H)

Toona australis, (F. Muell) Harms.
syn. *cedrella toona*, Roxb. var. *australis*, C.D.C.
Family: *Meliaceae*

Other names: red cedar, Indian cedar, Moulmein cedar, Queensland red cedar.

Distribution: Australia, Papua New Guinea and Irian Jaya.

General description: When mature, the timber is a rich reddish-brown with darker brown streaks. It has a spicy odour and is rather lustrous. The wood is straight grained with a moderately close but uneven texture. Weight about 450 kg/m^3 (28 lb/ft^3); specific gravity .45.

Mechanical properties: This is a relatively weak wood with a very poor steam bending classification in most properties.

Seasoning: The wood dries rapidly and care is required to avoid cupping and warping of thin stock and surface checking and collapse of thicker material. It should be kiln seasoned and allowed to condition. The trees are usually girdled and quickly converted to avoid degrade. The timber is stable in service.

Working properties: The timber is inclined to be woolly but works easily, except for quarter sawn material which may be difficult to obtain a smooth finish unless the cutting edges are sharp. The material nails, screws, glues and takes stain satisfactorily and provides a good finish.

Durability: Moderately durable and resistant to insect attacks. It is permeable for preservation treatment.

Uses: Furniture, superior joinery, doors, carriage work, musical instruments, cabinet linings, cigar boxes, boatbuilding superstructures, masts, oars and planking, toys, boxes, crates etc. Sliced into attractive decorative veneers with a fine silver grain ray figure, for doors, panelling, etc.

Note 1: Closely related spp. include *Melia azedarach, var australasica* producing '**white cedar**', also known as '**tulip cedar**' and '**golden cedar**' and *T. ciliata* producing **Burmese cedar**.

Note 2: Not a true cedar.

'AUSTRALIAN SILKY-OAK' (H)

Cardwellia sublimis, F. Muell.
Family: *Proteaceae*

Commercial names: northern silky oak (Aust). **Distribution:** Queensland, Australia.
General description: Pink to reddish-brown, toning down with age. Has large rays which produces a silver-grain figure on quartered surfaces. Narrow lines of gum ducts may be present. Straight grained, except where fibres pass around the rays, and moderately coarse textured, but even. Weighs 530 kg/m³ (33 lb/ft³); specific gravity .53.
Mechanical properties: Below average strength in all categories in relation to its density, especially in bending and compression strengths. Has a good steam bending classification.
Seasoning: Dries slowly with slight distortion, some surface checking, and splitting in thicker sizes. Drying must not be hurried and care taken to avoid degradation. Severe cupping of wide flat sawn boards can occur. There is medium movement in service.
Working properties: Works easily with hand and machine tools, but some difficulty will be experienced due to crumbling of the large ray cell walls, especially when planing or moulding, when a reduced cutting angle of 20° is required. The timber can be nailed, screwed, glued and stained satisfactorily, and a reasonable finish can be obtained.
Durability: Moderately durable, and moderately resistant to preservative treatment. Sapwood liable to attack by powder post beetle.
Uses: A medium quality timber for joinery and furniture, often as a substitute for oak. Suitable for cabinets and panelling, shopfitting and fancy goods. It has high resistance to abrasion and is excellent for block and strip flooring. Widely used in Australia for panelling and office fitting, and for building construction work. Rotary cut for plywood manufacture, and sliced for ornamental veneers suitable for panelling, etc. and marquetry.
Note 1: Not a true oak.
Note 2: Related spp. include *Grevillea robusta*, A. Cunn., producing **Grevillea** (UK) or **southern silky-oak** (Aust). (Also introduced into Africa, India, Sri Lanka).

AVODIRÉ (H)

Turraeanthus africanus, (Welw ex C.D.C) Pellgr.,
T. zenkeri, Harms, *T. Klainei*, Pierre,
T. vignei, Hutch & J. M. Dalz.
Family: *Meliaceae*

Other names: apeya (Ghana); apaya (Nigeria); engan (Cameroon); lusamba (Zaire); agbe (Ivory Coast); Esu (Congo). **Distribution:** Tropical West Africa.

General description: The heartwood darkens on exposure to a golden yellow, with a natural lustre or sheen with a moderate to fine texture. The grain is chiefly straight, but is often wavy or irregularly interlocked producing a very attactive mottled figure on quartered surfaces. Weight about 550 kg/m³ (34 lb/ft³); specific gravity .55.

Mechanical properties: This medium density wood has a very poor bending classification. It has medium bending strength and crushing strength, with low resistance to shock loads and very low stiffness.

Seasoning: It dries fairly rapidly and needs care to avoid warping, cupping or twisting. Existing shakes are liable to extend and some splitting occurs in and around knots. There is small movement in service.

Working properties: Works fairly easily with hand and machine tools but the interlocked grain tends to pick up in planing requiring the cutting angle to be reduced down to 15°. The French head is most suitable for moulding. Nailing should be pre-bored and the timber has good screwing and gluing properties. Quartered material tends to stain unevenly, but normally can be brought to a very good finish.

Durability: The wood is non-durable and not resistant to termites in West Africa. It is extremely resistant to preservative treatment although the sapwood is permeable.

Uses: Plain wood used for high-class joinery, office fitting, shop fitting, and plywood manufacture. Figured wood produces excellent sliced decorative veneers with a beautiful mottled figure for high grade cabinetmaking, flush doors, wall panelling, and is used extensively for marquetry work.

AYAN (H)

Distemonanthus benthamianus, Baill.

Family: *Leguminosae*

Commercial names: movingue (UK); Nigerian satinwood (USA and UK).

Other names: movingui (Benin); barré (Ivory Coast); ayanran (Nigeria); bonsamdua (Ghana); eyen (Cameroon); oguéminia (Gabon); okpe (Togo).

Distribution: Tropical West Africa.

General description: Heartwood darkens from golden-yellow to orange-brown, sometimes with darker streaks. The grain is straight to interlocked and sometimes wavy, producing a very attractive striped and mottled figure on quartered surfaces. It has a medium texture and may contain and excess of silica. The weight varies from 600–770 kg/m³ (37–48 lb/ft³), average about 680 kg/m³ (42 lb/ft³); specific gravity .68.

Mechanical properties: This hard wood with heavy density has a moderate wood bending classification, medium bending strength, high crushing strength, and low stiffness and resistance to shock loads. It has good strength compression along the grain.

Seasoning: It must be seasoned with care, and not left unprotected against sunlight or strong winds to avoid the risk of twisting or checking. There is small movement in service with good dimensional stability.

Working properties: The wood has a moderate to severe blunting effect on tools and offers medium to variable resistance in cutting due to amounts of silica in the wood, and gum tends to build up on sawblades. Glued joints hold perfectly, but the wood should be pre-bored for nailing. The grain needs to be well filled and will then provide an excellent finish.

Durability: The timber is moderately durable, showing fair resistance to termites in West Africa. The heartwood is resistant to preservation treatment.

Uses: Vehicle building, interior joinery, furniture and cabinetmaking and flooring. It is not suitable for use in kitchens or laundries because the yellow dye deposits in the pores are soluble in water and can cause staining. Selected logs are sliced to provide highly decorative mottled and striped veneer for panelling, cabinets, and marquetry.

BALAU (H)   *Shorea* spp. including: *S. glauca*, King; *S. maxwelliana*, King
Family: *Dipterocarpaceae*

Distribution: West Malaysia

General description: The heartwood is yellow-brown, varying to brown and dark reddish-brown, with an interlocked grain and a moderately fine and even texture. Weight averages 930 kg/m³ (58 lb/ft³); specific gravity .93.

Mechanical properties: Hard, heavy and very dense with a very high bending and crushing strength, and resistance to shock loads and high stiffness. It has a moderate steam bending classification requiring strong support on the outer face.

Seasoning: The timber dries very slowly with considerable degrade in thicker sizes, but distortion is not serious. Checking and splitting may be severe and existing shakes are liable to extend. Boards should be partially air dried before kilning. Movement is medium in service.

Working properties: The wood is moderately difficult to work with machines as the interlocked grain and toughness has a blunting effect on tools. Owing to the high density of the timber, the cutting angle should be reduced to 20° when planing. It is unsuitable for nailing or screwing, gluing results are variable and it is rarely necessary to stain the wood. It can be polished satisfactorily.

Durability: Very durable and immune from insect or fungal attack. Extremely resistant to preservation treatment.

Uses: Heavy constructional work, bridge and wharf construction, sleepers, boats, etc.

Note: Balau is separated into two types in Malaysia: **balau** and **red balau**. Red balau is produced principally from *S. guiso* and *S. kunstleri*, and is a purplish-red to dark red-brown timber; it is similar to balau but only moderately durable and weighs 850 kg/m³ (53 lb/ft³). Similar timbers also occur in Sabah, Brunei and Sarawak and are called **selangan batu**. Red selangan batu from Sabah (*S. guiso*, B1) weighs the same as red balau, and selangan batu from Sarawak, Brunei and Sabah (*S. laevis*, Ridl., *S. seminis*, V.Sl., and *S. superba*, Sym., (No. 1 grade) is the equivalent of balau. Balau and selangan batu are the most suitable for adverse conditions.

BALSA (H)

Ochroma pyramidale Urb,
syn. *(O. lagopus,* Sw) and *(O. bicolor,* Rowlee)
Family: *Bombacaceae*

Other names: guano (Puerto Rica and Honduras); lanero (Cuba); polak (Belize and Nicaragua); topa (Peru); tami (Bolivia).

Distribution: West Indies, Central America, tropical South America, particularly Ecuador.

General description: Most commercial timber is sapwood which is white to oatmeal in colour, with a pink-yellow tinge, often with a silken lustre. The central core heartwood in large logs is pale brown. The texture is fine and even and the grain is straight and open. The weight varies over a very wide range, from as little as 40 kg/m^3 (2½ lb/ft^3) up to 340 kg/m^3 (21 lb/ft^3). Most commercial material ranges between 100–250 kg/m^3 (6–16 lb/ft^3), and the average of most shipments is 160 kg/m^3 (10 lb/ft^3); specific gravity .16.

Mechanical properties: Balsa is the softest and lightest hardwood used commercially. It possesses excellent buoyancy and efficient insulation against heat, sound and vibration. This low density timber cannot be bent without buckling, but is strong in relation to its weight.

Seasoning: When green, balsa contains 200–400% moisture (and can absorb up to 792%). It has to be converted and dried very rapidly with heavy degrade. Kilning requires skilled care to avoid case hardening or toasting. It is usually treated with water repellent to prevent absorption. Once dry, it is stable in use with little movement.

Working properties: Very easy to work with thin, sharp-edged hand or power tools. The blunting effect is slight. Nails and screws easily but will not hold, so gluing is best method of fixing. It can be stained and polished but absorbs much material in the process.

Durability: The wood is perishable and liable to attack by beetle. It is permeable for preservation treatment.

Uses: Extensively used for heat, sound, and vibration insulation and buoyancy in rafts, lifebelts, floats, nets, buoys and water sports equipment. Also for protective packaging, toys and model making, and as core material in light-weight sandwich constructions.

BASSWOOD (H)

Tilia americana, L.
syn. *T. Glabra*, Vent., and
allied spp.
T. nigra, *T. latifolia* etc.
Family: *Tiliaceae*

Commercial names: American lime (UK); American whitewood (USA);
Other names: lime tree, American linden, whitewood, (USA).
Distribution: East coast of Canada and eastern U.S.A. More than half of total yield comes from the Great Lake States.
General description: Creamy-white to pale pinkish-brown, straight grained and fine, even texture due to uniform growth and lack of contrast between early and latewood zones. Weighs about 416 kg/m^3 (26 lb/ft^3); specific gravity .41.
Mechanical properties: This soft, light wood is weak and has a poor steam bending classification and very low strength properties.
Seasoning: Dries fairly rapidly with little distortion or degrade and with very little movement in service.
Working properties: Basswood works extremely easily with both hand and power tools, with low resistance to cutting and only a slight blunting effect on tools. It nails, screws and glues well and can be stained and polished without difficulty.
Durability: The timber is non-durable. Logs are liable to attack by longhorn beetle, and the sapwood by common furniture beetle. The wood is permeable for preservation treatment.
Uses: Hand carving, turnery, pattern making, drawing boards, piano keys, bee-hives, louvres, mallet heads, picture framing, match splints, wood wool, cooperage, high-class joinery, toys, constructional veneer and plywood, corestock for panels, chip baskets, small laminated articles, boxes, crates, laundry and dairy appliances. As it is free from odour it is also used for food containers.

BEECH, AMERICAN (H)

Fagus grandifolia, Ehrh.
Family: *Fagaceae*

Distribution: USA and Canada.

General description: The wood is reddish-brown and of coarser quality than European beech. It has conspicuous rays and tiny pores, is straight grained with a fine, even texture. It weighs 740 kg/m³ (46 lb/ft³); specific gravity .74.

Mechanical properties: Beech is classified as having excellent wood bending properties; it has high crushing strength, medium stiffness and resistance to shock loads. Similar in strength to European beech.

Seasoning: The wood dries fairly rapidly and well but with a strong tendency to warp, split and surface check. Considerable care must be taken during seasoning as it is subject to large shrinkage, checks and discolouration in addition to warping. Once dry, there is moderate movement in service.

Working properties: Beech works readily with most hand and machine tools, but there is a tendency for it to bind on the saw and to burn in crosscutting and drilling. It has good nailing and gluing properties and can be stained and polished to a good finish. It is an excellent wood for turnery.

Durability: Subject to attack by common furniture beetle and longhorn beetle. The wood is perishable, but permeable for preservation treatment.

Uses: Cabinetmaking and furniture making, both solid and laminated; flooring, turnery, brush backs, vehicle bodies, interior joinery, cooperage, domestic woodware and handles and veneers. It is particularly suitable for food containers as it does not impart taste or odour.

BEECH, EUROPEAN (H)

Fagus sylvatica, L.
Family: *Fagaceae*

Commercial names: English, Danish, French, etc., according to country of origin.

Distribution: Throughout central Europe and UK, also found in West Asia.

General description: The heartwood is very pale pink-brown. It is common practice on the continent to steam the timber which turns it to a reddish-brown tone. Some logs have a dark red kern or darker veining. Beech has a straight grain and fine, even texture. Average weight 720 kg/m³ (45 lb/ft³); specific gravity .72.

Mechanical properties: The steam bending properties are exceptionally good, even tolerant of knots and irregular grain. It has medium stiffness, high crushing strength and medium resistance to shock loads.

Seasoning: Dries fairly rapidly, but is classed as moderately refractory tending to warp, check, split and shrink. Care needed in air drying and kilning to avoid shrinkage. When dry there is a large movement in service.

Working properties: The ease of working varies with growth conditions and seasoning. Tough material or badly dried timber will bind on saws, burn when crosscut, and be difficult to plane. Beech offers medium resistance to hand and power tools, and has a moderate blunting effect on cutting edges. Pre-boring is necessary for nailing, it glues easily, stains well, and takes an excellent finish.

Durability: The wood is perishable, liable to attack by common furniture beetle and by death watch beetle in old buildings. Sapwood is affected by longhorn beetle. The timber is permeable for preservation treatment.

Uses: Cabinetmaking, high-class joinery, solid and laminated furniture, desks and work benches, chairmaking, shoe heels, sportsware, toys, bobbins, woodware, tool handles, turnery, musical instruments, domestic flooring, heavy construction, marine piling (when pressure treated), corestock and utility plywood. Sliced veneers have an excellent flecked figure on quartered surfaces, and broad rays on longitudinal surfaces, and are used for decorative veneering. More European beech is consumed in the UK than any other hardwood.

BEECH, JAPANESE (H)

Fagus crenata Bl., and
allied spp.
Family: *Fagaceae*

Other names: buna (Japan); Siebold's beech.

Distribution: Japan.

General description: The timber is derived from two or three closely related species of *Fagus*. The heartwood is pale pink brown in colour, with a straight grain and a fine, even texture. It weighs 620 kg/m³ (39 lb/ft³); specific gravity .62. It is more stable than central European beech.

Mechanical properties: The timber has medium density and bending strength, with medium stiffness and resistance to shock loads, and high crushing strength. It has high shear strength. The steam bending classification is excellent.

Seasoning: Tends to dry rapidly, tending to warp, check, split and shrink. Care is needed in drying as it is moderately refractory. Partially air drying before kilning is the best method. When dry, the timber is stable with small movement in service.

Working properties: The material offers medium resistance in cutting with a moderate blunting effect on cutters and a tendency to burn during drilling. A reduced cutting angle of 20°–30° in planing or moulding produces a smooth, clean finish. It has very good turning properties. May be necessary to pre-bore for nailing; it holds screws well and glues satisfactorily. Stains and polishes to a good finish.

Durability: Perishable and liable to attack by the common furniture beetle. It is permeable for preservation treatment.

Uses: Cabinetmaking, high-class joinery, furniture, flooring, turnery, tool handles, solid and laminated furniture, domestic woodware, chairmaking, shoe heels, sportsware, toys, bobbins, constructional work. It is pressure treated for exterior joinery, railway sleepers, marine piling. It is rotary cut for plywood manufacture and also used as corestock. Selected logs are sliced for decorative veneers and used for panelling, cabinet work and marquetry.

BELI (H)

Paraberlinia bifoliolata, Pellgr.
syn. *Julbernadia pellegriniana*, Troupin
Family: *Leguminosae*

Other name: awoura (Gabon).

Distribution: Tropical West Africa.

General description: The heartwood colour is light brown, with a darker, regular longitudinal striped figure, similar to zebrano, but not so well marked. The grain is interlocked, producing a striped figure on quartered surfaces, and the texture is medium to coarse. Weight between 750–850 kg/m³ (46–53 lb/ft³) average about 800 kg/m³ (50 lb/ft³); specific gravity .80.

Mechanical properties: This compact, medium density hardwood has medium strength in all categories and steam wood bending.

Seasoning: Dries rapidly and well with minimum degrade and kilns without difficulty with little risk of checking or twisting. There is large movement in service.

Working properties: Works fairly well with both hand and machine tools, but a reduced cutting angle of 20° in planing or moulding will reduce the tendency for the grain to tear on quarter sawn surfaces. The material takes nails and screws well, glues, stains and polishes satisfactorily.

Durability: Non-durable. Heartwood fairly resistant to attack by powder post beetle. Moderately resistant to preservative treatment.

Uses: Used locally for domestic flooring, boat building, agricultural implements, joinery and rotary cut for plywood manufacture; selected logs are sliced for decorative veneers for panelling, cabinets and furniture.

BERLINIA (H)

Berlinia spp., including:
B. bracteosa, Benth., *B. confusa*, Hoyle,
B. gradiflora, Hutch & Dalz.,
B. acuminata, Solander.
Family: *Leguminosae*

Commercial names: rose zebrano (UK); ebiara (Europe). **Other names**: ebiara (Gabon); ekpogoi (Nigeria); abem (Cameroon); melegbra (Ivory Coast); m'possa (Congo).

Distribution: Tropical West Africa.

General description: The heartwood varies from pink-red to dark red-brown, with dark purplish-brown irregular streaks or striped veins visible on quartered wood. The wood is interlocked and sometimes very irregular grained with dark coloured gum ducts which exude during drying. It has a coarse, open texture. The weight varies between 550–820 kg/m³ (34–51 lb/ft³), but averages 720 kg/m³ (45 lb/ft³); specific gravity .72.

Mechanical properties: This dense wood has a moderate steam bending classification with medium bending and crushing strength, but with low stiffness and resistance to shock loads.

Seasoning: Dries rather slowly and well, and is not subject to degrade, but exudation of gum and discolouration from mould growths which develop during kilning can be difficult. There is medium movement in service.

Working properties: There is moderate blunting effect on cutters due to interlocked or irregular grain. Works without excess difficulty with tungsten tipped saws. A reduced cutting angle of 20° is necessary for planing, and a French head, which may blunt rapidly, is best for moulding. Pre-boring is necessary for nailing. The wood glues, stains and finishes well.

Durability: Liable to severe attack by pinhole borers, and the sapwood to powder post beetles. It is moderately resistant to marine borers and termites in W. Africa. It is non-durable and resistant to preservative treatment.

Uses: General cabinetmaking and furniture, interior joinery, vehicle bodies, and structural purposes similar to oak. It produces highly decorative veneers for panelling and marquetry.

BIRCH, EUROPEAN (H)

Betula pendula, Roth, partly,
and *B. alba* L. (silver or white birch)
B. pubescens, Ehrh., partly,
and *B. alba*, L., and *B. odorata*, Bechst. (common birch)
(normally grouped and sold as European birch)
Family: *Betulaceae*

Commercial names: English, Finnish, Swedish birch according to origin. Also Karelian, masur, ice, flame, etc., according to figure displayed.

Distribution: Throughout Europe and UK, and Scandinavia.

General description: Cream-white to biscuit in colour, it is straight grained and fine textured, and lustrous. Flame and curly birch, ice birch etc., is caused by grain deviations. The flecked cambium figure of masur birch may be caused by external factors such as insect attack by the larvae of *Agromyzia carbonaria*, by chemical injury, climatic stress, or from internal genetic abnormalities. Weight varies from 600-700 kg/m^3 (37-43 lb/ft^3), specific gravity .66.

Mechanical properties: Has good steam bending properties but is not tolerant of pin knots. It has high bending and crushing strength with medium stiffness and resistance to shock loads.

Seasoning: Liable to fungal attack so must be dried very rapidly; there is a tendency to distort. Small movement in service.

Working properties: Works without difficulty with hand and power tools, but inclined to be woolly. To prevent tearing when planing crossgrained material or around knots reduce the cutting angle to 15°. There is a moderate blunting effect on cutters. Pre-bore for nailing near edges with irregular grain. Glues well and can be stained and polished to good finish.

Durability: The wood is perishable and subject to attack by common furniture beetle. It is moderately resistant to preservative treatment, but the sapwood is permeable.

Uses: High-class joinery, furniture drawer sides, legs and framing, cabinet interior fitments, upholstery framing, dowels, bobbins, brushes, brooms, and general turnery, flooring. It is the principal wood used for plywood in Finland and the U.S.S.R. Highly prized decorative veneers for panelling and marquetry. Impregnated for posts. Also used for ice cream spoons, etc.

BIRCH, JAPANESE (H)

Betula maximowicziana, Regel,
and allied spp. *B. platyphylla*, Subat
Family: *Betulaceae*

Other names: shira-kamba, shirakaba (Japan).

Distribution: Asia, China and Japan.

General description: The heartwood colour is bright yellow-red. The wood is fairly straight grained, and has a fine texture. The weight is about 670 kg/m^3 (41 lb/ft^3); specific gravity .67.

Mechanical properties: A hard, tough wood, with medium density, high bending strength and crushing strength, and medium stiffness and resistance to shock loads. It has a very good steam bending classification.

Seasoning: The material tends to air dry rapidly and to warp, and is liable to fungal attack unless the piles are well ventilated. Care is necessary to avoid degradation in kilning at low temperatures. There is medium to large movement in service.

Working properties: This material has only a moderate blunting effect on tool edges and works well with both hand and machine tools. There is a tendency for the wood to bind on saws, and tends to pick up the grain around knots when planing. Pre-bore when nailing near the edges; screw holding properties are good; the wood glues, stains and polishes very well.

Durability: Perishable and liable to attack by the common furniture beetle. The heartwood may contain pith flecks caused by insect attack. The heartwood is moderately resistant to preservative treatment, but the sapwood is permeable.

Uses: Suitable for furniture, interior joinery, upholstery frames, turnery, flooring for dance halls, gymnasia and light-duty factory flooring. It is rotary cut for plywood manufacture, and selected logs are sliced for decorative veneers for panelling and cabinet work. The birch twigs are used for brooms and descaling in steel rolling mills. Timber with incipient decay or dote is used for fancy articles, the black decay zone marks forming a decorative feature.

BIRCH, PAPER (H)

Betula papyrifera, Marsh.
Family: *Betulaceae*

Other names: American birch (UK); white birch (Canada).

Distribution: Canada and Eastern USA.

General description: Wide sapwood, creamy white in colour with a pale brown heartwood. Straight grained, and texture fine and uniform. Weighs about 620 kg/m³ (39 lb/ft³); specific gravity .62.

Mechanical properties: The wood has a moderately good bending classification, low stiffness, and medium crushing strength and resistance to shock loads.

Seasoning: Dries rather slowly with little degrade and small movement in service.

Working properties: The timber works well with most hand and power tools with moderate blunting of cutting edges. Curly grained material is liable to pick up in planing and a 20° angle should be used. It glues, stains and polishes well.

Durability: The wood is non-durable and the heartwood is moderately resistant to preservative treatment but the sapwood is permeable.

Uses: Mostly used as a turnery wood for dowels, spools, bobbins, hoops, domestic woodware, toys, agricultural implements. The best butts are selected for peeling into veneer for plywood or sliced into decorative veneers, depending on the degree of attractive figure present.

Note: Related spp. include:

B. occidentalis, Sarg, **western paper birch**, from Western Canada and the USA. It is slightly lighter in weight 610 kg/m³ (38 lb/ft³) but in all other respects is identical and often mixed with *B. papyrifera*.

BIRCH, YELLOW (H)

Betula alleghaniensis, Britt.
syn. *B. lutea*, Michx.f. (principally) and *B. lenta*, L.
Family: *Betulaceae*

Commercial names: hard birch, betula wood (Canada); Canadian yellow birch, Quebec birch, American birch (UK); grey, silver or swamp birch USA; *B. lenta*: sweet birch.

Distribution: Canada and USA.

General description: There is a wide range of colour differences in "unselected" parcels, but when stained will not show a marked difference between light yellow sapwood and reddish-brown heartwood. It is straight, close-grained, the texture fine and even. Weight about 710 kg/m³ (44 lb/ft³); specific gravity .71.

Mechanical properties: The wood bending classification is very good, with high bending strength, crushing strength and resistance to shock loads.

Seasoning: Dries rather slowly with little degrade; large movement in service.

Working properties: The wood works fairly easily with only a moderate dulling effect on cutters and finishes smoothly if straight grained. Curly grained material, or disturbed grain around knots requires a reduced cutting angle of 15°. It glues well with care and takes stain and polish extremely well. Its uniform, dense surface, free from large groups of pores, makes it unequalled as a base for white enamelling and guarantees a permanent smooth finish.

Durability: Liable to attack by common furniture beetle. Moderately resistant to preservative treatment, but the sapwood is permeable. The wood is perishable.

Uses: Furniture, high-grade joinery and flooring. Turnery, bobbins, shuttles, spools; cooperage, upholstery frames; high-grade plywood manufacture. Selected stock for highly decorative veneers for cabinets, panelling, marquetry, etc. Rotary cut veneers show a growth ring pattern of darker, reddish-brown veins.

Note: Curly grained or strongly figured varieties of these species are marketed in the UK as **Canadian silky wood**. North American specifications refer to "selected" and "unselected" and these refer to the *colour* and not the grade. Therefore sapwood may be called white birch (often confused with *B. papyrifera*) and the heartwood, red birch.

BLACKBEAN (H)

Castanospermum australe, A. Cunn.
Family: *Leguminosae*

Other names: Moreton Bay bean, Moreton Bay chestnut, beantree.
Distribution: Eastern Australia.
General description: The chocolate-brown coloured heartwood is figured with grey-brown streaks of parenchyma tissue surrounding large pores. Although generally straight grained it is sometimes interlocked. The texture is rather coarse. Weighs 700 kg/m³ (44 lb/ft³); specific gravity .70.
Mechanical properties: A hard, heavy wood with a very poor steam bending classification.
Seasoning: It is difficult to dry. Extreme care is required during air drying to avoid honeycombing and collapse. Very slow air drying prior to kilning is essential to avoid splitting. It has a marked tendency to degrade as the wood does not respond well to reconditioning treatment. Medium movement in service.
Working properties: The wood has a high resistance to the cutting edges of tools and a moderate blunting effect. The relatively softer patches of lighter coloured tissue tend to crumble during planing or moulding unless tools are kept very sharp. The greasy nature produces variable gluing results. Nailing and screwing are satisfactory and it can be stained and polished to an excellent finish.
Durability: Sapwood is liable to powder post beetle attack, and the heartwood is moderately resistant to termite attacks in Australia. The heartwood is extremely resistant to preservative treatment but the sapwood is permeable. The timber is durable.
Uses: High-class furniture making, cabinetmaking and joinery; turnery and carving and interior fittings. Heavy construction work, mallet heads, measuring instruments and electric appliances due to its insulating qualities. Sliced into highly decorative veneers for furniture and panelling.

BLACKBUTT (H)

Eucalyptus pilularis, Sm.
Family: *Myrtaceae*

Other names: yarri, New England ash, New England peppermint, Dundas blackbutt.
Distribution: Australia.
General description: pale-brown to brown, tinged pink. The grain is straight, occasionally interlocked or wavy, and with a moderately fine texture. Small scattered gum veins are characteristic. Weight varies, but on average is 880 kg/m^3 (55 lb/ft^3); specific gravity .88.
Mechanical properties: The wood has high bending and crushing strength and stiffness and has a poor steam bending classification.
Seasoning: Prone to check during drying and collapse may occur. Air drying before kilning is recommended.
Working properties: The wood has a moderate blunting effect on cutting edges, and for machining, a cutting angle of only 15° should be used for planing or moulding quartered material. Pre-boring necessary for nailing as the wood splits easily. Takes glue, stain and polish well for a good finish.
Durability: Very durable and extremely resistant to preservative treatment.
Uses: General construction, bridge decking, sleepers, flooring joists, posts and rails, measuring instruments, mallet heads, etc. Selected logs sliced for decorative veneers for cabinets or panelling.
Notes on related spp.
E. pilularis is the most important and is common to New South Wales and Queensland.
E. patens, Benth., produces **Western Australian blackbutt** or **yarri**. It is 30% weaker in strength than the other species.
E. andrewsii, Maid, and *E. campanulata*, R. T. Bak and H. G. Sm., produce **New England blackbutt**, or **New England ash**, or **peppermint** in NSW and Queensland.
E. dundasii, Maid, produces **Dundas blackbutt** in Western Australia.

BLACKWOOD, AFRICAN (H)   *Dalbergia melanoxylon*, Guill. & Perr.
Family: *Leguminosae*

Commercial names: Mozambique ebony (UK); mpingo (Tanzania).

Distribution: East Africa.

General description: Dark purple-brown with black streaks which predominate, giving an almost black appearance to the wood. Grain direction usually straight, but sometimes variable. Extremely fine, even textured and slightly oily to the touch. It is exceptionally hard and weighs 1,200 kg/m^3 (75 lb/ft^3); specific gravity 1.2.

Mechanical properties: This exceptionally heavy and dense wood is not used for steam bending purposes, but is very tough and strong in all categories.

Seasoning: Usually partially dried in log or billet form and then converted, end-coated and stacked under cover. Dries extremely slowly, and heart shakes are common. Great care in handling is required to avoid degrade. Small movement in service.

Working properties: The wood is difficult to work offering extreme resistance to cutting edges and very severe blunting effect. Stellite or tungsten carbide tipped saw teeth essential. In machining it tends to rise on the cutters. Pre-boring for nailing and screwing. Finishes exceptionally well.

Durability: Sapwood liable to attack by powder post beetle; the heartwood is very durable and extremely resistant to preservative treatment.

Uses: Musical instruments, especially woodwind; ornamental turnery, chessmen, carved figures, walking sticks, brushbacks, knife handles, truncheons, bearings and slides, pulley blocks, and inlay work. Its oiliness, resistance to climatic change, and ability to take an exceptional finish makes it preferable to ebony for these purposes.

BLACKWOOD, AUSTRALIAN (H)

Acacia melanoxylon, R.Br.
Family: *Leguminosae*

Other names: black wattle.

Distribution: Australia.

General description: The golden-brown to dark reddish-brown of the heartwood has regular chocolate-brown zones marking the growth rings. Mostly straight grained, but sometimes with interlocked or wavy grain producing beautiful fiddleback figure; medium and even texture and lustrous appearance. Weighs about 665 kg/m³ (41 lb/ft³); specific gravity .66.

Mechanical properties: Good wood bending properties, with medium stiffness and high crushing strength and resistance to impact.

Seasoning: The timber dries easily but with some tendency to cup unless the stack is weighted or removed with a final steaming treatment. There is small movement in service.

Working properties: It works satisfactorily with hand and power tools but a reduced cutting angle of 20° should be used for planing and moulding operations when interlocked or wavy grain is present. There is moderate blunting effect on cutting edges. Variable gluing properties; holds nails and screws well, and stains and polishes to an excellent finish.

Durability: The sapwood is liable to attack by powder post beetle and the heartwood by common furniture beetle and termites. A very durable wood and extremely resistant to preservative treatment.

Uses: A highly decorative timber in great demand for high quality furniture, shop, bank and office fitting, interior joinery and wall panelling, ornamental turnery, billiard tables, tool handles and gun stocks. Bentwork, cooperage, coach-building and boatbuilding. Sliced for beautiful decorative veneers used for plywood faces, flushdoors, and architectural panelling, marquetry, etc.

Note: Related spp. *A. mollissima*, R.Br., produces **wattle**, the bark of which is used for the extraction of tannin. The remaining timber is processed for uses similar to above.

BOMBANGA (H)

Macrolobium coeruleoides, De Wild.
syn. *Brachystegia laurentii*, Louis
Family: *Leguminosae*

Other names: léke, evène (Cameroon); yegna (Gabon); bonghei (Zaire).

Distribution: Tropical West Africa.

General description: The heartwood is yellow to light brown with a brown stripey figure, and with a coppery lustrous appearance. It is straight grained with a fine, even texture. The wood weighs 610 kg/m³ (38 lb/ft³); specific gravity .61.

Mechanical properties: The wood is of medium density and has a good steam bending classification; it has low stiffness but medium bending and crushing strengths and resistance to shock loads.

Seasoning: The timber dries easily with no tendency to check or warp, but may exude gum if the process is hurried. There is small movement in service.

Working properties: Bombanga works well and easily with both hand and machine tools with only a moderate blunting effect on tools. It nails, screws, glues and stains easily and can be brought, after sanding, to an excellent silken finish.

Durability: The wood is non-durable, moderately resistant to preservative treatment but the sapwood is permeable.

Uses: Furniture, interior fitments, interior construction, and cabinets. Peels and slices easily for plywood faces and for decorative veneering for wall panelling, flushdoors, etc.

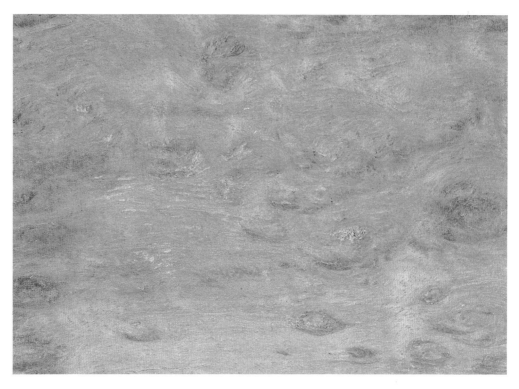

BOX, WHITE TOPPED (H)

Eucalyptus quadrangulata, Sm.
Family: *Myrtaceae*

Commercial names: white topped box (UK and Australia).

Distribution: Western Australia.

General description: The heartwood colour varies from light yellow-brown to a darker tan colour. The grain is interlocked and the texture is medium to coarse but even. The timber weighs 990 kg/m³ (61 lb/ft³); specific gravity .99.

Mechanical properties: This timber has high bending and crushing strength, medium stiffness and resistance to shock loads. It has a poor steam bending classification.

Seasoning: It is difficult to season with a marked tendency to distort and shrink; some collapse may occur if kiln drying from green. Partial air drying before kilning and final reconditioning treatment are recommended. There is small movement in service.

Working properties: It has a severe blunting effect on tools and is fairly difficult to work. Straight grained material finishes cleanly in most operations but the majority of interlocked material requires a reduced cutting angle. It turns very well. The wood is unsuitable for plywood manufacture due to its weight. Can be nailed with care, and glues, stains and polishes to a good finish.

Durability: Durable. Resistant to Lyctus attack when used in exposed conditions. Extremely resistant to preservative treatment.

Uses: Widely used as a turnery wood for mauls, mallets, handles, shuttles, etc. Domestic flooring, bridge and wharf decking and heavy construction. Selected logs are sliced for decorative veneers.

Note 1: Not a true box (*Buxus* spp)

Note 2: Closely related spp. include *E. moluccana*, syn. *E. hemiphloia* producing **grey box.**

BOXWOOD, EUROPEAN (H)

Buxus sempervirens, L.
Family: *Buxaceae*

Commercial names: box; Iranian, Persian, Turkish, etc., boxwood, according to country of origin (UK).

Distribution: The United Kingdom, southern Europe, Asia Minor and Western Asia.

General description: The timber is compact and pale yellow in colour. The grain is fairly straight to slightly irregular, with a very fine and even texture. Weight varies from 830–1140 kg/m^3 (52–71 lb/ft^3), average about 910 kg/m^3 (57 lb/ft^3); specific gravity .91.

Mechanical properties: This very heavy, dense wood has good steam bending properties, high stiffness, and good crushing strength and resistance to shock loads.

Seasoning: Dries very slowly with pronounced tendency to surface checks. Liable to severe end splitting if dried in the round; end coatings should be applied or the billets converted. Should be dried under covered storage. There is small movement in service.

Working properties: Cutting resistance is high and it is rather hard to work with moderate blunting effect on cutting edges. Pre-boring is necessary for nailing. Gluing, staining and polishing give good results.

Durability: Heartwood may be attacked by common furniture beetle, but the timber is durable; the sapwood permeable for preservative treatment.

Uses: Boxwood is an excellent carving and turning wood; used for textile rollers, shuttles, pulley blocks, skittles, croquet mallets, tool handles, rulers, engraving blocks, parts of musical instruments, chessmen, and extensively used for boxwood inlay lines, bandings and stringings, and for inlay motifs in veneer form.

Note: Related spp. include *B. macowani*, Oliv., **East London Boxwood** and a number of botanically unrelated spp. including *Gossypiospermum praecox* – **Maracaibo boxwood** *Phyllostylon brasiliensis* – **San Domingo boxwood** *Gonioma kamassi* – **Knysna boxwood**.

BRAZILWOOD (H)

Caesalpinia echinata, Lam.
syn. *Guilandina echinata*, Spreng
Family: *Leguminosae*

Other names: bahia wood, para wood, pernumbuco wood, (UK, USA); Brazil ironwood, pau ferro* hypernic, brasilette, brasilete, brasiletto. **Distribution:** Brazil.

General description: The heartwood colour is bright, vivid orange-red, maturing upon exposure to red-brown. It has a variegated stripey to marble-like figure, sometimes accentuated by pin knots. It is usually straight to interlocked grained with a fine, compact, smooth texture with a natural lustre. Weight from 1200–1280 kg/m^3 (75–80 lb/ft^3). Specific gravity 1.2.

Mechanical properties: This extremely hard, tough resilient wood has high strength properties in all categories.

Seasoning: Needs to be dried slowly and with care to avoid checking and degradation.

Working properties: It is sometimes difficult to work, with a severe blunting effect on cutting edges, and a reduction of the cutting angle to 15° is required for planing or moulding quartered stock. It needs pre-boring for nailing, has good screw holding properties and can be glued, stained and polished to a brilliant lustrous finish, often showing a snakelike ripple. Lacquer finishes preserve the beautiful colour.

Durability: Very durable and resistant to insect attack and decay.

Uses: World famous as a dye wood and also greatly prized for best quality violin bows because of its resilience. Ornamental turnery, gun stocks, exterior joinery, panelling, and inlaywork. Exterior structural work, dock and wharf building, jetties and piling. Heavy duty parquet flooring. Selected logs sliced for decorative veneers for cabinets, furniture, etc.

Note 1: *Libidibia sclerocarpa*, from the Guianas and Tropical South America is also produced as **pau ferro**. It is purple-brown to black in colour, weighs 1120 kg/m^3 (701 lb/ft^3); s.g. 1.1. Used for heavy constructional work, dock piling, etc.

Note 2: *Caesalpinia granadillo* Pitt, and allied species from Venezuela produces **partridgewood**, known as '**Maracaibo ebony**' (UK) and **granadillo** (Venezuela).

BUBINGA (H)   *Guibourtia demeusei*, (Harms) J. Léon, principally,
also including *G. pellegriniana*, J. Léon,
G. tessmannii, (Harms) J. Léon
Family: *Leguminosae*

Commercial names: African rosewood, kevasingo (rotary) (UK)
Other names: essingang (Cameroon); kevazingo, buvenga (Gabon).
Distribution: Chiefly from the Cameroon and Gabon, also from Zaire.
General description: The wood is medium red-brown with lighter red to purple veining. The grain is straight or interlocked. In some logs the grain is very irregular and these are converted by peeling into rotary cut veneers called kevasingo. The texture is moderately coarse but even. The weight ranges from 800–960 kg/m^3 (50–60 lb/ft^3), average 880 kg/m^3 (55 lb/ft^3); s.g. .88.
Mechanical properties: The timber has low steam bending qualities and exudation of gum pockets is troublesome.
Seasoning: Dries easily except for gum exudation, with little degrade, and is stable in service.
Working properties: The timber works easily with both hand and machine tools, although gum pockets may cause difficulty. Interlocked and irregular grained material tends to tear or pick up and a reduced cutting angle of 15° is necessary for planing or moulding. There is a moderate to severe blunting effect on cutting edges which must be kept sharp. Nailing requires pre-boring; gluing may be difficult due to gum pockets, but the wood stains easily and can be brought to an excellent finish.
Durability: It is moderately durable but liable to common furniture beetle attack. The sapwood is permeable and the heartwood is resistant to preservative treatment.
Uses: It is an excellent turnery wood, and used for knife handles, brush backs, fancy goods. The chief use is for sliced decorative veneers for cabinets and panelling, particularly the rotary cut kevasingo, with a wild, swirling, veined figure.

BUTTERNUT (H)

Juglans cinera, L.
Family: *Juglandaceae*

Commercial name: white walnut.

Distribution: Canada and USA.

General description: The heartwood is medium dark brown in colour but not as dark as black American walnut which it otherwise resembles. It is straight grained with a coarse but soft texture. It weighs around 450 kg/m³ (28 lb/ft³); specific gravity .45.

Mechanical properties: It has a low wood bending classification and is generally lower in all strength properties than black American walnut.

Seasoning: Dries rather slowly with little degrade. Medium movement in service.

Working properties: It is easily worked with both hand and power tools. There is little resistance to cutting edges which must be kept very sharp because of the softness of the wood. The wood nails, screws and glues well, and can be stained and brought to an excellent finish.

Durability: The timber is non-durable and liable to attack by the common furniture beetle. It is only moderately resistant to preservative treatment, the sapwood being permeable.

Uses: High-class and utility joinery, interior trim for boats, superstructures, cabinet fitments, furniture, and for boxes and crates. It is an excellent carving wood. It is sliced as decorative veneer and used as a substitute for black American walnut for furniture and wall panelling.

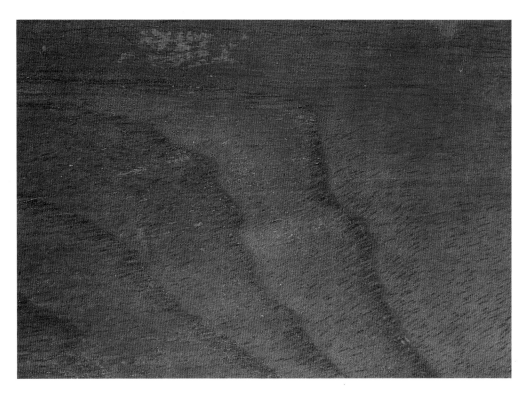

CALANTAS (H)

Toona calantas, Merr & Rolfe
syn. *Cedrela calantas*, Merr & Rolfe.
Family: *Meliaceae*

Other name: kalantas (Philippines).

Distribution: Philippines.

General description: The heartwood colour is from light to dark red, with straight to interlocked grain and with a moderately coarse texture. The wood has a cedar-like scent due to exudation of an essential oil in the form of resin, sometimes found on the surface of the wood. Weight about 448 kg/m³ (28 lb/ft³); specific gravity .44.

Mechanical properties: Moderately strong, and with medium steam bending properties.

Seasoning: Seasons easily, but care is required when drying thick material to avoid degrade in the form of checking or collapse.

Working properties: Works well with both hand or machine tools, but the timber is inclined to be woolly and very sharp cutting edges are necessary. Gluing and finishing can be a problem if gum exudation occurs, but with care and when filled, the material can be stained and polished to an excellent finish.

Durability: Calantas is durable, and amenable to preservative treatment.

Uses: Joinery, furniture making, carving, piano cases, cigar boxes, paddles and light oars and boat and ship interiors.

Note: A closely related species *Azadirachta integrifolia*, Merr, known in the Philippines as **maranggo**, produces curly or bird's eye calantas, which is slightly harder and heavier and darker in colour and has the same uses as calantas except for cigar boxes.

CEDAR (S)   (1) *Cedrus atlantica*, (Endl.) Carr.
                                        (2) *C. deodara*, (Roxb.) G. Don.
                                        Family: *Pinaceae*

Other names: (1) Atlas cedar, Atlantic cedar (2) deodar cedar (India and UK).
Distribution: (1) Algeria and Morocco (2) N. India. (Those grown in the UK are mostly ornamental).
General description: The heartwood is light brown in colour, with a pungent cedar odour. The growth rings are clearly marked by the contrasting earlywood and dense latewood zones. The grain is usually straight, especially in *C. deodara*, but the *C. atlantica* grown under parkland conditions may be knotty with grain disturbances. The texture is medium to fine. Weight 580 kg/m^3 (36 lb/ft^3); specific gravity .58.
Mechanical properties: These timbers have low bending strength and resistance to shock loads, low stiffness and crushing strength. This brittle timber has a very poor steam bending classification.
Seasoning: Dries quite easily but with a tendency to warp. There is medium movement in service.
Working properties: Easy to work with very little dulling effect on cutters although knots and in-growing bark pockets may be troublesome. If cutters are kept sharp, a good, clean finish is obtainable. The material takes nails and screws well; glues, stains and takes paint or varnish for a good finish.
Durability: Durable. Liable to attack by pinhole borer and longhorn beetle. The heartwood is resistant to preservative treatment and the sapwood varies from permeable to moderately resistant.
Uses: Suitable for joinery, construction, bridges, garden furniture, gates, fences and doors, and railway sleepers according to grade of timber.

CEDAR OF LEBANON (S)

Cedrus libani, A. Rich.
syn. *C. libanotica*, Link.
Family: *Pinaceae*

Other name: true cedar. **Distribution:** Middle East.

General description: The heartwood is strongly scented and resinous with contrasting growth rings marked by the darker dense latewood zones. There may be grain disturbance around knots in parkland timber, but selected grades are straight grained with medium to fine texture. There may be in-growing bark pockets in the wood – a feature of true cedars. Weight 560 kg/m^3 (35 lb/ft^3); specific gravity .56.

Mechanical properties: This soft, brittle timber has a low bending strength and stiffness, resistance to shock loads and crushing strength. It also has a very poor steam bending classification due to resin exudation.

Seasoning: The timber dries easily with only a slight tendency to warp and there is medium movement in service.

Working properties: Easy to work with hand or machine tools, with little blunting effect on cutters. Large knots and in-bark may cause difficulty when machining. Nails and screws hold well and the wood stains, varnishes, paints or polishes to a good finish.

Durability: Durable. Liable to attack by pinhole borer and longhorn beetle and *Sirex*. The heartwood is resistant to preservative treatment and the sapwood moderately resistant.

Uses: Suitable for joinery, doors and interior decoration from selected grades, and is used locally for building. Timber grown in the UK is usually park grown and very knotty and used mainly for garden furniture, gates, fences and exterior work. Selected logs are sliced for decorative veneers suitable for architectural wall panelling, and plywood faces.

Note: There are nearly 50 references in the Bible to the Cedars of Lebanon. The Lebanon has created a Cedars of Lebanon National Park near Basharri, 84 miles north of Beirut.

'CELERY TOP PINE' (S)   *Phyllocladus rhomboidalis* L.C. and
                                                              A. Rich
                                          syn. *P. asplenifolius*, (Labill.)
                                                             Hook f.
                                            Family: *Podocarpaceae*

Distribution: Tasmania.

General description: The heartwood colour is pale yellow, with clearly defined growth rings. It is straight grained, with a fine, even texture. Weight about 640 kg/m³ (40 lb/ft³); specific gravity .64.

Mechanical properties: It is strong, stable and tough and has medium to high strength in all categories, with a moderate bending rating.

Seasoning: The timber dries readily with little degrade. There is medium movement in service.

Working properties: The wood works well with hand or machine tools and takes glue, stain and varnish well.

Durability: The material is moderately durable, and permeable for preservation treatment.

Uses: Carriage building, joinery, cabinet work, agricultural implements, fencing, carpentry, and also used in the round as masts for small vessels. Selected logs sliced for veneers.

Note 1: Not a true pine.

Note 2: A closely related species *P. hypophyllus* occurs in Papua New Guinea and weighs 540 kg/m³ (33 lb/ft³). It is used for similar purposes.

CEREJEIRA (H)

Amburana cearensis, (Fr.Allem) A.C.Sm.
syn. *Torresia cearensis*, Allem.
Family: *Leguminosae*

Commercial name: amburana (USA).

Other names: cerejeira rajada, cumaré (Brazil); palo trebol (Argentina).

Distribution: Central and South America, chiefly in Brazilian eastern states.

General description: A uniform yellow to medium-brown with an orange-pink tint. Straight to irregular grain and a coarse texture. It is faintly scented. Weighs 600 kg/m^3 (37 lb/ft^3); specific gravity .60.

Mechanical properties: It has good strength properties in relation to its weight and moderate steam bending classification.

Seasoning: Care is needed in drying to avoid degradation as the wood is subject to high tangential shrinkage; it is stable in service.

Working properties: The material works well with both hand and machine tools, with only a moderate blunting effect on tools. Cutting edges must be kept sharp and a reduced angle of 20° should be used where irregular grain is present. Pre-boring is necessary for nailing or screwing as there is a tendency to split. Glued joints hold well; stains easily and when filled gives an excellent finish.

Durability: The wood is durable and not subject to insect attack. It is extremely resistant to preservative treatment.

Uses: It is used for carpentry, joinery, domestic flooring, vehicle bodies and for boat building. Sliced veneers for decorative veneering and architectural panelling, doors, etc.

CHERRY, AMERICAN (H)

Prunus serotina, Ehrh.
Family: *Rosaceae*

Commercial names: black cherry (Canada and USA); cabinet cherry (USA).

Other names: rum cherry; whisky cherry; wild cherry.

Distribution: In small quantities or scattered trees in deciduous forest areas in Canada and USA.

General description: Heartwood varies from rich red to reddish-brown, with a fine, straight, close grain with narrow brown pith flecks and small gum pockets, and with a smooth texture. Weighs about 580 kg/m³ (36 lb/ft³); specific gravity .58.

Mechanical properties: The timber has good wood bending properties, low stiffness, and medium strength and resistance to shock loads.

Seasoning: Dries fairly rapidly, with little degrade if care is taken to avoid a moderately large amount of shrinkage during seasoning. There is medium movement in service.

Working properties: The wood works easily with both hand and power tools with only moderate blunting effect on cutting edges. It nails, glues, stains and takes an excellent polish.

Durability: Sapwood is liable to attack by common furniture beetle, and heartwood moderately resistant to preservative treatment. The wood is moderately durable.

Uses: Pattern making, tobacco pipes, musical instruments, furniture and cabinetmaking, high-class joinery, boat interiors, backing blocks for mounting printing plates. It is an excellent turnery and carving wood. Selected logs are converted into decorative veneers for furniture, cabinets, wall panelling, flushdoors etc.

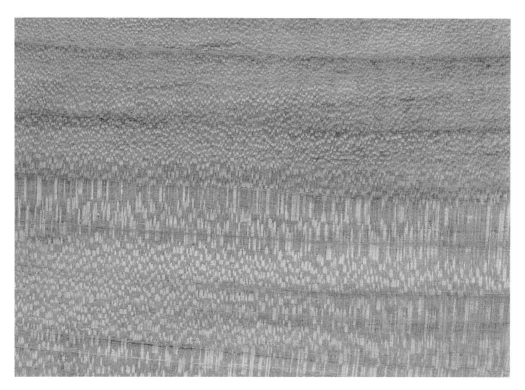

CHERRY, EUROPEAN (H)

Prunus avium, L.
syn: *Cerasus avium*, Moench.
Family: *Rosaceae*

Commercial names: gean, wild cherry, mazzard, fruit cherry (UK).
Other names: merisier (France); kers (Netherlands); kirsche (Germany).
Distribution: Europe, including the UK, Scandinavia and W. Asia and N. Africa.
General description: The heartwood is pale pinkish-brown, straight grain, and a fairly fine, even texture. Weight about 610 kg/m^3 (38 lb/ft^3); specific gravity .61.
Mechanical properties: The timber has a very good wood bending classification, with medium bending and crushing strength, also medium shock resistance but low stiffness ratings. Its strength properties are similar to oak.
Seasoning: Dries fairly rapidly with a strong tendency to warp. There is a medium amount of movement in service.
Working properties: There is a moderate blunting effect on cutting edges and straight grained material finishes very well. However, a cutting angle of 20° should be used on crossgrained material which tends to tear. The wood nails, glues and stains well and can be brought to an excellent finish.
Durability: The sapwood is liable to attack from the common furniture beetle, but the wood is almost immune from attack by powder post beetle. The heartwood is moderately durable and resistant to preservative treatment.
Uses: Generally used in small sections due to its tendency to warp. Cabinetmaking and furniture, panelling and decorative joinery. It is excellent for turnery and is used for domestic ware, shuttle pins, toys and parts of musical instruments. When sliced, it is available as a highly decorative veneer for furniture, doors and wall panelling.

CHERRY, JAPANESE (H)

Prunus japonica, L.
Family: *Rosaceae*

Other names: yama-zukura, kaba-zakura (Japan)

Distribution: Japan.

General description: The timber is pale pinkish-brown in colour maturing to a mahogany colour. The grain is usually straight, and with a fine, even texture. Weight is about 630 kg/m³ (39 lb/ft³); specific gravity .63.

Mechanical properties: The timber has medium bending and crushing strengths, and resistance to shock loads, with low stiffness giving it a very good steam bending classification.

Seasoning: Dries fairly readily but with a pronounced tendency to warp. There is a medium movement in service.

Working properties: There is a moderate blunting effect on cutting edges, and when interlocked or irregular grain is present a reduction of the cutting angle to 20° is advised for planing or moulding. The material holds nails and screws well, may be glued, stained and polished to an excellent finish.

Durability: Moderately durable. Susceptible to attack by the common furniture beetle, and liable to termite attack. Resistant to preservative treatment, but the sapwood is permeable.

Uses: High-class decorative joinery, cabinetmaking, and domestic woodware. Parts of musical instruments, toys, shuttle pins. It is excellent for turnery. Also used for engraving blocks. Selected logs sliced for decorative veneers for panelling, and furniture.

CHESTNUT, AMERICAN (H)

Castanea dentata, Borkh.
Family: *Fagaceae*

Other names: wormy chestnut.
Distribution: Eastern Canada and USA.
General description: The heartwood is pale brown in colour with wide growth rings producing a pronounced figure on longitudinal surfaces. It is generally similar to oak in appearance except that the absence of broad rays means that chestnut does not have the "silver ray" figure of oak. A fungal disease known as chestnut blight severely affects the tree resulting in wormy chestnut. Weight 480 kg/m^3 (30 lb/ft^3); specific gravity .48.
Mechanical properties: Chestnut has a low bending strength, medium crushing strength and very low stiffness and resistance to shock loads, and has a moderate steam bending classification.
Seasoning: It is difficult to season and has a tendency to collapse or honeycomb or retain patches of moisture. There is small movement in service.
Working properties: It is liable to blue stain if in contact with ferrous metals, and, as it is rich in tannin, can corrode metals in contact with it under damp conditions. It is easy to work with hand or machine tools; nails and glues well, and stains and polishes to an excellent finish.
Durability: The heartwood is durable; sapwood is liable to attack by powder post beetle and common furniture beetle. It is extremely resistant to preservative treatment.
Uses: Used in sound form for furniture, office desks and equipment, coffins, tanks, posts and sleepers. Wormy chestnut is used for furniture and picture frame mouldings, and sliced for decorative veneers. At one time it was used as corestock for plywood manufacture.
Note: Closely related species *Castanea sativa*, produces **sweet chestnut**.

CHESTNUT, HORSE (H)

Aesculus hippocastanum, L.
Family: *Hippocastanaceae*

Distribution: United Kingdom and Europe.

General description: Creamy-white to yellowish when mature. It is often spiral, cross, or wavy grained, with a fine, close uniform texture caused by fine rays and minute pores, often with a ripple or mottle on longitudinal surfaces caused by the storied rays. Trees felled in early winter are extremely white in colour, but if felled later in season the colour varies from yellow to light brown. It weighs 510 kg/m^3 (31 lb/ft^3); specific gravity .51.

Mechanical properties: The material has low bending strength, very low stiffness, and medium crushing strength. It has a good wood bending classification and bends well if free from knots and air dried, but tends to rupture on the inner compressed face if in the green state.

Seasoning: The wood dries rapidly and well but with some tendency to distort and the ends to split. It should be end racked immediately after conversion. Kilning should be carried out at low temperature. There is small movement in service.

Working properties: Easy to work with both hand and machine tools, with only a slight blunting effect, but it tends to tear in planing and sawing. The wood nails, screws, glues and stains easily and can be brought to a good finish.

Durability: Sapwood liable to attack by the common furniture beetle. The heartwood is perishable, but permeable to preservative treatment.

Uses: Its uses are dependent upon the dried quality of the wood. Cabinetmaking, furniture, carving and turnery, brush backs, dairy and kitchen utensils, fruit storage trays and racks, moulder's patterns, and hand pieces of racquets. Utility joinery, boxes and crates etc. It is also sliced for decorative veneering, and used for chemically treated harewood and dyed woods for inlays and marquetry work.

Note: *A. octandra*, Marsh, produces **buckeye** (USA).

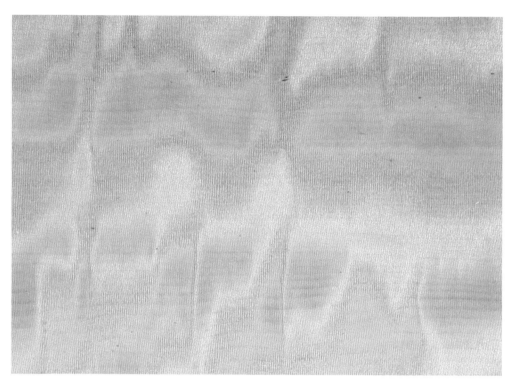

CHESTNUT, JAPANESE HORSE (H)

Aesculus turbinata, B1.
Family: *Hippocastanaceae*

Other names: Tochi, tochi-noki (Japan).

Distribution: Japan.

General description: The heartwood is golden brown in colour unlike its European counterpart. The grain is wavy or crossed and the texture is fine and uniform. It weighs 590 kg/m³ (36 lb/ft³); specific gravity .59.

Mechanical properties: The material has a good steam bending classification, low stiffness, and with medium crushing strength and resistance to shock loads.

Seasoning: The material dries rapidly with some distortion and end splitting. It should be stacked with plenty of air circulating between the boards or end racked. Kilning requires a low temperature. There is small movement in service.

Working properties: The wood works easily with both hand and machine tools, with a slight blunting effect on cutting edges. The use of sharp, thin edged cutters is advised, with a reduced cutting angle for a very good finish. The material nails, screws, glues and stains well and provides an excellent finish.

Durability: The heartwood is liable to attack by common furniture beetle and is perishable, but permeable to preservative treatment.

Uses: It is excellent for turnery and wood carving. Dairy and kitchen utensils, food containers and fruit storage trays. Selected logs containing mottled figure and incipient decaying yellow patches of discoloured wood enclosed by black zone markings are highly prized for decorative work for cabinets and furniture. Sliced logs are used for decorative veneering, panelling etc.

CHESTNUT, SWEET (H)

Castanea sativa, Mill.
syn. *C. vesca*, Gaertn.
Family: *Fagaceae*

Commercial names: Spanish chestnut, European chestnut.

Distribution: United Kingdom, Europe and Asia Minor.

General description: The colour is pale brown to biscuit similar to oak, but without the silver grain figure of oak due to finer rays. The grain is from straight to spiral. Texture is coarse. Ring shakes are liable to be present in old trees. Weight around 540 kg/m^3 (34 lb/ft^3); s.g. .54.

Mechanical properties: This wood of medium density has low bending strength, medium crushing strength, and very low stiffness and resistance to shock loads. If bent in the green state is liable to rupture on the inner face. Air dried wood has a good steam bending classification, although intolerant of pin knots.

Seasoning: It is difficult to dry. It dries slowly with a marked tendency to collapse and honeycomb and retain patches of moisture, and does not respond well to reconditioning treatments. There is small movement in service.

Working properties: Due to its acidic character it tends to corrode metal in contact with it under damp conditions, and blue-black iron stains are likely to appear in the wood if in contact with iron compounds in moist conditions. There is only slight blunting effect on tools and the material is easy to work with hand or power tools. It nails, screws, stains and polishes well.

Durability: Sapwood liable to powder post beetle and furniture beetle attack. The heartwood is durable and extremely resistant to preservative treatment.

Uses: Furniture, turnery, coffin boards, ornamental bowls, kitchens utensils, cleft fencing, stakes, and hop poles. Casks of chestnut staves are used for oils and fats, fruit juices, cheap wines, barrel hoops, walking sticks and umbrella handles. Selected logs are sliced into decorative veneers.

Note: Other spp. include *C. dentata*, Borkh., **American Chestnut**.

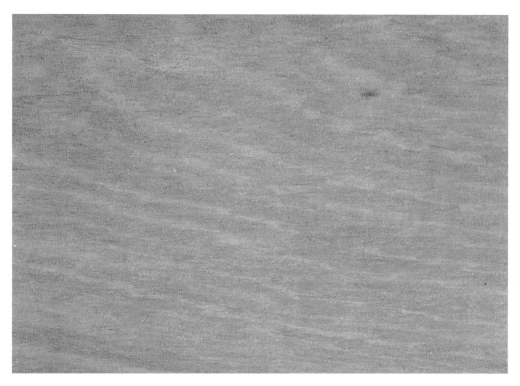

COACHWOOD (H)

Ceratopetalum apetalem, D.Don.
Family: *Cunonaceae*

Commercial name: scented satinwood
Distribution: Australia.
General description: Light brown to pink brown, darkening upon exposure. The grain is mostly straight, close and rather short, and the texture, fine and even. Weight about 630 kg/m^3 (39 lb/ft^3); specific gravity .63.
Mechanical properties: In most strength properties it is similar to European beech, with medium bending strength, stiffness and shock resistance and high crushing strength. Its steam bending rating is good.
Seasoning: The material dries fairly rapidly, with a tendency to split and warp. It requires slow and careful seasoning to avoid shrinkage. There is a medium amount of movement in service.
Working properties: The wood works fairly easily with both hand and power tools and gives a smooth finish in planing or moulding. There is a tendency to chip at the exit of tools in drilling and mortising, and it tends to split when nailed unless pre-bored. It glues well and and takes stain, and provides an excellent polish.
Durability: The timber is non-durable, subject to powder post beetle attack, but the wood is permeable for preservation treatment.
Uses: The numerous fine rays produce an attractive flecked figure on quartered surfaces, and the fine texture and smooth finish makes the wood ideal for furniture and cabinetmaking. Used also for mouldings, sporting goods, gun stocks, musical instruments, flooring, skirtings, bobbins, shoe heels, boat building and wall panelling. It is also used as plywood corestock, and sliced as a decorative veneer for cabinets and panelling.

COCOBOLO (H)

Dalbergia retusa, Hemsl, and allied species
Family: *Leguminosae*

Other name: granadillo (Mexico).

Distribution: West coast of Central America.

General description: The heartwood colour varies from rich red to an attractive variegated appearance of yellow, orange and red streaks and zones, which mature upon exposure to a mellow orange red. The grain is irregular and variable, but has a fine uniform texture. It is a hard timber weighing from 990 to 1200 kg/m³ (61–75 lb/ft³), average about 1100 kg/m³ (68 b/ft³); specific gravity about 1.10.

Mechanical properties: This very heavy, tough, strong timber has high mechanical strength in all categories but these are unimportant due to the purposes for which the timber is used.

Seasoning: The wood dries out very slowly, with a marked tendency to split and check. There is small movement in service.

Working properties: Works fairly well with both hand and machine tools, with a moderate blunting effect on cutting edges which must be kept very sharp. A reduced cutting angle is required for planing or moulding, and the surface can be rendered very smooth to the touch. It can be nailed and screwed easily, but it difficult to glue. It takes stain and can be brought to an excellent finish.

Durability: Very durable and resistant to preservative treatment.

Uses: Turnery, brushbacks, cutlery handles, small tool handles, truncheons, small trinkets and fancy goods, wooden jewellery and similar small decorative items. Sliced into very beautiful figured veneers for inlay work and decorative purposes on furniture.

COPAIBA (H)

Guibourtia langsdorfii, Desf.
syn. *Copaifera langsdorfii*, Desf.
Family: *Leguminosae*

Commercial name: pau de oleo (Brazil).
Other names: copahyba, copaiba jutahy, copaiba marimary (Brazil).
Distribution: Grows mainly in Brazil, also in Paraguay and Peru.
General description: Heartwood is reddish-brown with darker streaks, and lustrous. The grain is fairly straight or wavy, and the texture is medium-fine and uniform. The weight varies from 760–840 kg/m^3 (47–52 lb/ft^3), average 800 kg/m^3 (50 lb/ft^3); specific gravity .80.
Mechanical properties: This strong, tough timber has good steam bending properties, crushing strength and resistance to shock loads, but exudation of resin is likely during steaming.
Seasoning: It is difficult to air dry without degrade, but kiln drying is satisfactory if carried out very slowly at low temperatures to avoid checking and twisting. There is small movement in service.
Working properties: Works well with hand and power tools, with only a slight blunting effect on cutting edges which need to be kept sharp where wavy grain is present. It works into a very smooth surface finish, takes nails, screws, and glues well. Staining and polishing produces an excellent finish.
Durability: Resistant to insect and fungal attacks, and is durable in exposed situations.
Uses: Essential oils such as copal and copaiba resin are obtained from this species, and used in the paint industry. The wood is extensively used for furniture and cabinetmaking, interior joinery, general and ship building, domestic flooring and skirtings. It is also sliced for decorative veneering for wall panelling.
Note: *Copaifera officinalis*, (H), from Central America and *Copaifera guianensis*, from Brazil, are related species, with similar characteristics.

CORDIA, LIGHT AMERICAN (H)

(1) *Cordia alliodora*, Chan.
syn. *(C. gerascanthus)*
(2) *Cordia trichotoma*, Allab.
Family: *Boraginaceae*

Other names: (1) salmwood (British Honduras); Ecuador laurel, princewood (UK); cyp, cype, bocote, solera, ziricote and canaletta (USA); (2) louro (Brazil); peterebi (Argentina).

Distribution: West Indies and Tropical America.

General description: The heartwood is dull golden brown in colour with variegated irregular markings and an attractive ray flecked figure on quartered surfaces. It is straight grained, with a medium coarse texture. Weight 550 kg/m³ (34 lb/ft³); specific gravity .55.

Mechanical properties: Possesses medium strength properties in all categories and a good steam bending classification.

Seasoning: Dries easily without much degrade. There is medium movement in service.

Working properties: Works easily with both hand and machine tools, with a slight blunting effect on tool edges; can be finished smoothly and cleanly in most machining operations. Takes nails and screws well, glues, stains and polishes to a good finish.

Durability: Moderately durable, resistant to preservative treatment and the sapwood is permeable.

Uses: Cabinets and furniture, interior joinery, boat decking, vehicle bodies, light construction. Selected logs sliced for veneers suitable for panelling and furniture.

CORDIA, WEST AFRICAN (H)

(1) *Cordia abyssinica*, R.Br.
(2) *C. millenii*, Bak. (3) *C. platythyrsa*, Bak.
Family: *Boraginaceae*

Other names: (1) mukumari (Kenya); mringaringa (Tanzania); (2) mugoma (Kenya); mukeba (Uganda); (2 and 3) omo (Nigeria).

Distribution: Mainly Kenya, Tanzania and Nigeria.

General description: The colour varies from rich golden brown, with a pinkish tint, and darker streaks. The grain is irregular to interlocked, which, combined wtih medium sized rays, produces an attractive striped, mottled ray figure on quartered surfaces. Texture is moderately coarse. Weight about 430 kg/m^3 (27 lb/ft^3); specific gravity .43.

Mechanical properties: A light density wood, with low bending strength, very low stiffness and resistance to shock loads, and medium crushing strength. Steam bending is poor.

Seasoning: Dries rapidly and well with only a slight tendency to bow and twist. A high temperature kiln schedule is needed to remove moisture from the centre of the timber. There is small movement in service.

Working properties: The material is easy to work with hand or machine tools, with only slight blunting effect on cutting edges. Sharp tools are needed to prevent the surface from becoming woolly, and care is necessary to avoid tearing the interlocked grain. The wood nails and screws well, glues without difficulty, and when filled, can be stained and polished satisfactorily.

Durability: The heartwood varies from very durable to moderately durable as brittleheart is fairly common in this species, and the outer heartwood is tougher. It is reported to be free from insect or fungal attack. The heartwood is resistant to preservative treatment.

Uses: Furniture and cabinetmaking and joinery where strength is unimportant. It is used for library fittings, interior fitments and general utility joinery. Locally for making traditional drums because of its resonant properties, and sounding boards. Also for canoe making and boatbuilding. Peeled for plywood corestock and sliced for decorative veneers for panelling etc.

COURBARIL (H)

Hymenaea courbaril, L.
Family: *Leguminosae*

Commercial names: locust (West Indies); West Indian locust (UK, USA).

Other names: jutaby, jatoba, jatai amerelo, jatai vermelho (Brazil); locust (Surinam); copal (Equador); marbre (Guadaloupe); guapinal (Mexico); algarrobo (Puerto Rico).

Distribution: Central and South America and West Indies.

General description: The heartwood is salmon red to orange-brown marked with dark brown and russet brown streaks. The wood has a golden lustre. The grain is commonly interlocked with a medium to coarse texture. Weight 910 kg/m^3 (56 lb/ft^3); specific gravity .91.

Mechanical properties: Very strong, hard and tough with a very good bending classification.

Seasoning: Rather difficult to dry, tends to be rapid with moderate surface checking and warping and a liability to case harden. Slow drying will overcome these tendencies. There is small movement in service.

Working properties: Moderately difficult to work because of its high density. It nails badly but has good screw holding; glues well. It has a moderate blunting effect on tools which must be kept sharp, and a reduced cutting angle of 20° will provide a smooth finish on the interlocked grain. The wood stains well but does not take a high polish.

Durability: Moderately durable, but non-durable when a high proportion of sapwood is present. It is very resistant to termites and extremely resistant to preservative treatment.

Uses: Furniture, cabinetmaking, joinery and turnery. Its high shock resistance makes it ideal for tool handles and sports goods; excellent for flooring, stair treads, ships planking, gear cogs, wheel rims, looms, general building construction. Used for steam bent boat parts in place of oak. Lock gates in waters free from marine borers. Second growth timber has a wide sapwood of greyish-pink colour, and is sliced for decorative veneers for panelling and furniture.

Note: *Hymenaea davisii,* Sandw., grows in Guyana and is similar in all other respects.

CYPRESS (S)

Cupressus lindeyi, (C. lusitanica Mill),
C. macrocarpa, Gord. *C. sempervirens*, Linn.
Family: *Cupressaceae*

Commercial names: East African cypress, etc. according to origin.

Distribution: *C. lindeyi*: Mexico, Honduras, Guatemala, East Africa. *C. macrocarpa*: N. America, Australasia, East and South Africa. *C. sempervirens*: Mediterranean countries, Asia Minor and Himalayas.

General description: The heartwood is orange to pinkish-brown. It is straight grained with a fairly fine, even texture. The growth rings are marked by an inconspicuous narrow band of latewood. Although classed as "non-resinous", resin cells are present and may appear as brown streaks or flecks. The cedar-like scent gradually fades in time. The wood weighs 450 kg/m^3 (28 lb/ft^3); specific gravity .45.

Mechanical properties: Although the timber is strong in relation to its weight, it has a poor steam bending classification due to knots, which appear scattered over its surface.

Seasoning: The timber dries easily with little degrade, and there is small movement in service.

Working properties: The wood works without difficulty with hand and machine tools with only a slight blunting effect on cutting edges, but the knots are troublesome. Straight grained material finishes cleanly, but disturbed grain tears and end grain breaks away at the tool exit and extra care should be taken by reducing the cutting angle. It nails, screws and glues well, and gives satisfactory results with the usual finishing treatments.

Durability: The timber has a high resistance to insect and fungal attack.

Uses: It is a strong, durable softwood used for structural work, especially suitable where the timber is in contact with the ground and for external work generally. Shipbuilding, farmhouse-style dining room furniture, linings for wardrobe doors and trunks.

Note: Related spp: *C. torulosa*, **Himalayan cypress**; *C. benthamii*, **Arizona cypress**.

DAHOMA (H)

Piptadeniastrum africanum, (Hook.f.) Brenan
syn. *Piptadenia africana*, Hook.f.
Family: *Leguminosae*

Commercial names: dahoma (UK and USA); dabéma (France, Germany, Italy).
Other names: banzu (Zaire); ekhimi, agboin (Nigeria); toum (Gabon); ka-bari (Sierra Leone); mpewere (Uganda); atui (Cameroon); dabéma (Ivory Coast).
Distribution: Tropical rain forests of West, Central and East Africa.
General description: The heartwood is a uniform yellow-orange to golden-brown. The wood is broadly interlocked with a coarse texture, but inclined to be woolly. Weighs from 560–780 kg/m^3 (35–48 lb/ft^3), average about 690 kg/m^3 (43 lb/ft^3); specific gravity .69.
Mechanical properties: This heavy density timber has medium bending strength, low stiffness and shock resistance, but high crushing strength; it has only a moderate bending classification as it is inclined to distort severely during steaming and bending operations. It is not possible to use in small sections, but selected pieces bend well.
Seasoning: Difficult to dry, some material has tendency to collapse and distort, and this cannot be removed by reconditioning treatment. It dries slowly and needs careful handling, especially thicker material. There is medium movement in service.
Working properties: The interlocked grain and fibrous texture affect machining. There is a moderate blunting effect in sawing and overheating in boring and mortising operations. Nailing is satisfactory if pre-bored and it glues and finishes well. Fine dust can cause irritation.
Durability: Sapwood is liable to attack by powder post beetle, it is moderately resistant to termites. The heartwood is durable and resistant to preservative treatment, and the sapwood moderately resistant.
Uses: Vehicle body building; building construction, heavy work benches, domestic flooring, door and window frames, naval and railway construction, fresh water piling. Should not be used in small sizes where strength is important, such as ladder rungs.
Note: The Ugandan name **mpewere** includes closely allied species *Newtonia buchanani*, Gilb.

DANTA (H)

Nesogordonia papaverifera, (A. Chév) Capuron
syn. *Cistanthera papaverifera*, (A. Chév).
Family: *Tiliaceae*

Commercial name: kotibé (Europe). **Other names:** otutu (Nigeria); kotibé (Ivory Coast); ovoué (Cameroon); olborbora (Gabon); eprou (Ghana); tsanya (Zaire).

Distribution: West Africa.

General description: Reddish-brown timber with lustrous surface similar to dark mahogany with an interlocked grain, a fine texture with a greasy feel when planed. Weighs 740 kg/m^3 (46 lb/ft^3); specific gravity .74. The appearance is sometimes marred by the presence of small sound pin knots and dark streaks of scar tissue.

Mechanical properties: Has a high bending strength and crushing strength, medium resistance to shock loads and a low stiffness factor. The sapwood is inclined to be brittle in bending, but the heartwood is generally suitable for bends of moderate curvature. A strong, elastic timber with properties similar to European ash, but weaker in resistance to impact.

Seasoning: Dries rather slowly but well, with little degrade. Over-rapid drying should be avoided as there is a tendency to warp and case harden with some ribbing of the surface, and knot splitting during kilning. There is medium movement in service.

Working properties: Interlocked grain affects machining operations and there is a moderate blunting of cutting edges. Pre-boring is advisable for nailing. It glues well and when stained and polished offers a good finish.

Durability: Liable to attack by powder post beetle and moderately resistant to termites in West Africa. The heartwood is durable and resistant to preservative treatment and the sapwood is moderately resistant. Moderately durable to marine borers.

Uses: Vehicle bodywork, furniture, cabinetmaking, shop fittings and flooring. Bench tops, tool handles, boat building and as an excellent turnery wood and an etching timber for graphic arts. Also used in plywood manufacture and as a decorative veneer.

DEGAME (H)

Calycophyllum candidissimum, DC.
Family: *Rubiaceae*

Other names: degame lancewood (UK); lemonwood (USA).

Distribution: Cuba, Central America, tropical South America.

General description: The wide sapwood is white to light brown in colour with a small light olive brown variegated heartwood. The grain varies from straight to very irregular, with an exceedingly fine and uniform texture.

Mechanical properties: It is a hard, heavy, tough and resilient timber with a very good bending classification, high bending and crushing strength and medium stiffness. Weighs 820 kg/m³ (51 lb/ft³); specific gravity .82.

Seasoning: Dries well with little degrade and small movement in service.

Working properties: It is not difficult to work, offering only slight blunting of cutting edges. Holds nails and screws well; glues, stains and polishes very well.

Durability: Non-durable; the heartwood is non-resistant to decay.

Uses: Excellent for carving. Used as an alternative to lancewood (*Oxandra lanceolata*) for turnery, tool handles, the top joints of fishing rods, archery bows, billiard cues, superior joinery and cabinet work.

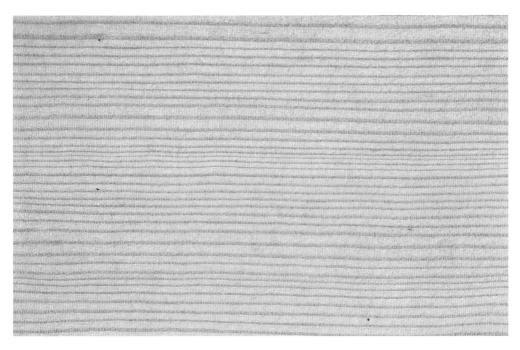

DOUGLAS FIR (S)

Pseudotsuga menziesii, (Mirb) Franco
syn. *P. taxifolia*, (Lamb) Britten ex Sudw.,
and *P. douglasii*, (Lind) Carr.
Family: *Pinaceae*

Other names: British Columbian pine, Columbian pine (UK); Oregon pine (USA).

Distribution: USA and Canada. Also planted in the UK, New Zealand and Australia.

General description: The heartwood is a light reddish-brown shade, and the contrast between earlywood and latewood provides a prominent growth ring figure which shows as an abrupt colour contrast on plain sawn timber and rotary cut veneers. The wood is straight grained but sometimes with wavy or spiral grain and with a uniform medium texture. Weight 530 kg/m³ (33 lb/ft³); specific gravity .53.

Mechanical properties: Timber from Pacific coastal districts is heavier, harder and stronger than from mountain areas, the latter being equivalent to timber from the UK. It has high stiffness and crushing strength, medium resistance to shock loads and high bending strength.

Seasoning: The timber dries rapidly and well without much checking or warping, but knots tend to split and loosen. There is small movement in service. Resin canals tend to bleed and show as narrow brown lines on longitudinal surfaces.

Working properties: The wood works readily with hand and machine tools, but with a blunting effect on cutters which must be kept sharp. Hard, loose knots can be troublesome. Pre-bore for nailing; screws and glues satisfactorily. It stains effectively and finishes well following preparation. Material with high resin content should be kiln dried for varnished or painted interior surfaces.

Durability: Moderately durable, but subject to attack by pinhole borer, longhorn beetle and jewel beetle. Resistant to preservative treatment, especially American mountain-grown timber.

Uses: More veneer and plywood are produced from this species than any other timber. Also for heavy construction work, laminated arches and roof trusses, interior and exterior joinery, poles, piles, paper pulp, vats and tanks. Dock and harbour work, marine piling, ship building, mining timber, railway sleepers, slack and tight cooperage. **Note:** Not a true fir.

EAST AFRICAN CAMPHORWOOD (H)

Ocotea usambarensis, Engl.
Family: *Lauraceae*

Other names: camphor, muzaiti, muura, munganga, mutunguru.

Distribution: Kenya and Tanzania.

General description: The timber darkens on exposure to deep brown, and although it has a distinct scent of camphor, it should not be confused with Borneo or Sabah true camphorwood. Straight to interlocked grain, producing an attractive striped figure when quartercut. The texture is moderately fine and even. Weight varies from 510–640 kg/m³ (32–40 lb/ft³), average 590 kg/m³ (36 lb/ft³); specific gravity .59.

Mechanical properties: This medium density wood has only moderate bending qualities as it tends to distort and is intolerant of pin knots. For its weight, it has extremely good strength properties. It has low stiffness and resistance to shock loads, and medium crushing strength.

Seasoning: Needs care in air drying to avoid warping and twisting if the process is too rapid. Kilning can be carried out slowly and with little degrade, and only small movement in service.

Working properties: Works easily with both hand and machine tools, but needs care in planing or moulding quarter sawn surfaces due to interlocked grain. There is a slight blunting effect on cutting edges. The wood nails, screws and glues satisfactorily, stains easily and can be brought to a very good finish. Selection of straight grained timber is essential as many logs are ill-shaped with twisted grain and large logs may have rotten cores.

Durability: Resistant to insect attack and extremely resistant to preservative treatment, but the sapwood is permeable. A very durable wood.

Uses: Furniture, interior and exterior joinery, flooring, panelling, vehicle building, cabinet work. It should not be used for kitchens because of the camphor-like odour.

EBONY, AFRICAN (H)

Diospyrus crassiflora, Hiern.
D. piscatoria, Gürke.
Family: *Ebenaceae*

Other names: Cameroon ebony, Kribi ebony, Gabon ebony, Madagascar ebony, Nigerian ebony, etc., according to country of origin (UK).

Distribution: Limited range in Southern Nigeria, Ghana, Cameroon and Zaire.

General description: Marketed in Great Britain as short billets of heartwood only. Some billets have an uneven grey to black colour with black stripes, but selected billets are jet black. The grain is straight to slightly interlocked and the texture is very fine. *D. crassiflora* is believed to be the blackest wood that grows. Weight from 1,000–1,030 kg/m³ (63–64 lb/ft³); s.g. 1.03.

Mechanical properties: This very heavy density timber has a good steam bending classification and very high bending and crushing strength, with high stiffness and resistance to shock loads.

Seasoning: The billets dry fairly rapidly and well with little degrade and with small movement in service.

Working properties: This is a very hard wood to work with either hand or machine tools, with severe blunting effect on cutting edges. In planing, a reduced angle of 20° is required when irregular grain is present, with an increase in pressure bar and shoe pressures advised to prevent the wood from riding or chattering on cutters. Pre-boring is necessary for nailing and screwing, gluing is good, and it can be polished to an excellent finish.

Durability: Very durable. *D. crassiflora* highly resistant to termites and *D. piscatoria* moderately resistant, and both species extremely resistant to preservative treatment.

Uses: Tool, cutlery and knife handles, door knobs, butt ends of billiard cues, facings of tee squares, piano and organ keys, organ stops, violin finger boards and pegs, parts of bagpipes and other musical instruments, turnery, brush backs and fancy articles; inlaid work, inlay lines and stringings. It is occasionally available as a sawcut veneer for the repair of antiques.

EBONY, MACASSAR (H)

Diospyros celebica, Bakh.
syn. *Diospyros macassar*, A. Chév.
Family: *Ebenaceae*

Commercial names: Macassar ebony, Indian ebony (UK and USA); coromandel, calamander wood (UK). **Other names:** tendu, temru, tunki, timbruni (India and Celebes).

Distribution: The Celebes Islands.

General description: The heartwood is dark brown to black, streaked throughout with bands of greyish-brown, yellow-brown or pale-brown. The grain is mostly straight, but may sometimes be irregular or wavy. The texture is fine and even. Weight about 1090 kg/m^3 (68 lb/ft^3); specific gravity 1.09.

Mechanical properties: This is an exceptionally heavy, dense, hard wood. The black heart tends to be brittle, and this species is used mostly for decorative purposes, where strength properties are of minor importance.

Seasoning: The timber is difficult to dry. The trees are usually girdled for two years before felling, and a further six months air drying in plank or scantling and stored under cover. It should be well protected against too rapid drying to avoid checking and degradation. There is very small movement in service.

Working properties: The material is hard to work with hand or machine tools as the wood is of a brittle nature. There is severe blunting of cutting edges. Pre-boring is necessary for nailing and it is difficult to glue. The wood takes an excellent finish.

Durability: Liable to attack by forest longhorn beetle and moderately resistant to termites. The wood is very durable and extremely resistant to preservation treatment.

Uses: Selected pieces are used for cabinet work, brush backs, walking sticks, and sapwood used for tool handles, etc. Also used for snuff boxes, musical instruments, inlay work, billiard cues and excellent for turnery. Also sliced for highly decorative veneers.

Note: Related spp. include: *Diospyros ebenum*, Koen, from Sri Lanka, "true" ebony, *D. tomentosa*, Roxb., and *D. melanoxylon*, Roxb., from India, *D. marmorata*, Park, from Andaman Islands

EKKI (H)

Lophira alata, Banks ex Gaertn.f.
Family: *Ochnaceae*

Other names: kaku (Ghana); azobé (UK and Ivory Coast); bangassi (Cameroon); akoura (Gabon); eba (Nigeria); hendui (Sierra Leone); red ironwood (USA).

Distribution: Tropical West Africa.

General description: Dark red to deep chocolate-brown with conspicuous white deposits in the pores giving a speckled appearance. Grain is usually interlocked, and the texture coarse and uneven. Weight 950–1120 kg/m^3 (59–70 lb/ft^3), averaging 1025 kg/m^3 (64 lb/ft^3); s.g. 1.02.

Mechanical properties: This exceptionally heavy density wood, has very high bending and crushing strength, and high stiffness and resistance to shock loads. It is probably too tough for steam bending.

Seasoning: It is extremely refractory and dries very slowly with severe splitting and possible distortion, notably surface checking and end splitting. Should be piled very carefully. Large movement in service.

Working properties: Very difficult to work with hand tools but possible with machine tools. The blunting of cutters is severe. For planing, a strong cutting edge is required with sharpness angle 40–45° obtained by reducing the clearance angle or cutting angle or both. The timber must be held very firmly to prevent chatter. Tends to char in boring, and pre-boring is necessary for nailing. Glues satisfactorily and can be stained and polished normally.

Durability: Ekki is very durable and very resistant to decay; it is one of Africa's most durable woods. Moderately resistant to attack by termites in Africa and extremely resistant to preservative treatment.

Uses: Suitable for heavy construction, all marine work, wharves, bridge building and decking, railway sleepers, very heavy duty flooring. Also for rollers, wagon work and superior joinery. Its acid resistance makes it ideal for filter press plates and frames. A wider range of uses is limited by the difficulty of machining.

ELM, AMERICAN WHITE (H)

Ulmus americana, L.
Family: *Ulmaceae*

Other names: American elm (in part) (Canada and USA); soft elm, water elm, swamp elm (USA); orhamwood (Canada).

Distribution: Canada and USA.

General description: The heartwood is medium reddish-brown in colour. The grain is usually straight but sometimes interlocked, the texture coarse and rather woolly. Weight about 560 kg/m^3 (35 lb/ft^3); specific gravity .56.

Mechanical properties: The wood has medium density, and medium bending and crushing strengths, very low stiffness and high resistance to shock loads. It has a very good steam bending classification.

Seasoning: Dries readily with medium degrade and movement in service.

Working properties: It is fairly easy to work if cutting edges are kept sharp, and there is a moderate blunting effect on tools. Nails and screws well, and takes glue, stain and polish.

Durability: Trees and logs are liable to attack by forest longhorn beetle and the heartwood is non-durable. The heartwood is moderately resistant to preservative treatment but the sapwood is permeable.

Uses: It is used in boat and shipbuilding for keels, gunwales, bilge stringers, and in dock and harbour work for fenders and rubbing strips. Agricultural implements, chair rockers, gymnasium equipment, vehicle body work, ladder rungs, sleigh runners, staves and hoops for slack cooperage, coffins, church pews, furniture and chairs, cheese boxes. It is sometimes rotary cut for plywood manufacture, and sliced into decorative veneers for panelling, cabinets and furniture. Generally, white elm is used for many of the same purposes as rock elm, provided that slightly lower strength properties are taken into account.

Note: Related spp. *U. fulva*, Michx., producing **slippery elm** and botanically associated spp. *Celtis occidentalis* L., producing **hackberry**, (Eastern USA) are marketed with white elm.

ELM, DUTCH AND ENGLISH (H)

(1) *Ulmus hollandica*, Mill.
var. *hollandica*.
(2) *Ulmus procera*, Salisb., (*U. campestris* Auct. angl.)
Family: *Ulmaceae*

Commercial names: (1) Dutch elm (2) English elm. **Other names:** (1) cork bark elm (UK); (2) red elm, nave elm (UK); (1–2) orme (France); iep (Netherlands); ulme (Germany).
Distribution: (1) Europe and the UK. (2) Mainly in England and Wales.
General description: The heartwood colour is a dull brown, with the annual rings distinct due to large earlywood pores, giving a coarse texture to the wood. Tends to be of irregular growth and crossgrained. Dutch elm is usually of a more even growth and straighter grained than English elm. Average weight 550 kg/m³ (34 lb/ft³); specific gravity .55.
Mechanical properties: Both are of medium density with low bending and crushing strengths, very low stiffness and resistance to shock loads. (1) is 40% tougher than (2). Dutch elm has very good steam bending properties but English elm has a tendency to distort during setting.
Seasoning: Both dry fairly rapidly with a very great possibility of distortion and a liability for collapse to occur. The pile should have closely spaced sticks and be heavily weighted. The degrade can be reduced by reconditioning. There is medium movement in service.
Working properties: Not an easy timber to work as it tends to bind on the saw and pick up in planing and moulding. There is a moderate blunting effect on tools which should be kept sharp. (1) provides a better finish than (2) owing to a milder grain. They accept nails and screws without splitting; gluing is good, and the material stains and polishes or waxes to a high finish.
Durability: The timber is non-durable and subject to insect attack; it is moderately resistant to preservative treatment, but the sapwood is permeable.
Uses: Cabinet work, chairs and settee frames, Windsor chairs, turnery, bentwood backs, and for domestic flooring. It is extensively used for coffin making, boat building, dock and harbour work, weatherboarding. Selected logs are sliced for decorative veneers.
Note: Related spp. include: *U. laciniata*, Mayr., and *U. davidiana*, Planch, var. *U. japonica* (Rehd) Nakai, **Japanese elm**. *U. glabra*, Huds. non Mill, **wych elm**.

ELM, ROCK (H)   *Ulmus thomasii*, Sarg. (*U. racemosa*, Thom)
Family: *Ulmaceae*

Other names: Canadian rock elm, cork elm (Canada and UK); cork bark elm, hickory elm (USA).

Distribution: Eastern Canada and USA.

General description: The heartwood colour is light brown, with a straight grain and moderately fine texture – the finest textured wood of all the elms. It weighs from 620–780 kg/m³ (39–49 lb/ft³) averaging at about 700 kg/m³ (43 lb/ft³); specific gravity .70.

Mechanical properties: A heavy density timber with medium bending and crushing strengths, very low stiffness but very high resistance to shock loads. It has very good steam bending properties. The earlywood pores of rock elm can hardly be seen without a lens on end grain surfaces, whereas other elms are quite distinct.

Seasoning: Requires care in drying as it tends to check and twist. It kilns rather well with little degrade. There is medium movement in service.

Working properties: Rock elm is denser and therefore more difficult to machine than other elms. It has a moderate blunting effect on cutters and tends to burn with all saws, and char in boring, cross cutting or mortising. It can be nailed, screwed, glued satisfactorily, and stained and polished to a very good finish.

Durability: Non-durable. The sapwood is liable to attack by powder post beetle and the heartwood is resistant to preservative treatment.

Uses: Rock elm has outstanding toughness and resistance to shock loads, making it suitable for many boat building purposes, such as stern posts, ribs, general framing, keels, rubbing strips, especially those which are submerged in water. Also for wheel hubs, chair rockers, gymnasium equipment, agricultural implements, vehicle body work, ladder rungs, sleigh runners, etc. Under water parts for dock and wharf construction. Selected stock sliced for decorative veneers.

ELM, SMOOTH LEAVED (H)

Ulmus carpinifolia, Gled.
syn. *U. nitens*, Moench
U. foliacea, Gilib.
Family: *Ulmaceae*

Commercial names: French elm, Flemish elm, common elm.
Distribution: Europe and the UK.
General description: The heartwood is a dull reddish-brown colour, relatively straight grained, with some tendency to cross grain due to irregular growth rings and large earlywood pores which give a coarse texture. Weight 580 kg/m³ (36 lb/ft³); specific gravity .58.
Mechanical properties: This medium density wood has low bending and crushing strengths, with very low stiffness and resistance to shock loads. It has a very good steam bending classification but is intolerant of pin knots and is inclined to warp during the setting process.
Seasoning: Dries rapidly with a marked tendency to distort or collapse in thick sizes. Degrade can be reduced by kiln reconditioning. There is medium movement in service.
Working properties: Reasonably easy to work with hand and machine tools but with a moderate blunting effect on cutters. Nailing, gluing, staining and polishing are satisfactory.
Durability: Non-durable and liable to insect attack. Moderately resistant to preservative treatment, but the sapwood is permeable.
Uses: Furniture and cabinets, chairs and settee frames, turnery, salad bowls, etc., domestic block flooring, coffin making and boat building. When treated it is used for dock and harbour work for keel blocks, cappings, etc. Selected logs are sliced for decorative veneers.
Note: Related spp. include **wych elm**, *Ulmus glabra*, Huds. non Mill. (*U. montana*, Stokes). Other names: mountain elm, Scotch elm, white elm; grows in the UK.

ESIA (H)   *Combretodendron macrocarpum*, (P. Beauv) Keay
syn. *C. africanum*, Exell.
Family: *Lecythidaceae*

Commercial names: abalé (Italy); essia (France and Germany);
Other names: owewe (Nigeria); abalé (Ivory Coast); minzu (Congo and Zaire); abine (Gabon); abing (Cameroon).
Distribution: Tropical West Africa.
General description: The heartwood is reddish-brown with darker veins or streaks giving the wood a speckled appearance. The grain tends to be interlocked and the texture moderately coarse. Weight 800 kg/m³ (50 lb/ft³); specific gravity .80.
Mechanical properties: This very heavy, dense hardwood has high bending strength and crushing strength, medium stiffness and resistance to shock loads, and therefore a very poor bending classification.
Seasoning: The material dries slowly with strong tendency to check and split. Distortion, end splitting, surface checking and serious shakes are likely to occur. It is impracticable to kiln dry and air drying must be very slowly and carefully undertaken. Large movement in service.
Working properties: The wood has a high resistance to tools and a moderate blunting effect on cutting edges causing overheating of saws, and thicker gauge saws are recommended. In planing, a reduced cutting angle of 20° will prevent tearing. When filled, the wood stains and polishes satisfactorily.
Durability: The wood is moderately resistant to termites in Africa. The heartwood is durable and extremely resistant to preservative treatment although the sapwood is permeable.
Uses: Because of the serious degrade which occurs in drying, this abundant species is used mainly for heavy, rough construction work, railway sleepers, etc., in the countries of origin. It is also employed for mining timber, agricultural implements and marine piling. However, selected logs are sliced to produce a most attractive decorative veneer with a conspicuous ray figure which is used for panelling.

ETIMOÉ (H)

Copaifera salikounda, Heck.
Family: *Leguminosae*

Other names: olumni (Gabon); allihia, nomatou (Ivory Coast); entedua (Ghana); buini, gum copal, salikunda (Sierra Leone).

Distribution: West Africa.

General description: The colour of the heartwood varies from light reddish-brown to grey-brown with a pinkish hue, often veined with a reddish stripe. The grain is straight to interlocked and the texture is fine and even. Weight range varies from 750–800 kg/m³ (46–50 lb/ft³), average about 770 kg/m³ (48 lb/ft³); specific gravity .77.

Mechanical properties: This hard, very strong and resilient timber has medium bending and crushing strength, low stiffness and resistance to shock loads. It has a moderate steam bending classification, due to exudation of resin during the steaming process.

Seasoning: Dries rather slowly but well with minimum degrade. There is small movement in service.

Working properties: The timber works fairly easily with both hand and machine tools with only a moderate blunting effect on cutting edges. A reduction of the cutting angle to 20° when planing or moulding quartered stock is advised. Pre-boring necessary when nailing close to the edges, but holds screws well; glues well and stains and polishes to a good finish.

Durability: Moderately durable; subject to attack by powder post beetle but has a high natural resistance to decay. Resistant to preservative treatment.

Uses: Suitable for flooring, ship and boat building, vehicle bodies, joinery, turnery, heavy construction. Selected material used for furniture making and sliced for decorative veneers for panelling, cabinets and furniture.

FIR, JAPANESE (S)

Abies mariesii, Mast.
Family: *Pinaceae*

Other name: todo matsu (Japan).
Distribution: Japan.
General description: The heartwood is a pale buff-reddish colour, rather darker in colour than most species of true fir due to darker latewood bands, and is coarser in texture than spruce. Usually straight grained. It weighs 420 kg/m^3 (26 lb/ft^3); specific gravity .42.
Mechanical properties: The timber has medium bending and crushing strengths, with low stiffness and resistance to shock loads and a poor steam bending classification.
Seasoning: Dries well with little degrade.
Working properties: Works easily with hand or machine tools with little blunting effect on cutters. Sharp cutting edges are necessary to avoid tearing. Knots are liable to fall out in machining processes. The material finishes cleanly. It nails well, stains easily and gives good results with paint, varnish or polish.
Durability: Non-durable. Damage by pinhole borer is possible. Resistant to preservative treatment.
Uses: Suitable for building, interior finishing, general carpentry and box making.
Note: Often sold mixed with yezo-matsu, **Japanese spruce** and used for similar purposes.

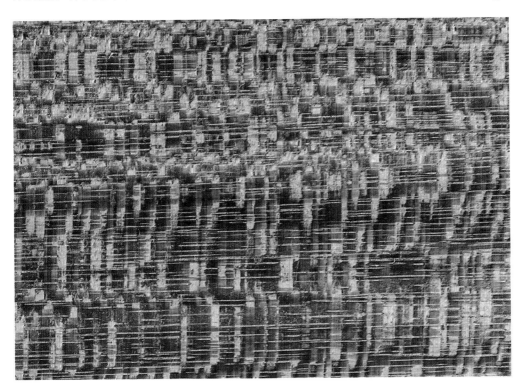

FREIJO (H)

Cordia goeldiana, Hub.
Family: *Boraginaceae*

Other names: frei jorge (Brazil); cordia wood, jenny wood (USA).

Distribution: Brazil, mainly in the Amazon basin.

General description: The heartwood is golden brown to dark brown, similar to teak, and on quartered surfaces the rays produce a lighter figure than the background tissues. It is straight grained, and the texture medium and uniform and of medium density. The weight varies from 400–700 kg/m³ (25–44 lb/ft³) but averages 590 kg/m³ (37 lb/ft³); specific gravity .59.

Note: The example illustrated is quarter sawn.

Mechanical properties: Medium strength properties in all categories, but has a poor steam bending classification, although bends of a moderate radius of curvature are possible with selected wood and used for cooperage in Brazil.

Seasoning: Dries readily and well with little distortion and only a slight tendency for end splitting. There is small movement in service.

Working properties: Works easily with hand and machine tools, but with a moderate blunting effect on cutting edges which must be kept sharp to avoid tearing the grain during planing or moulding. It requires support in end grain working, mortising, boring, etc., to prevent breaking away. Nailing and screwing are satisfactory and the material glues, stains and polishes well if the grain is well filled.

Durability: Freijo is durable. The sapwood is liable to attack by powder post beetle and the heartwood is resistant to preservative treatment.

Uses: Suitable for panelling, cabinets, furniture and fitments, boat building, decking, vehicle manufacture, interior and exterior joinery, and cooperage. Selected logs sliced for decorative veneers.

FUSTIC (H)

Chlorophora tinctoria, Gaud
Family: *Moraceae*

Other names: moral, moral fino (Ecuador); yellowwood (West Indies); tatajuba (Brazil)*

Distribution: West Indies and Tropical and South America.

General description: This wood was originally a source for dyestuffs in addition to its use as commercial timber. The heartwood is a golden yellow, sometimes with darker streaks, which matures after seasoning to a russet brown colour. It is usually straight grained to interlocked, with a moderately coarse texture. Weight about 880–960 kg/m^3 (55–60 lb/ft^3); specific gravity .92.

Mechanical properties: The wood has medium bending and crushing strengths, medium resistance to shock loads, and stiffness. It has a poor steam bending classification as the dye is soluble in water and will stain badly.

Seasoning: The timber dries slowly with very little degrade and there is small movement in service.

Working properties: It works well with hand or machine tools, with only a slight blunting effect on cutting edges, and may be nailed, screwed, glued, stained and polished to a high lustrous finish.

Durability: The wood is durable and very resistant to decay and preservation treatment.

Uses: Carpentry and heavy construction for civil and marine purposes, wheelwright's work and boat building; selected logs are sliced for veneers.

Note: The name **tatajuba** is used in Brazil for **fustic**, and also for species of *Clarisia*. It should not be confused with *Bagassa guianensis* Aubl., and *B. tiliaefolia* (Desv.) R. Ben, from the same family. (See tatajuba).

GABOON (H)

Aucoumea klaineana, Pierre.
Family: *Burseraceae*

Commercial names: okoume (France); gaboon (UK); combogala (Congo).

Other names: angouma (Gabon); mofoumou, n'goumi (Equatorial Guinea).

Distribution: Equatorial Guinea, Gabon and the Congo Republic.

General description: The heartwood is light pinkish-brown. The grain is straight to shallowly interlocked or slightly wavy, of medium texture which is uniform and even. The weight varies from 370–560 kg/m³ (23–35 lb/ft³) but averaging 430 kg/m³ (27 lb/ft³); specific gravity .43.

Mechanical properties: It is a weak, light density timber with a poor wood bending classification, low bending strength, very low stiffness, and medium crushing strength.

Seasoning: The wood dries rapidly and well with little degrade in either air or kiln drying. Medium movement in service.

Working properties: The timber contains silica and causes a moderate to severe blunting effect on tools. It works fairly easily with hand or machine tools, but is inclined to be woolly and cutting edges must be kept sharp. A reduced angle of 20° is necessary for planing to prevent tearing. The wood nails satisfactorily and glues well, and stains and polishes to a lustrous surface.

Durability: Logs are liable to attack by forest longhorn beetle and sapwood by powder post beetle. The heartwood is non-durable to marine borers. It is resistant to preservative treatment.

Uses: Gaboon is used extensively for the manufacture of plywood, blockboard and laminboard. It is usually rotary cut for laminated work, but selected logs are sliced into mottled and striped decorative veneers for cabinets and panelling. Solid timber is used for interior frame construction, sports goods, cigar boxes, packing cases, and as a substitute for mahogany in furniture making for edge lipping, facings, mouldings, etc.

GEDU NOHOR (H)

Entandrophragma angolense, (Welw.) C. DC.
including:
E. macrophyllm, A. Chév., *E. dolicarpum*, Harms.,
E. acuminata, Pellegr., *E. lucens*, Hoyle.
Family: *Meliaceae*

Other names: edinam (UK and Ghana); tiama (France, Ivory Coast); kalungi (Belgium, Zaire); gedu lohor, gedu noha (Nigeria); edoussie (Cameroon).

Distribution: West, Central and East Africa.

General description: Plain, dull reddish-brown, but occasional logs are pinkish-brown. Regularly interlocked grain with a medium-coarse texture. The surface is lustrous. The weight is about 540 kg/m³ (34 lb/ft³); specific gravity .54.

Mechanical properties: This medium density wood has a low bending strength and resistance to shock loads; very low stiffness and medium crushing strength and the steam bending classification is poor.

Seasoning: The timber dries fairly rapidly with a marked tendency to distort and must be carried out slowly to avoid checking etc. There is only small movement in service.

Working properties: The wood works easily with both hand and machine tools but tends to tear during planing and moulding due to the interlocked grain unless the cutting angle is reduced to 15°. It has a moderate blunting effect on cutting edges and a tendency to char in mortising. Nailing and screwing are satisfactory and it stains and finishes well.

Durability: The sapwood is liable to attack by powder post beetle, and the logs are non-resistant to termites in West Africa. The heartwood is moderately durable. The sapwood is resistant and the heartwood extremely resistant to preservative treatment.

Uses: The timber is related to sapele, but of plainer appearance and used for similar purposes in furniture manufacturing. Also for interior and exterior joinery, shop and office fitting and flooring. In boatbuilding for planking, cabins and ship's furniture; vehicle building, railway carriage construction and for coffins. Plain rotary cut veneers used for plywood manufacture, and sliced decorative veneers for panelling and furniture.

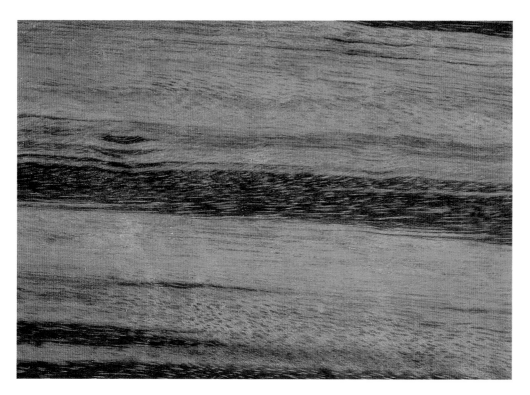

GONÇALO ALVES (H)

Astronium fraxinifolium, Schott.
and *A. graveolens*, Jacq.
Family: *Anacardiaceae*

Commercial names: zebrawood (UK); tigerwood (USA). **Other names:** *A. fraxinifolium*: urunday-para, mura, bois de zebre; *A. graveolens*: chibatao, guarita, urunday, aderno.
Distribution: Brazil.
General description: The timber is reddish-brown in colour, richly mottled and with dark brown streaks and spots similar to rosewood. It has an irregular, interlocked grain, with alternating layers of hard and soft material. The wood is of medium texture, and weighs 950 kg/m^3 (59 lb/ft^3) when dry; specific gravity .95.
Mechanical properties: This hard, heavy, dense wood is strong in all categories and is not used for steam bending.
Seasoning: It is a difficult timber to dry, with a distinct tendency to warp and check and should be air dried slowly. There is small movement in service.
Working properties: The timber is rather difficult to work, with a moderate to severe blunting effect on tools which should be kept sharp. The contrasting layers of hard and soft material together with irregular or interlocked grain requires a reduced cutting angle of 15° for best results. Pre-boring necessary for nailing, but it holds screws well, glues easily and finishes with a high natural polish.
Durability: Not subject to beetle attack, and highly durable. Extremely resistant to preservative treatment.
Uses: High-class furniture and cabinetmaking, excellent for turnery, fancy goods and decorative work. Sliced veneers are used for architectural panelling and face veneering.
Note: *A. graveolens*, is usually straight grained, of medium texture, and slightly plainer than *A. fraxinifolium*; weighs 897 kg/m^3 (56 lb/ft^3), and is used for general construction, exterior joinery and turnery.

GREENHEART (H)

Ocotea rodiaei, Mez.
Family: *Lauraceae*

Other names: demerara greenheart (Guyana); black, brown, yellow and white greenheart.

Distribution: Principally Guyana; also Surinam and Venezuela.

General description: This evergreen tree varies considerably in colour, from yellow-green, golden yellow, light olive, dark olive, yellow-brown, dark brown to black. Decayed or defective logs have a yellow colour. The grain is straight to interlocked or roey. The texture fine and even, lustrous and cold to the touch. Weight 1030 kg/m³ (64 lb/ft³); specific gravity 1.03.

Mechanical properties: Exceptionally heavy density, and very high bending and crushing strengths; very high stiffness and high resistance to shock loads. It has a moderate steam bending classification although requiring extra efficient support on the outer face.

Seasoning: Dries very slowly with considerable degrade with checking and end splitting. Boards over 1″ (25 mm) thickness should be partly air dried before kilning. Existing shakes liable to extend and splitting of knots may occur. Medium movement in service.

Working properties: Difficult to work and with moderate blunting effect on cutters, but a fine, smooth lustrous surface can be obtained. A cutting angle of 20° is necessary in planing operations owing to the high density of the wood and interlocked grain; cross or end grain material may break out or splinter and these splinters are poisonous. It requires pre-boring for nailing and gluing results are variable. Staining is rarely necessary but the wood polishes to a good finish. Its low acid content provides a very low corrosive effect on nails, spikes or metal fastenings.

Durability: Very durable. Excellent resistance to marine borers. Sapwood liable to attack by pinhole borers, but the heartwood is immune. Extremely resistant to preservative treatment.

Uses: Suitable for all marine construction work including ship construction. Also for bridges, heavy duty flooring, chemical vats, billiard cue butts, turnery, fishing rods, longbows etc.

GUAREA (H)

(1) *Guarea cedrata*, Pellgr.
(2) *G. thompsonii*, Sprauge and Hutch.
Family: *Meliaceae*

Commercial names: (1) white guarea, obobonufua (Nigeria); scented guarea (UK); (2) black guarea, obobonekwi (Nigeria). **Other names:** obobo (Nigeria); bossé (France and Ivory Coast); diambi (Zaire); ebanghemwa (Cameroon); divuiti (Gabon).
Distribution: Tropical West Africa.
General description: (1) The heartwood is a pale pinkish-brown mahogany colour, with a fine texture and cedar-like scent. (2) Similar colour but darkens to a better mahogany colour. Straight grained and of silky appearance. The texture is even, compact and quite fine. Both have straight to interlocked grain but (1) produces a mottled or curly figure and (2) is straighter in grain and plainer in figure. (1) weighs 580 kg/m³ (36 lb/ft³) and (2) weighs 620 kg/m³ (39 lb/ft³); specific gravity .58 and .62 respectively.
Mechanical properties: Both types are of medium density and low resistance to shock loads. The steam bending classification of (1) is good, but it cannot be bent successfully if small knots are present, (2) is inclined to distort during setting and has only a moderate classification.
Seasoning: Both types dry fairly rapidly with little tendency to warp. Kiln drying requires care to avoid resin exudation and (2) requires greater care as it is liable to split. There is small movement in service.
Working properties: Moderate blunting effect on cutters. Nailing: (1) satisfactory, and (2) pre-boring required. Resin deposits can make gluing difficult but with care gluing properties are good. When finishing, care is needed to avoid resin exudation in warm atmospheres, but otherwise good. Fine dust can cause irritation.
Durability: Very durable timbers; extremely resistant to preservative treatment, although the sapwood is permeable.
Uses: Furniture, cabinetmaking, sports goods, shop fitting, boat building, high-class joinery and vehicle construction; marine piling in non-teredo waters. Rotary cut for plywood manufacture, and sliced for decorative veneering.

GUM, AMERICAN RED (H)

Liquidambar styraciflua, L.
Family: *Hamamelidaceae*

Commercial names: Note: heartwood marketed separately from sapwood. **Heartwood**: gum, sweet gum, bilsted (USA); satin walnut* (UK). **Sapwood**: sap gum (USA); hazel pine (UK).
Distribution: USA.
General description: The sapwood is wide and creamy white in colour. The well-defined heartwood varies from pinkish-brown to deep red brown, often with darker streaks with a mottled or marbled appearance and with a satiny lustre. It has a fine, even, uniform texture, and the grain is generally irregular. Weight 560 kg/m^3 (35 lb/ft^3); specific gravity .56.
Mechanical properties: The wood has a very low steam bending classification, but with medium strength in all categories.
Seasoning: The timber dries rapidly with a strong tendency to warp and twist. It requires great care in drying to avoid degradation. It is very susceptible to atmospheric changes when in use and tends to shrink, swell, twist or split, often to excess, but quarter sawn boards are less liable to distort in service.
Working properties: The wood is easy to work with both hand and machine tools with only slight resistance to cutting edges. It nails, screws and glues well, takes stain easily and can be brought to a smooth excellent finish.
Durability: Non-durable and subject to insect attack. The heartwood is moderately resistant to preservative treatment but the sapwood is permeable.
Uses: Widely used in the USA for cheaper furniture, doors, interior trim, joinery, and for plywood manufacture, boxes, crates, chip baskets, and small laminated items. Sliced veneers are used for wall panelling and decorative veneering. It is also a source of storax or styrax, a pathological balsam product formed in the bark by wound stimulation.
Note: The name satin walnut used in the UK is misleading and should be discontinued.

GUM, RED RIVER (H)

Eucalyptus camaldulensis, Dehnh.
syn. *E. rostrata*, Schlecht.
Family: *Myrtaceae*

Commercial names: Murray red gum, Queensland blue gum, red gum.
Distribution: Australia.
General description: The heartwood colour varies according to location and age, from pink to red. The grain is interlocked and frequently wavy which produces a fiddleback figure when quarter cut. The texture is close and even. The wood is resinous with frequent gum pockets. The surface is often distinctly mottled. Weight 825 kg/m³ (51 lb/ft³); specific gravity .82.
Mechanical properties: The timber has excellent strength properties but is not used for steam bending due to the exudation of gum.
Seasoning: Dries well, but care should be taken to avoid longitudinal shrinkage during seasoning, and gum pockets causing distortion or degrade. There is small movement in service.
Working properties: The wood is difficult to work with both hand and machine tools due to the presence of gum. The interlocked grain requires a reduced cutting angle of 20° to prevent tear out, and cutting edges have to be kept very sharp. The wood should be pre-bored for nailing; it holds screws well but is rather difficult to glue without treatment. Can be brought to a good finish.
Durability: It is very durable with a natural high resistance to termites and marine borers and extremely resistant to preservative treatment, but the sapwood is permeable.
Uses: Piling, shipbuilding, mining timbers, constructional purposes, weatherboards. Ideal for flooring, paving blocks, and stair treads and for constructions which remain in water or damp soil for long periods. Sliced quartered veneers are used for panelling and decorative veneering.

GUANACASTE (H)

Enterolobium cyclocarpum
Family: *Mimosaceae*

Other names: jenisero, parota, kelobra, rain tree.

Distribution: Guatemala, British Honduras and Mexico.

General description: The heartwood is walnut brown with darker variegated streaks, with a greenish cast. Straight and roey grain, sometimes interlocked. Texture is medium to coarse and rather lustrous. Vessel lines prominently visible on longitudinal surfaces. Weight is 520–600 kg/m^3 (32–37 lb/ft^3); specific gravity .55.

Mechanical properties: This material has low strength in all categories and a poor bending classification.

Seasoning: Air seasons rapidly with little tendency to warp or split. Small movement in service.

Working properties: Works easily with hand or machine tools and finishes smoothly. Saws readily and planes well even on interlocked grain on quartered surfaces. There is a moderate blunting effect on cutting edges. Nailing and screwing properties are good; glues, stains and polishes very well. Sawdust has an unpleasant odour and may cause skin irritation.

Durability: Perishable. Heartwood resistant to termites, but susceptible to pinhole borers. Although very durable in fresh water the timber is permeable for preservative treatment.

Uses: Furniture and cabinet work, ship and boat building, interior trim, blockboard, joinery, draining boards, food containers, pattern making. Veneers for plywood, and sliced veneers, especially crotches and swirls for decorative veneering.

HACKBERRY (H)

Celtis occidentalis, L.
Family: *Ulmaceae*

Other names: sugarberry, bastard elm, hack-tree, hoop ash, nettletree (USA).

Distribution: Southern Canada and Eastern USA.

General description: There is little difference between the sapwood and heartwood which is yellow-grey to light brown with yellow streaks. It is subject to blue sap stain. It has irregular grain, occasionally straight and sometimes interlocked; distinct rays, with a fairly fine and uniform texture, and rather fissile. Weighs 640 kg/m³ (40 lb/ft³); specific gravity .64.

Mechanical properties: Has good elastic and shock resisting properties, medium bending and crushing strengths, very low stiffness and a very good steam bending classification.

Seasoning: Dries readily with little degrade and with medium movement in service.

Working properties: Cutting edges should be kept sharpened to overcome a moderate blunting effect on tools, but the material works well with hand and machine tools. A reduction to 20° is necessary when planing interlocked grain. It nails and screws well, glues, stains and polishes satisfactorily.

Durability: Non-durable; liable to attack by forest longhorn and Buprestid beetle. Moderately resistant to preservative treatment, but the sapwood is permeable.

Uses: Furniture, cooperage, vehicle bodies, sports and gymnasium equipment. (Hackberry is often marketed with white and slippery elm and shares similar uses). Rotary cut for plywood manufacture and selected logs sliced for decorative veneer.

Note: Closely related is **African celtis** known as esa (Ghana); ita, ohia (Nigeria); principally: *Celtis adolfi-friderici*, Engl., *C. mildbraedii*, Engl., *C. zenkeri*, Engl. (*C. soyauxii*, Engl.)

HEMLOCK, JAPANESE (S)

(1) *Tsuga sieboldii*, Carr
(2) *T. diversifolia*
(3) *T. chinensis*
(4) *T. yunnanensis*
Family: *Pinaceae*

Other name: tsuga (Japan).

Distribution: *T. sieboldii* is the principal species growing in Japan, also (2) (3) and (4) occur in China. All have similar characteristics.

General description: The heartwood colour is pale brown with darker latewood bands having a reddish or purplish cast. It has a straight to crossed grain and a rather coarse texture. The average weight is 470 kg/m³ (29 lb/ft³); specific gravity .47.

Mechanical properties: The timber has low bending and crushing strength, low resistance to shock loads and very low stiffness. It has a poor steam bending classification.

Seasoning: Difficult to dry as it tends to twist. Careful piling is recommended. There is medium movement in service.

Working properties: Works readily with both hand and machine tools, with little blunting effect on cutting edges. The knots are hard and brittle. The softness of the earlywood requires thin edged, sharp tools. Requires pre-boring for nailing; holds screws well and gluing is satisfactory. The material gives good results with polish, paint or varnish.

Durability: Non-durable. Logs subject to attack by pinhole borer and common furniture beetle. Resistant to preservative treatment.

Uses: General construction, carpentry and joinery. Selected logs sliced for decorative veneers for cabinets and panelling.

Note: Eastern hemlock, *Tsuga canadensis*, known as **white hemlock** in Canada and the USA, is very similar in characteristics to Japanese hemlock. It is used for inferior work such as paling boards, outsheds etc. and the bark is a source of tannin extract and wood pulp.

HEMLOCK, WESTERN (S)

Tsuga heterophylla, (Rof) Sarg.
Family: *Pinaceae*

Commercial names: Pacific hemlock, British Columbian hemlock (USA, UK); Alaska pine (Canada). **Other names:** hemlock spruce.

Distribution: Canada and USA and introduced into the UK.

General description: The heartwood is pale brown, with darker coloured latewood bands with a reddish-purple cast, producing a well marked growth ring figure on plain sawn surfaces showing as a short purplish line. The wood is straight grained, non-resinous and non-tainting, with a lustrous surface, and a fine, even texture. Weight about 500 kg/m^3 (31 lb/ft^3); s.g. .50.

Mechanical properties: This timber closely resembles the weight and strength properties of Scots pine. It has medium bending and compressive strength, and low hardness and stiffness.

Seasoning: The timber has a very high moisture content which may be difficult to extract from thick planks and needs care in drying. It kiln dries satisfactorily although there is a tendency towards fine surface checking. There is small movement in service.

Working properties: The wood works easily with both hand and machine tools with little dulling effect on cutters, although the knots are fairly hard and brittle; tools must be kept sharp. Pre-boring is necessary for nailing near the ends of boards. It can be glued, stained and polished well and gives good results with paint and varnish.

Durability: The timber is non-durable and susceptible to insect attack. It is resistant to preservative treatment but the sapwood is permeable.

Uses: Large baulk sizes of this species are shipped worldwide for general construction, carpentry and joinery; also for broom handles, vehicle bodies, railway sleepers, wood pulp, quality paper newsprint, plywood manufacture, and sliced veneers for panelling and decorative veneering.

Note: Related spp. include: *T. canadensis*, **white hemlock** (Canada and USA) *T. sieboldii*, Carr., and *T. diversifoia*, **Japanese hemlock** *T. chinensis* and *T. yunnanensis*, **Chinese hemlock**

HICKORY (H)   (1) *Carya glabra*, (Mill.) Sweet *(Hicoria glabra*, Brit.*)*
(2) *C. tomentosa*, Nutt. *(C. alba*, K. Koch., *Hicoria alba*, Brit.*)*
(3) *C. laciniosa*, Loud *(Hicoria laciniosa*, Sarg.*)*
(4) *C. ovata* (Mill.) K. Koch. *(Hicoria ovata*, Brit.*)*
Family: *Juglandaceae*

Other names: (1) pignut hickory (2) mockernut hickory (3) shellbark hickory (4) shagbark hickory, red or white hickory (USA).

Distribution: S. Eastern Canada and Eastern United States.

General description: The heartwood is brown in colour or reddish brown and sold as red hickory, and the sapwood sold separately as white hickory. Typically straight grained, but may be wavy or irregular, with a rather coarse texture. The weight is from 700–900 kg/m^3 (45–56 lb/ft^3) but averages about 820 kg/m^3 (51 lb/ft^3); specific gravity .82.

Mechanical properties: Density and strength varies according to the rate of growth. It has excellent steam bending properties. With high bending strength and crushing strength, high stiffness and very high shock resistance, this outstanding combination of strength properties earns it a very good classification.

Seasoning: Dries rapidly with little tendency to warp or twist, but with a risk of shrinkage.

Working properties: A rather difficult wood to work, with moderate to severe blunting of cutters. A reduction of cutting angle to 20° necessary when planing irregular grain. Pre-boring for nailing is required, and gluing can be difficult. Stains and polishes to a good finish.

Durability: Non-durable. Trees and logs liable to attack by forest longhorn beetle. Sapwood liable to attack by powder post beetle. Moderately resistant to preservative treatment.

Uses: Striking-tool handles, hammers, picks, axes etc., and for spokes and felloes for wheels, chairs, ladder rungs, shunting poles, vehicle bodies. Sports goods such as shafts for golf clubs, lacrosse sticks, laminae in tennis racquets, baseball bats, backs of longbows, skis, tops of heavy sea fishing rods, drum sticks etc. Used for plywood faces and sliced for decorative veneers.

Note: Other spp. include *C. illinoensis*, K.Koch. and *C. aquatica*, Nutt. produces **Pecan** (USA).

HOLLY (H)

Ilex spp. including
I. aquifolium, L. *I. opaca*
Family: *Aquifoliaceae*

Distribution: *I. aquifolium*: UK Europe and Western Asia; *I. opaca*: USA. Also grown in Guinea and Brazil. (175 different species grow around the world).

General description: The heartwood is cream-white, sometimes with a greenish-grey cast with little or no figure. The grain tends to be irregular but with a fine even texture which is velvet smooth to the touch. Weight about 800 kg/m^3 (50 lb/ft^3); specific gravity .80.

Mechanical properties: Due to the small sections obtainable, this is not a timber used for steam bending although it is hard, heavy and tough in all strength categories.

Seasoning: Fairly difficult timber to dry as it has a marked tendency to distort and for end splitting to occur if dried in the round. It is best converted to small dimensions and dried very slowly with the top of the pile weighted down. There is a large movement in service. Holly should be cut in winter, converted and dried before summer to avoid discolouration.

Working properties: Difficult to saw because of the irregular grain, and for a smooth finish the cutting edges must be kept really sharp and the cutting angle reduced to 15°. There is a moderate blunting effect on tools and high resistance to working with hand tools. It can be nailed, screwed and glued satisfactorily; it stains readily and provides an excellent finish.

Durability: The wood is perishable and liable to insect attack, but it is permeable to preservative treatment.

Uses: Used as a substitute for boxwood and dyed as a substitute for ebony. It is an excellent turnery wood. Used for engraving blocks, small musical instruments, keys for pianos and organs, brush backs, and cut into inlay lines and stringings for furniture decoration. Sliced or sawcut veneers are used for marquetry inlay motifs (wreaths, sprays, shells, fans, etc.) for reproduction furniture and the repair of antiques.

'HOOP PINE' (S)

Araucaria cunninghamii, Ait. ex D.Don.
Family: *Araucariaceae*

Distribution: Australia and Papua New Guinea.

General description: The timber is similar in appearance to Parana pine, (*A. angustifolia*) but without the pinkish streaks. The heartwood is yellow-brown to darker brown with a pinkish tinge. It is straight grained, with texture very fine and uniform. The wood is generally marked by leaf traces which sometimes produces an attractive bird's eye figure. Weighs 560 kg/m³ (35 lb/ft³); specific gravity .56.

Mechanical properties: The bending strength and stiffness are medium to low, with medium crushing strength and resistance to shock loads. It is not used for steam bending.

Seasoning: The material dries rapidly and well without degrade. There is small movement in service.

Working properties: Works fairly easily with both hand or machine tools but the cutting edges must be kept very sharp to avoid the grain around knots tearing and picking up. Nails and glues well, and can be brought to a good finish with the usual finishing treatments.

Durability: Non-durable and susceptible to attack by the common furniture beetle. The heartwood is moderately resistant to preservative treatment but the bulk of the sapwood is permeable.

Uses: Battery separators, broom handles, cabinetmaking, turnery, dowels, furniture, linings, flooring, light construction, pattern making, joinery, mouldings, matchboxes and wood pulp. It is rotary cut for plywood manufacture and selected logs are sliced for decorative veneers.

Note: Not a true pine.

HORNBEAM, EUROPEAN (H)

Carpinus betulus, L.
Family: *Betulaceae*

Other names: charme (France); haagbeuk (Netherlands); hainbuche (Germany).

Distribution: Europe including the UK, Asia Minor and Iran.

General description: The heartwood colour is dull white with greyish streaks and a flecked figure on quartered surfaces due to broad rays. The grain is commonly irregular, with a fine, even texture. Weight 750 kg/m³ (47 lb/ft³); specific gravity .75.

Mechanical properties: This heavy density wood has high bending and crushing strength, with medium stiffness and resistance to shock loads. It has a very good steam bending classification and is suitable for most types of bending; excellent shear strength and splitting resistance.

Seasoning: Dries very well with little degrade. There is a large movement in service.

Working properties: There is high resistance in cutting and a moderate blunting effect on cutting edges, normal in relation to its density. It machines well and turns to a smooth finish. When nailing, the wood may need pre-boring but glues satisfactorily, and stains and polishes to a high finish.

Durability: Perishable. Logs liable to attack by forest longhorn beetle, sapwood by the common furniture beetle. The wood is permeable to preservative treatment.

Uses: Suitable for piano actions, and for clavichords and harpsichords, violin bridges, cogs, pulleys, dead-eyes, mallets and pegs. Drum sticks, billiard cues, skittles, Indian clubs, brushbacks and general turnery. Makes an excellent alternative to maple for light industrial flooring due to its high resistance to wear. Sliced for veneers.

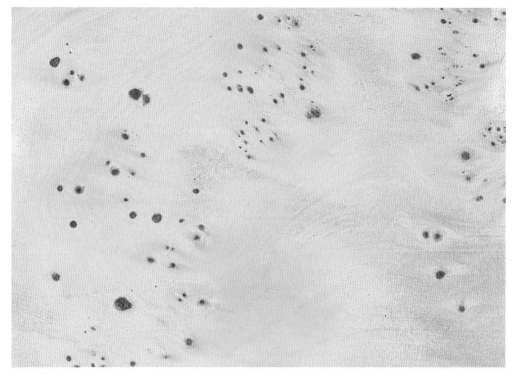

'HUON PINE' (S)

Dacrydium franklinii, Hook
Family: *Podocarpaceae*

Other names: macquerie pine.

Distribution: Tasmania.

General description: The heartwood is a creamy-white to pale pinkish-brown with a straight grain and extremely fine texture with very distinct growth rings. It weighs about 530 kg/m^3 (33 lb/ft^3); specific gravity .53.

Mechanical properties: The wood has low stiffness and resistance to shock loads, medium bending and crushing strengths and a very poor steam bending rating.

Seasoning: The timber dries readily with a slight tendency for surface checking. There is medium movement in service.

Working properties: This fragrant softwood is easily wrought with hand or machine tools, with only a very slight blunting effect on cutters. It planes and moulds cleanly, but may tend to split on nailing and require pre-boring. The wood takes glue, stain and polish easily and can be brought to a good finish.

Durability: It is durable, resistant to insect attack and permeable to preservation treatment.

Uses: Cabinet work, joinery, boat planking and building, furniture; selected logs are sliced for decorative veneers.

Note 1: Not a true pine.

Note 2: Closely related to *D. cupressinium*, Soland, from New Zealand known as **rimu** or **red pine**, which also weighs 530 kg/m^3 (33 lb/ft^3).

IDIGBO (H)

Terminalia ivorensis, A. Chév.
Family: *Combretaceae*

Commercial names: framiré (France, Ivory Coast); emeri (Ghana, UK).
Other names: black afara (Nigeria); bajii, bajee (Sierra Leone).
Distribution: West Africa.
General description: Heartwood is pale yellow-brown, showing a zonal figure originating in the growth rings – like plain oak – and sometimes with a light pinkish cast. The grain is straight to slightly irregular or interlocked. The texture is medium to fairly coarse and uneven. The weight is variable owing to the prevalence of light-weight brittleheart in the inner core-wood; also liable to thunder shakes. Weight from 480–620 kg/m^3 (30–39 lb/ft^3). Average sound material 560 kg/m^3 (35 lb/ft^3); specific gravity .56.
Mechanical properties: Very poor steam bending classification, medium crushing strength, low bending strength and very low stiffness and resistance to shock loads.
Seasoning: The wood dries rapidly and well with little checking or distortion. It is very stable with only small movement in service.
Working properties: The slightly interlocked grain tends to pick up in planing and reduced cutting angle of 20° is advised, but generally works well. Material containing brittleheart or compression failures are liable to crumble when cut on end grain. There is a slight blunting effect on tools. Nails, screws and glues well and a good finish is obtainable when filled. When moist, its acidic properties tend to corrode metals.
Durability: Sapwood liable to attack by powder post beetle. Moderately resistant to termites. The heartwood is durable and extremely resistant to preservative treatment; the sapwood is moderately resistant.
Uses: Used in furniture and high-class joinery for interior and exterior work, and general carpentry and joinery and construction work. Rotary cut material is used for plywood manufacture and sliced for decorative veneers for panelling. It should not be used in damp conditions due to natural staining properties if in contact with iron compounds.

IMBUIA (H)

Phoebe porosa, Mez.
Family: *Lauraceae*

Commercial names: imbuya, imbuia amarela, canela imbuia, embuia (Brazil); Brazilian walnut* (USA and UK).

Distribution: Brazil (usually grown in association with *Araucaria*, Parana pine).

General description: The heartwood is yellow-olive to chocolate brown, with variegated streaks and stripes. The grain is usually straight but often wavy or curly, with fine and even growth rings visible to the naked eye. Fine to medium texture. The weight is about 660 kg/m³ (41 lb/ft³); specific gravity .66.

Mechanical properties: The material is not strong and has a very low wood bending classification and is chiefly used for its very decorative appearance. It is moderately stable, fairly hard and heavy.

Seasoning: Dries rapidly and requires care to avoid warping. It should be kiln dried slowly to avoid degrade. The natural spicey, fragrant scent is mostly lost in drying. There is small movement in service.

Working properties: It is easy to work with both hand and machine tools, offering only slight resistance to cutting edges and finishes very smoothly. There is a tendency for the grain to pick up in planing or moulding operations which can be eliminated by using a reduced cutting angle of 20°. The material nails, and holds screws well, has good gluing properties and can be stained and polished to an excellent finish. Machining dust can be an irritant.

Durability: The wood resists attacks by wood boring insects, and the heartwood is durable. It is moderately resistant to preservation treatment but the sapwood is permeable.

Uses: In Brazil it is used for high-class furniture and cabinetmaking and superior joinery. Also for high-grade flooring, panelling and gunstocks. Quality veneers are exported to Europe for panelling and decorative veneering.

***Note:** This name is likely to cause confusion and has been discontinued in the trade.

'INDIAN ALMOND' (H)

Terminalia catappa
Family: *Combretaceae*

Distribution: India.

General description: The heartwood is pinkish-yellow with brownish-red variegated streaks and stripes. The grain is twisted and interlocked but the surface is lustrous, although the texture is moderately coarse. The timber weighs about 650 kg/m³ (40 lb/ft³); specific gravity .65.

Mechanical properties: The timber has low bending and crushing strength, very low stiffness and resistance to shock loads. This produces a very poor steam bending classification.

Seasoning: The timber tends to dry rapidly with a strong tendency to split and shake, and care is needed in seasoning to avoid degrade. Partial air drying is recommended. There is small movement in service.

Working properties: The twisted and interlocked grain causes severe blunting of tools and the cutting edges should be kept sharp. A reduction of 20° in the cutting angle is necessary for smooth planing or moulding. Nailing and screwing are satisfactory and it takes glue well. It can be stained and polished to a very good finish.

Durability: The wood is subject to insect attack and is non-durable. The heartwood is resistant to preservative treatment but the sapwood is permeable.

Uses: This decorative wood is used for interior joinery, shop and office fitting, furniture and doors. Locally it is used for general light construction and interior trim. Selected logs are sliced for decorative veneers suitable for panelling and furniture.

Note: Not a true almond.

'INDIAN LAUREL' (H)

Terminalia alata, Roth.
T. coriacea, Wright & Arn. *T. crenulata*, Roth.
formerly *T. tomentosa* (W & A)
Family: *Combretaceae*

Other names: taukkyan (Burma); asna, mutti, sain, (India); cay (Sri-Lanka); hatna (Indonesia); neang (Khmer Rep.).

Distribution: India, Burma, Sri Lanka, also Pakistan and Bangladesh.

General description: The heartwood varies from light brown with few markings to dark brown with irregular darker streaks or lines. The wood is fairly straight grained to irregular or interlocked; coarse textured, very heavy, compact and elastic. The weight varies between 740–950 kg/m^3 (46–59 lb/ft^3), averaging 860 kg/m^3 (53 lb/ft^3); specific gravity .86.

Mechanical properties: A strong, hard wood with medium bending strength and stiffness, and high crushing strength.

Seasoning: This is a highly refractory timber to dry, being liable to surface checking, warping and splitting. The timber should be converted green during the rainy season and allowed to air dry very slowly in stick. Kiln drying should be carried out slowly and may give more satisfactory results, but there is a tendency for distortion, splitting or checking to occur. Medium movement.

Working properties: Difficult to work with hand tools, and moderately hard to machine with a blunting effect on cutting edges, particularly when irregular or interlocked grain is present. Sawdust can be an irritant. Pre-boring is necessary for nailing, but holds screws well and glues firmly though may be difficult due to natural oil content. Finishing processes are satisfactory.

Durability: Logs are liable to attack by forest longhorn beetle and sapwood by powder post beetle. Resistant in teredo infested water and excellent for use in non-teredo water. The heartwood is moderately durable. The wood is resistant to preservative treatment, but the sapwood is permeable.

Uses: Locally for marine construction and piling, boat-building, posts, pitprops etc. Widely used for furniture and cabinetmaking, joinery, brush backs, police batons and tool handles. It is an excellent turnery wood. Sliced veneers are produced for panelling and decorative veneering.

Note: Not a true laurel.

IPÊ (H)

Tabebuia serratifolia, (Vahl) Nicholson.,
also *T. ipê*, Standl., *T. guayacan*, Memsl.
Family: *Bignoniaceae*

Commercial names: pau d'arco, ipê tabaco (Brazil); bethabara (Caribbean).

Other names: yellow poui (Trinidad); hakia, ironwood (Guyana); groenhart, wassiba (Surinam); lapacho (Argentina); ébène vert (Fr. Guiana); amata prieto (Mexico).

Distribution: Central and South America and the Caribbean.

General description: The heartwood is olive-brown with lighter or darker streaks. The grain is straight to irregular with a low to medium lustre. The pores, appearing as fine yellow dots, or, on longitudinal surfaces as yellow lines, contain yellowish lapachol powder which turns deep red in alkaline solutions. The material is fine textured and appears oily; fine ripple marks may be present. Weight varies between 960–1200 kg/m^3 (60–75 lb/ft^3); specific gravity 1.08.

Mechanical properties: The material has very high strength in all categories, but is resistant to wood bending and has only a moderate classification. It is a strong, tough, resilient wood.

Seasoning: The material dries rapidly with slight warping, cupping, twisting and end surface checking. A slow kiln drying schedule is recommended. There is very small movement.

Working properties: The wood is difficult to work, especially in sawing, and has a severe blunting effect on cutting edges. A reduced cutting angle of 15° should be used for planing or moulding. Pre-boring required for nailing; holds screws well and stains and polishes well. Machine dust is an irritant.

Durability: Ipê has a very high resistance to all insect and fungal attacks and is very durable. Extremely resistant to preservative treatment.

Uses: The material is ideal for bridge building, naval construction and dock work, exterior construction, etc. It is also used for turnery, factory flooring, decking, vehicle bodies, tool handles, archery bows, walking sticks and fishing rods, and carpentry and cabinet work. Selected logs provide highly decorative veneers for panelling.

IROKO (H)

Chlorophora excelsa, (Welw) Benth, Hook.f.,
C. regia, A. Chév.
Family: *Moraceae*

Commercial name: kambala (Europe). **Other names:** mvulu (E. Africa); odum (Ghana); kambala (Zaire); tule, intule (Mozambique); moreira (Angola); band (Cameroon).

Distribution: West and East Africa.

General description: Golden-orange to brown, lighter vessel lines are conspicuous on flat sawn surfaces. The material may contain large, hard deposits of calcium carbonate in cavities, and the wood around them may be darker in colour. The grain is interlocked and sometimes irregular and the texture rather coarse, but even. The weight is 640 kg/m^3 (40 lb/ft^3); s.g. .64.

Mechanical properties: This medium density wood has a moderate steam bending classification, with medium bending and crushing strength, very low stiffness and resistance to shock loads.

Seasoning: Dries fairly rapidly and well without much degrade and there is a tendency for stick marks to show during drying. There is a small movement in service.

Working properties: The material works satisfactorily with hand and machine tools but with a moderate to severe blunting effect on cutting edges when calcareous stone deposits are present. A reduction of cutting angle to 15° is necessary for a smooth finish in planing quarter sawn surfaces due to interlocked grain. The wood nails and screws well, glues satisfactorily, and when the grain is filled, an excellent finish can be obtained.

Durability: The sapwood is liable to attack by powder post beetle, but is highly resistant to termites in Africa. The heartwood is very durable, and is extremely resistant to preservative treatment. The sapwood is permeable.

Uses: Ship and boat building, interior and exterior joinery; laboratory benches, furniture making and carving. It is a structural timber suitable for piling and marine work, and for domestic flooring. Also for plywood manufacture and sliced for wall panelling, flush doors and decorative veneering.

IVORYWOOD, RED (H)

Rhamnus zeyheri, Sond.
Family: *Rhamnaceae*

Commercial names: red ivorywood, pink ivory.
Other names: mnai (E. Africa); umgoloti, umnini (S. Africa); m'beza (Zimbabwe); mulatch-ine, pau preto, mucarane (S.E. Africa); sungangona (Mozambique).
Distribution: South and South East Africa, particularly Mozambique.
General description: The heartwood is yellow-brown with a red-gold lustre. The pore structure is fine and the growth rings have alternate light and dark coloured areas giving a characteristic pink-red striped figure. The grain is straight to interlocked or irregular and the texture moderately fine and even. Weight about 900 kg/m³ (56 lb/ft³); specific gravity .90.
Mechanical properties: This very hard, heavy, tough wood is exceptionally strong in most categories, but has a low steam bending classification as it can only be bent to a large radius of curvature.
Seasoning: Difficult to air dry without degrade; kilning should be carried out very slowly and carefully to prevent serious distortion caused by unusually high differential shrinkage. There is a large movement in service.
Working properties: Fairly difficult to work with hand tools, and has a medium to severe blunting effect on all tools which should be kept very sharp. Quarter sawn wood tends to pick up in planing, and a reduced cutting angle of 20° is recommended. The material should be pre-bored for nailing, but holds screws and glues well, stains easily and sanded surfaces can be brought to a high polish.
Durability: The timber is non-durable and subject to attack by insects. It is extremely resistant to preservation treatment although the sapwood is permeable.
Uses: The wood is used for furniture and interior joinery, light-duty flooring, vehicle bodies, and as a mining timber. It is also excellent for turnery and carving, chessmen, instruments and inlaying. Selected logs are sliced to display the attractive rope figure suitable for wall panelling and as a decorative veneer.

IZOMBE (H)

Testulea gabonensis
Family: *Ochnaceae*

Distribution: Gabon principally, and throughout the equatorial forests of West Africa.

General description: The heartwood varies from orange-yellow and grey-yellow to pinkish-yellow with a greyish hue. It is straight grained with a fine, even texture. The vessel cells sometimes contain a dark gum. The weight is 800 kg/m³ (50 lb/ft³); specific gravity .80.

Mechanical properties: It has high bending and crushing strength, medium stiffness and resistance to shock loads, with a moderate steam bending classification.

Seasoning: Seasons well with little degrade, although the sapwood is liable to blue sapstain. There is small movement in service.

Working properties: Works easily with hand and machine tools, glues, stains and polishes well.

Durability: A hard, durable wood; resistant to impregnation.

Uses: Heavy construction, flooring, furniture and cabinets, veneer and plywood, boxes for precision instruments, joinery, including doors and windows, carving, turnery and pattern making.

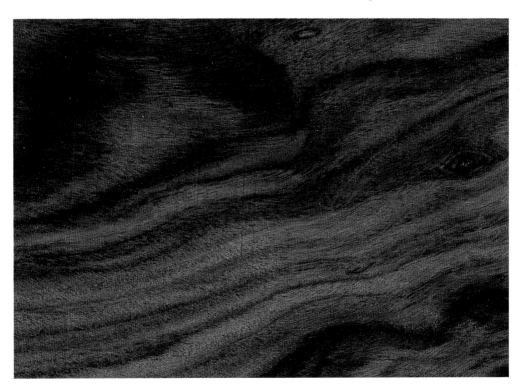

JACARANDA PARDO (H)

Machaerium villosum, Veg.
Family: *Leguminosae*

Other names: jacaranda amarello, jacaranda do cerrado, j. escuro, j. do mato, j. paulista, j. pedra, j. roxo (Brazil).

Distribution: Brazil.

General description: The heartwood is similar in most respects to Brazilian rosewood except that it is lighter in hue between pink-brown to violet-brown, and not so highly figured. It has an undulating grain, a coarse texture, and is fibrous. Weight averages 850 kg/m³ (53 lb/ft³); specific gravity .85.

Mechanical properties: This straight grained material has a moderate steam bending classification, and high strength properties in other categories.

Seasoning: Air dries slowly with a tendency to check.

Working properties: Rather difficult to work and causes severe blunting of cutting edges. The cutting angle should be reduced to 20° when planing or moulding quartered stock to prevent the grain picking up.

Durability: Very durable and resistant to preservation treatment.

Uses: Furniture and cabinetmaking, interior trim, cutlery handles, fancy woodware, decorative veneers for panelling and marquetry.

JARRAH (H)

Eucalyptus marginata, Donn. ex. Sm.
Family: *Myrtaceae*

Distribution: West and South West Australia.

General description: Heartwood is a rich dark brownish-red, sometimes marked by short, dark brown radial flecks on the end grain and boat shaped flecks on flat sawn surfaces which enhance its decorative value. These marks are caused by the fungus *Fistulina hepatica*. Gum veins or pockets may also be present. The grain is usually straight but often interlocked or wavy. The texture is even but moderately coarse. The weight varies from 690–1040 kg/m^3 (43–65 lb/ft^3) but averages about 800 kg/m^3 (50 lb/ft^3); specific gravity .80.

Mechanical properties: This very heavy timber has a moderate steam bending classification, with medium bending strength and high crushing strength. Satisfactory bends of moderate radius can be made using straight grained material.

Seasoning: Partial air drying before kilning is recommended with low temperatures and high humidities advisable, especially in thick sizes, to avoid distortion. There is medium movement in service.

Working properties: The material is rather difficult to work with hand tools, and fairly hard to machine with high resistance to cutting edges and a moderate blunting effect. A reduced cutting angle of 15° is advised to prevent wavy or interlocked grain from tearing out. Pre-boring necessary for nailing and screwing. Gluing properties are good and the wood polishes very well.

Durability: The heartwood is very durable and highly resistant to insect attack and preservative treatment but the sapwood is permeable. In some logs the vessels can be penetrated but the fibres cannot.

Uses: All marine work, ship building, heavy construction, sleepers, shingles, weatherboards, rafters, joists, flooring, chemical vats and filter presses, agricultural implements, interior fittings, furniture, and tool handles. Selected logs are sliced for panelling and decorative veneering.

JELUTONG (H)

Dyera costulata, Hook.f.
Family: *Apocynaceae*

Other names: jelutong bukit, jelutong paya (Sarawak).

Distribution: Malaya and Indonesia.

General description: The colour of the heartwood is creamy-white to straw, but may be stained by fungi after tapping for latex. Latex traces may be seen on tangential surfaces as large lens-shaped bodies although they are usually eliminated in conversion into smaller dimensions. The grain is almost straight, the texture fine and even and of plain appearance. Weight varies from 420–500 kg/m^3 (26–31 lb/ft^3) average 460 kg/m^3 (29 lb/ft^3); specific gravity .46.

Mechanical properties: This wood of medium density has low bending and crushing strengths and very low stiffness and has a poor steam bending classification.

Seasoning: It is relatively easy to dry with little tendency to check or distort, but staining may be troublesome. In air drying, free circulation of air is necessary to ensure the quick drying of the surface. It may be difficult to extract moisture from the centre of thick stock before staining occurs. There is small movement in service.

Working properties: Easy to work with hand or machine tools, with only a slight blunting effect on cutting edges. Finishes cleanly and smoothly and takes nails and screws well. Can be glued easily and takes stains, varnish or polish very well.

Durability: Non-durable. Sapwood liable to attack by powder post beetle. Logs are non-resistant to termites in Malaya. It is permeable to preservative treatment.

Uses: Jelutong is used for pattern making as an alternative to yellow pine; drawing boards, wood carving, wooden clogs, handicraft work, matches, core stock for plywood and flush doors, light-weight partitions, interior joinery and fitments. Selected, latex-free material is used for battery separators. The other main use for the latex extracted from the wood is for the manufacture of chewing gum.

JEQUITIBA (H)

Cariniana pyriformis, Miers.
C. legalis, O. Ktze.
Family: *Lecythidaceae*

Commercial names: jetquitiba rosa, abarco (Brazil).

Other names: albarco, abarco (Colombia); bacu (Venezuela).

Distribution: Brazil, Colombia and Venezuela.

General description: The heartwood varies from yellow-pink to orange red-brown marked with darker brown streaks. The material is straight grained with a fine to medium texture, with distinct rays. The weight is variable from 496–688 kg/m^3 (31–43 lb/ft^3) but a fair average is 580 kg/m^3 (36 lb/ft^3); specific gravity .58.

Mechanical properties: The wood is of medium density, with a medium steam bending classification; very low stiffness, medium crushing strength and low shock resistance.

Seasoning: The material dries rapidly and well without difficulty and is fairly easy to kiln without degrade. There is very small movement and the wood is very stable.

Working properties: Works well with both hand and machine tools with only a slight blunting effect on cutting edges, which must be kept very sharp to avoid raising the grain and woolly surfaces. May require pre-boring for nailing, but glues, stains and polishes well.

Durability: The heartwood is durable and extremely resistant to preservative treatment although the sapwood is permeable.

Uses: Widely used in South America for general construction, carpentry, interior construction, joinery and cabinetmaking. It is used in ship building instead of mahogany. Also used for planking and superstructures in boatbuilding. Selected logs are used for veneer and plywood and for sliced decorative veneers. Not always favoured in veneer mills because of split logs.

KAATOAN BANGKAL (H)

Anthocephalus chinensis, (Lamk.) Rich. ex Walp.

Family: *Rubiaceae*

Commercial names: Anthocephalus.
Other names: magalablab, manuluko, (Bagobos) sapuan (Manayas)
Distribution: Philippines, Borneo, Sumatra, Malaya and India.
General description: The wood is soft and light; sapwood is indistinct from heartwood which is cream coloured. It is straight grained and the texture varies from moderately fine to moderately coarse. The growth rings are not sharply defined, the pores are barely visible and the rays are not visible to the naked eye. Weight approx. 400 kg/m^3 (25 lb/ft^3); s.g. .40.
Mechanical properties: The steam bending classification is poor although the timber has medium strength properties.
Seasoning: The wood seasons very easily by kiln drying with very little degrade in the form of loosening of knots, warping and collapse.
Working properties: It is relatively easy to work with little blunting effect on cutters, and an excellent quality planed surface is obtained with a 30° cutting angle. Boring qualities are fair. Fuzziness on the side grain can be minimised by keeping the tool bit very sharp. Mortising quality is poor. Light pressing of the chisel bit on the wood reduces crushing and tearing. It is an excellent turning wood. Gluing is easy, and the wood sands and takes stain and varnish very well with minimum finishing material.
Durability: It is perishable, but amenable to preservative treatment.
Uses: Light construction, pencil slats, wooden clogs, woodcarving, wood turning, veneer and plywood manufacture, pulp and paper making, match splints and boxes, fibre and particle board manufacture.
Note: *Nauclea orientalis*, (L) L., (*Sarcocephalus cordatus*, Miq) produces **kanluang** (Thailand and Burma), **bangkal** (Philippines), and is not related to kaatoan bangkal.

KAHIKATEA (S)

Podocarpus dacrydiodes, A. Rich.
syn. *Dacrycarpus dacrydiodes*
Family: *Podocarpaceae*

Commercial names: New Zealand white pine, white pine.

Distribution: New Zealand.

General description: The timber grown on hill sites has a high proportion of yellow heartwood, but timber from lowland sites and swamp areas is comprised almost entirely of creamy-white sapwood providing long, clear lengths in wide widths for sawing. Straight grained, with a fine even texture. Weight 465 kg/m³ (29 lb/ft³); specific gravity .46.

Mechanical properties: The material is of low density, but for its weight has moderate strength properties in all categories and suitable for steam bending to moderate curves.

Seasoning: The material dries easily and well, but there is a danger of sap-stain during air drying. There is small movement in service.

Working properties: The timber works easily and well with both hand and machine tools. It holds nails and screws well, glues and finishes smoothly to a surface ideal for painting, varnishing or polishing.

Durability: The sapwood is non-durable and subject to insect attack. The heartwood is moderately durable, and moderately resistant to preservative treatment.

Uses: In New Zealand it is classed as a group 1 material for building purposes. It is used for building construction, scaffold planks, fascia boards, weatherboards (when treated), flooring, framing, joinery, kitchen furniture, boat building, domestic woodware, mouldings, casks and boxes. It is an excellent turnery wood. Also used in manufacture of ice cream spoons and toothpicks, cocktail sticks etc. Selected logs converted into plywood and decorative veneers. It is not recommended for exterior use with stain or a dark finish.

Note: Related *podocarpus* spp. include: *P. ferrugineus*, D. Don., **miro** (NZ) *P. spicatus*, R.Br., **matai**, also known as **mai** or **black pine** (NZ) *P. totara*, D. Don., Ex Lamb and *P. hallii*, T. Kirk, **totara** (NZ). Also *Dacrycarpus imbricatus*, Blume de Laub. syn. *Podocarpus imbricatus*, R. Br. known as **igem** in the Philippines.

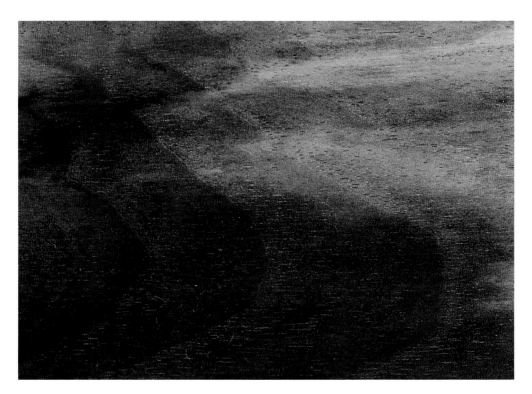

KAKI (H)

Diospyros kaki, L.f.
Family: *Ebenaceae*

Other names: Chinese persimmon, Japanese ebony (UK & USA).

Distribution: Japan and China.

General description: This timber has a commercially valuable, very wide straw-coloured sapwood, and a dense black heartwood streaked with orange-yellow, brown, grey or salmon pink, either separately or combined, which gives the wood a very decorative appearance. Planed surfaces have a cold, marble-like feel. The grain is straight and the texture fine and even. Average weight 830 kg/m³ (52 lb/ft³); specific gravity .83.

Mechanical properties: Bending and crushing strengths are high, with medium stiffness and resistance to shock loads. It is not usually employed for steam bending.

Seasoning: Dries readily with a tendency to check. There is a small movement in service.

Working properties: The material has a moderate blunting effect on cutting edges which must be kept sharp. A reduced cutting angle of 20° will help to get the exceptionally smooth surface that is obtainable. Nailing requires pre-boring and gluing may be difficult. It produces a very fine finish.

Durability: Durable and resistant to preservative treatment.

Uses: In Japan, the timber is highly valued for ornamental work of all kinds and small tables. The straw-coloured sapwood is used for golf club heads, turnery, textile shuttles, shoe lasts, etc. Suitable for any purpose requiring a very heavy, close, compact wood with ability to wear smoothly. Selected logs are sliced for decorative veneers for cabinets or panelling, but large sizes are not freely available. It is too heavy for plywood manufacture.

KAPUR (H)

(1) *Dryobalanops aromatica*, Gaertn. F.,
(2) *D. oblongifolia*, Dyer, (3) *D. lanceolata*, Burck.,
(4) *D. beccarii*, Dyer, (5) *D. fusca*, V.Sl.
Family: *Dipterocarpaceae*

Commercial names: (1) kapur. (2) keladan. (1+2) Malaysian kapur. (1+3) Sarawak kapur. (3) and (4) Sabah kapur, Sabah kapor. (1) and (2) Sumatra kapur. (1) and (3) Kalimantan kapur. (1–5) Indonesian kapur (from Borneo).

Other names: Borneo camphorwood (UK); kapoer (Indonesia); petanang (Malaya).

Distribution: Malaysia, Indonesia and S.E. Asia.

General description: The wood is a uniform light to deep red-brown, with a camphor-like odour. It is straight grained to shallowly interlocked with a fairly coarse but even texture, and has resin filled continuous gum ducts in concentric lines. The weights vary between 790 kg/m³ (49 lb/ft³) and 700 kg/m³ (43 lb/ft³); specific gravity averaging .77.

Mechanical properties: This heavy density material has high bending strength and crushing strength, with medium stiffness and shock resistant qualities. It has only a moderate steam bending classification and steaming produces resin exudation.

Seasoning: Dries rather slowly but well, with slight tendency to cup and twist, with a possibility of end splitting and surface checking in thicker material. There is medium movement.

Working properties: The wood works well with both hand and machine tools with a moderate blunting effect on cutting edges and severe blunting when interlocked grain is present. The material nails, screws, stains and polishes satisfactorily.

Durability: The sapwood is liable to attack by powder post beetle. The heartwood is very durable and extremely resistant to preservative treatment, but the sapwood is permeable.

Uses: Blue stain may occur if wood is in contact with iron compounds in damp conditions. Its acidic character may induce corrosion in metals. The sapwood contains yellow colouring which may stain fabrics. It is excellent for external structural purposes, farm buildings, wharf decking, exterior joinery, e.g. windows, doors and stairways; cladding, outdoor garden seats, flooring, vehicle floors, fittings and furniture making. Above water line for docks, wharves, bridges. Used for plywood manufacture and selected logs for sliced decorative veneers for panelling.

KARRI (H)

Eucalyptus diversicolor, F. Muell.
Family: *Myrtaceae*

Distribution: S. Western Australia.

General description: Heartwood colour is reddish-brown, paler in colour than jarrah when fresh but maturing to a more uniform brown. (See note below). The grain is interlocked with some wavy grain, the texture is even and moderately coarse. Heavy density with the weight about 880 kg/m³ (55 lb/ft³); specific gravity .88.

Mechanical properties: High bending and crushing strengths and stiffness with medium resistance to shock loads. The steam bending classification is good, but the timber is intolerant of pin knots. It is also fire resistant.

Seasoning: Needs great care in drying as checks become severe and very deep in adverse conditions, checking most severely on the tangential face. Distortion is liable in thin stock. In kilning from green condition, low temperatures and high humidities are advised. Partial air drying before kilning produces best results. There is large movement in service.

Working properties: Difficult to work with hand tools, and with machines a moderate to severe blunting effect on cutters. In planing and moulding a cutting angle of 15° is necessary to avoid picking up the grain. Pre-bore for nailing. It can be glued, stained and polished satisfactorily.

Durability: The wood is durable. The heartwood is extremely resistant to preservative treatment but the sapwood is permeable.

Uses: Structural and constructional work for bridges, wharves, superstructures, shipbuilding, wagon work, flooring, joists, rafters and beams, furniture and cabinet work, interior trim. In plywood making care is needed to avoid excessive buckling of the veneers during drying. Also used for solid bent work, and sleepers, poles and piles, after treatment. Karri is inferior to jarrah for underground use and for situations in contact with water as in dock and harbour works.

Note: To distinguish between karri and jarrah, a dry heartwood splinter test is used. After burning, a thick white ash is formed with karri, while jarrah burns to a black, ashless charcoal.

KATSURA (H)
Cercidiphyllum japonicum, Sieb & Zucc.
Family: *Trochodendraceae*

Distribution: Japan.

General description: The heartwood has a light nut-brown colour, with an occasional thin light coloured line, caused by a narrow band of parenchyma marking the growth rings. The logs selected for timber are mostly straight grained, and the texture is fine and even. It is soft, compact and light in weight, about 470 kg/m^3 (29 lb/ft^3) at 12% moisture content; specific gravity .47.

Mechanical properties: The wood has medium bending and crushing strength with low stiffness and resistance to shock loads. It has a moderately good steam bending classification.

Seasoning: Dries easily and well without degrade. There is small movement in service.

Working properties: Katsura is very easy to work and machine as its soft, but compact nature lends itself to moulding and carving where there is a need for sharp arrises to remain intact and not chip out. Nails, screws, glues well and can be brought to an excellent finish.

Durability: Non-durable. Liable to insect attack, but permeable for preservative treatment.

Uses: Furniture, cabinets and panelling, high-class joinery, lacquered work, delicate mouldings, carving, engraving, cigar boxes. Selected logs sliced for decorative veneers for panelling, cabinets and marquetry.

KAUVULA (H)

Endospermum medullosum, L.S.Sm.
Family: *Euphorbiaceae*

Other names: New Guinea basswood (Papua New Guinea); endospermum, sasa, hongopo (Solomon Islands).

Distribution: Papua New Guinea, Solomon Islands and Fiji.

General description: The heartwood colour matures from cream-yellow to straw-biscuit upon exposure. The grain is usually straight, but may also be interlocked or wavy and the texture moderately coarse and even. The weight is about 440 kg/m^3 (27 lb/ft^3); specific gravity .44.

Mechanical properties: A soft, weak wood, with very low strength properties and unsuited to construction work. It has a very poor steam bending classification.

Seasoning: Dries well with low shrinkage. There is small movement in service.

Working properties: The wood works easily with hand and machine tools, although inclined to be woolly due to the interlocked or wavy grain which may cause some difficulty in planing or moulding unless the cutting angle is reduced to 20°. The straight grained material provides a clean, smooth finish. It takes nails and screws easily, glues well, and may be stained and polished to a good finish.

Durability: It is a non-durable wood, liable to insect attack, but is permeable for preservation treatment.

Uses: Selected grades are used for furniture and cabinetmaking, light framing, lining, internal joinery, flooring for light domestic use, and turnery. It is also used for plywood manufacture and for decorative veneers for panelling, doors, etc.

KEMPAS (H)

Koompassia malaccensis, Maing.
Family: *Leguminosae*

Other names: impas (Sabah).

Distribution: Malaysia, Sumatra and Borneo.

General description: The heartwood colour is orange-red to brown with numerous yellowish lines or streaks caused by parenchyma tissue surrounding the pores. The grain is usually interlocked, but often spiral or wavy grain is present. The surface is moderately lustrous, and texture coarse but even. Abnormal veins of very hard rock-like tissue, usually discarded during conversion, may be found in converted stock. These veins are about 6mm wide and may extend about one metre along the grain, and are a source of mechanical weakness, limiting the strength properties and leading to degrade in drying. Brittleheart is occasionally present. The timber is acidic and could cause the corrosion of some metals. Weighs on average 880 kg/m³ (55 lb/ft³); specific gravity .88. May sometimes weigh up to 1,000 kg/m³ (62 lb/ft³).

Mechanical properties: It has high strength properties and moderate steam bending rating.

Seasoning: The timber dries reasonably well but where zones of abnormal tissue are present, there is a great tendency to split.

Working properties: Machining properties vary with occasional severe blunting of tool edges due to hardness and fibrous texture; with interlocked grain a 20° cutting angle is necessary for planing. Pre-boring for nailing is advised. It takes glue, stain and polish satisfactorily, and when filled produces a good finish.

Durability: The timber is durable but subject to insect attack; it is resistant to preservative treatment, although the sapwood is permeable.

Uses: Heavy constructional work, bridge building, and shingles from selected stock; core stock for plywood. When treated is used for railway sleepers.

Note: A closely related species *Koompassia excelsa*, Taub. produces **tualang**, which is dark brown in colour with a striped figure on quartered surfaces and with similar uses to kempas.

KEYAKI (H)

Zelkova serrata, Makino,
syn. Z. *acuminata*, Planch., also
Z. *carpinifolia*, syn. Z. *crenata*
Family: *Ulmaceae*

Other names: keaki, kilkova keaki.

Distribution: Z. *serrata* grows in China and Japan; Z. *carpinifolia* grows in Iran and the Caucasus and now introduced into the UK.

General description: The heartwood is light golden brown and lustrous, otherwise very similar in general appearance to elm with its coarse texture. The grain varies from straight to irregular and wavy. Weight 625 kg/m^3 (39 lb/ft^3); specific gravity .62.

Mechanical properties: The material is chiefly used for its decorative values, but it is a hard, tough, resilient wood, very strong in all categories for its weight. It has a good steam bending classification for selected material.

Seasoning: Dries rapidly and requires care to prevent distortion and degradation. Best results are when partially air dried and completed in the kiln to prevent undue shrinkage. Medium movement in service.

Working properties: The wood works well with both hand and machine tools, with moderate blunting effect on cutters due to wild grain in some stock. The material nails, screws, glues satisfactorily, and provides an excellent, smooth finish.

Durability: Very resistant to insect and fungal attack, and moderately resistant to preservative treatment. It is durable.

Uses: In China and Japan the wood is used for building and maintenance of temples and is a protected tree reserved for this purpose. For centuries it has been used for lacquer works, cabinetmaking, carvings, and for highly polished columns in temples. Plain wood is used for structural work, shipbuilding, light construction, high-class joinery, carving, and turnery. Very large burrs are obtained from trees which may be up to 1,000 years old, and highly decorative figured wood features delicate bird's eyes, outlined with fine fringes and distinct rays. These selected stocks are sliced into greatly treasured decorative veneers.

KERUING (H)   *Dipterocarpus* spp.
Family: *Dipterocarpaceae*

More than 70 species of *dipterocarpus* produce timber of the keruing type, known by distinctive names according to their country of origin. The principal species are as follows:

Malaysian/Sarawak/Sabah/Indonesian **keruing**, and Malaysian **gurjun**: *D. cornutus*, Dyer; *D. costulatus* V.Sl; *D. crinitus*, Dyer; *D. sublamellatus*, Foxw.

Indian/Andaman **gurjun**: *D. grandiflorus*, Blanco; *D. indicus*, Bedd; *D. macrocarpus*, Vesque.

Sri Lanka **hora** or **gurjun**: *D. zeylanicus*, Thw. Philippines **apitong**, *D. grandifloris*, Blanco.

Burma **gurjun**, Burma **kanyin**, Thailand **yang**: *D. alatus*, Roxb; and *D. turbinatus*, Gaertn.f.

Khmer Republic **dau**: *D. alatus*, Roxb; *D. costatus*, Gaertn.f; *D. dyeri*, Pierre; *D. intricatus*, Dyer; and *D. obtusifolius*, Teijsm. ex Miq.

Burma **eng**, (or **in**) and Thailand **eng** or **pluang**: *D. tuberculatus*, Roxb.

General description: These evergreen trees vary in colour from pinkish-brown to dark brown heartwood, often with a purple tint. The grain is straight to shallowly interlocked, and texture is moderately coarse but even. Some species contain oleo-resin which exudes, especially on the end grain. The weight varies between 640–960 kg/m^3 (40–60 lb/ft^3), average 740 kg/m^3 (46 lb/ft^3), except *D. tuberculatus* which weighs 880 kg/m^3 (55 lb/ft^3); specific gravity averaging .74 and .88 respectively.

Mechanical properties: These species are high in bending and crushing strengths and in stiffness, but with only medium resistance to shock loads. Gurgun is unsuitable for steam bending. Keruing from Sabah and eng from Burma have moderate steam bending properties, but both suffer from resin exudation during the steaming process.

Seasoning: These timbers dry slowly and are difficult to dry uniformly from the centre outwards in thick stock or quartered stock. High temperatures will cause resin exudation. Distortion, especially cupping, is considerable and slight collapse may occur. There is high shrinkage in drying and large movement in service.

Working properties: These vary according to species but blunting is from moderate to severe when the wood also contains silica. Tungsten carbide saws are advised. Straight grained stock machines cleanly but with a fibrous finish. Planing requires a reduced cutting angle of 20° on interlocked grain. Resin adhering to tools, machines, and fences can be troublesome. Nailing is satisfactory and gluing results are variable. The timbers stain well, but varnishing or polishing require care due to the resin.

Durability: Moderately durable. Sapwood liable to attack by powder post beetle. They are moderately resistant or resistant to preservative treatment. Reported to be non-resistant to termites.

Uses: Heavy and light construction, wharf decking, bridges, flooring in domestic and public buildings, but not heavy-duty floors. Vehicle building, sills, wagon sides and floors, and exterior joinery when treated, although liable to exude resin if exposed to strong sunlight.

KINGWOOD (H)

Dalbergia cearensis, Ducke.
Family: *Leguminosae*

Commercial names: violet wood, violetta (USA); bois violet (France).
Other names: violete (Brazil).
Distribution: South America, chiefly Brazil.
General description: The heartwood has variegated colours with a background of rich violet-brown, shading almost to black with streaks of violet-brown, dark violet and black, sometimes with golden yellow, presenting an unmistakeable appearance. Usually straight grained, uniformly fine textured and lustrous. It weighs 1,200 kg/m^3 (75 lb/ft^3); specific gravity 1.2.
Mechanical properties: Although very strong and tough in all strength categories, kingwood is chiefly used for decorative purposes as its use is restricted by the small sizes available.
Seasoning: Drying is rapid and care is needed to avoid a slight tendency to checking and splitting. The material kilns without degrade.
Working properties: Works well with both hand and machine tools with a moderate dulling effect on cutters. If cutting edges are kept sharp a very smooth finish is obtainable. Nails and screws hold well, and the wood can provide a fine, natural waxy finish.
Durability: The timber is durable and extremely resistant to preservative treatment.
Uses: Extremely popular with antique restorers, as "bois violet" was widely used by leading ébènistes during the reigns of Louis XIV and XV of France, and throughout the Georgian periods in England. Chiefly used today in sliced veneer form for inlays and marquetry, oyster veneering, and in solid form for making inlay bandings, turnery, and fancy goods.

KIRI (H)

Paulownia tomentosa, C. Koch.,
syn. *P. imperialis*, Sieb & Zucc.,
P. fargesii
Family: *Scrophulariaceae*

Other names: foxglove tree (UK).
Distribution: *P. tomentosa* occurs in Japan, and *P. fargesii* in China, and both are very similar in all characteristics.
General description: The heartwood varies in colour from silver-grey to a light brown or nut brown, sometimes with a reddish cast. It has a very fine straight grain and smooth even texture. Very light, weighing only 320 kg/m³ (20 lb/ft³); specific gravity .32.
Mechanical properties: Weak in all strength properties, which are unimportant in the uses to which it is best suited.
Seasoning: Dries rapidly and well with little degrade.
Working properties: This timber is easily worked with hand or machine tools and produces an excellent smooth finish. It glues, stains and polishes very well.
Durability: Non-durable, subject to insect attack but permeable to preservative treatment.
Uses: Kiri is highly valued in Japan for a wide range of uses including cabinet and drawer linings, musical instruments, clogs, floats for fishing nets, and for peeling into exceptionally thin "scale veneers", mounted on paper and printed to produce special visiting cards – especially from the silver-grey coloured wood.

KOA (H)

Acacia koa
Family: *Leguminosae*

Distribution: Hawaiian Islands.

General description: The heartwood is reddish to dark brown with regular dark brown zones marking the growth rings showing as black lines on longitudinal surfaces. The grain is interlocked, sometimes wavy or curly, producing fiddleback figure. The texture is medium and even and the surface is lustrous. The wood weighs 670 kg/m^3 (41 lb/ft^3); specific gravity .67.

Mechanical properties: The material has medium bending strength and stiffness, high crushing strength and good resistance to shock loads.

Seasoning: Dries fairly easily without undue degrade. Any tendency to cup can be overcome by final conditioning in the kiln. There is small movement in service.

Working properties: Works fairly easily with both hand and machine tools, but for end grain working the cutting edges must be kept sharp as the material has a moderate blunting effect. A reduced cutting angle of 20° is recommended for planing or moulding when curly grain is present. The wood takes nails and screws well, but gluing properties may be variable. Provides an excellent finish.

Durability: The wood is durable, resistant to insect and fungal attack; extremely resistant to preservative treatment.

Uses: The world-famous Hawaiian ukuleles are made from koa. It is also used for high-grade cabinets and fine furniture, musical instruments, gunstocks, interior joinery, shop and bank fittings, bent work in boat building, coachwork etc., but chiefly produced as a highly decorative veneer, with fiddleback figure, for architectural panelling and decorative face veneering.

KOKKO (H)

Albizia lebbek, Benth.
Family: *Leguminosae*

Other names: siris (India); "East Indian Walnut" (UK).
Distribution: India, Burma and the Andaman Islands.
General description: The heartwood is a mid-brown colour with striking dark brown markings which are irregular, and with a deeply interlocked or irregular grain, often wavy, and a very coarse but even texture. The weight averages about 635 kg/m^3 (39 lb/ft^3); specific gravity .63.
Mechanical properties: This medium density timber has medium bending and crushing strengths, and medium resistance to shock loads and low stiffness. It has a good steam bending classification.
Seasoning: Logs are usually converted in green condition to avoid heart shakes developing, and then dries under cover to avoid surface checking. Ends should be sealed to prevent end splitting. Kiln drying from green is satisfactory. Medium movement in service.
Working properties: Rather difficult to work due to a woolly texture and irregular or interlocked grain which tends to pick up in planing and moulding, requiring a reduced cutting angle. Cutters have to be kept very sharp and there is a moderate blunting effect on cutting edges. Nails, screws, glues and finishes well if the grain is suitably filled.
Durability: Moderately durable also moderately resistant to preservative treatment.
Uses: Solid furniture and panelling, carving, boat building, casks, structural purposes. Chiefly used as sliced decorative veneers for cabinets and panelling, with an attractive walnut-like appearance.

KWILA (H)

Intsia bijuga (Colebr) O.Ktze.
Family: *Leguminosae*

Other names: hintzy (Madagascar); ipil (Philippines).

Distribution: S.E. Asia, Malaysia, Australasia.

General description: The heartwood is brown to dark brown in colour. The grain is slightly interlocked and the texture is moderately coarse. Yellow deposits in the vessels are a common feature of the wood. There is a characteristic scent which persists after seasoning. It is non-siliceous, sometimes lustrous. Average weight is about 800 kg/m³ (50 lb/ft³); specific gravity .80, although timber from Papua New Guinea is a little lighter.

Mechanical properties: Kwila has high bending strength, crushing strength and stiffness, with medium resistance to shock loads. It has a poor steam bending classification due to exudation of oil.

Seasoning: Kwila dries well with little distortion. Sealing is advised to prevent end checking. Air drying to 30% moisture content before kilning keeps degrade to a minimum. It has low shrinkage values and is stable. There is small movement in service.

Working properties: The wood can be worked with hand or power tools but there is a severe blunting effect on cutting edges. A reduction of the cutting angle to 20° will aid planing or moulding quartered surfaces. The timber tends to split when nailed, but holds other fastenings well. May need treating before gluing; it takes stain, polish and paint well, but oily patches may adversely affect the finish.

Durability: Durable. The sapwood is subject to insect attack; the heartwood is resistant to preservative treatment, but the sapwood is permeable.

Uses: Furniture, joinery, shop fitting, boat keels and framing, decking, wharf and bridge construction, general construction, non-impact tool handles, interior fittings, flooring, sills, poles and mining timbers. Selected logs are sliced for decorative veneers for furniture and panelling.

LAMPATI (H)

Duabanga grandiflora, Ham
D. sonneratioides, (H)
syn. *Lagerstroemia grandiflora*, Roxb.
Family: *Lythraceae*

Commercial names: lampatia (UK); phay (Europe).

Other names: duabanga, kochan (India); kalam (Burma); kendata (Malaysia); bong-su, phay sung (Indonesia).

Distribution: India and the Himalayan regions of Indonesia and Burma.

General description: Heartwood is pale grey to yellow-brown in colour, streaked with irregular brown markings and fairly lustrous. The grain is straight, often wavy and interlocked and the texture is coarse and non-uniform. Quarter cut surfaces display an ornamental fleck and very decorative appearance. Weight 410 kg/m³ (25 lb/ft³); specific gravity .41, but varying with origin and growth conditions.

Mechanical properties: Moderately light wood with good strength properties in relation to its weight, but with a poor steam bending classification.

Seasoning: The trees are usually girdled before felling, and the timber requires to be kilned very slowly to avoid checking and twisting. There is medium movement in service.

Working properties: The timber works easily with hand and machine tools, with slight bunting effect. Its gluing, nailing and screwing properties are good. It stains well and can be brought to an excellent finish.

Durability: It is non-durable and subject to insect attack, but is not resistant to preservative treatment and may be used in teredo infested waters when treated.

Uses: In the solid it is used for light joinery work, matchboarding, furniture, tea chests and mouldings, etc. Its chief use is in plywood manufacture and selected logs are sliced for very attractive decorative veneers for panelling and veneering.

LARCH, EUROPEAN (S)

Larix decidua, Mill
syn. *L. europaea*, D.C.
Family: *Pinaceae*

Distribution: Europe, particularly the mountain areas of the Alps, UK, W. Russia.

General description: The resinous heartwood is pale red-brown to brick red in colour, with clearly marked annual rings. The wood is straight grained, contains knots, and has a fine uniform texture. Weight about 590 kg/m³ (37 lb/ft³); specific gravity .59.

Mechanical properties: Air dried timber is about 50% harder than Baltic redwood, and slightly stronger in bending strength and toughness, and similar properties in crushing and impact strengths.

Seasoning: Larch dries fairly rapidly with a tendency to distort and for knots to split and loosen. It may be kiln dried very satisfactorily. There is small movement in service.

Working properties: Works well with most hand and machine tools but knotty material can cause severe blunting of cutting edges. It saws and machines cleanly in most operations although loosened knots may be troublesome. Nailing causes splitting and pre-boring is essential. It takes stain, paint or varnish well.

Durability: The wood is moderately durable and subject to insect attack. The heartwood is resistant and the sapwood moderately resistant to preservative treatment.

Uses: Pit props, posts, transmission poles, piles, boat planking, exterior work in contact with the ground. Door and window frames, flooring, staircases, ship building. As larch is harder and tougher than most conifers, it is used in preference where durability and strength are prime requirements. Sliced as decorative veneers.

Note: Other spp. include:
L. laricina, (Du Roi) K.Koch., **Tamarack larch** (Canada & USA)
L. occidentalis, Nutt, **Western larch** (Brit. Columbia and W. USA)
L. russica, (Endl) Sabine, ex. Trautr., syn. *L. sibirica*, Ledeb., **Siberian larch** (N.E. Russia).

LARCH, JAPANESE (S)

Larix kaempferi, (Lamb) Carr.,
syn. *L. leptolepis*, (Sieb & Zucc) Endl.
L. dahurica, Gord.
Family: *Pinaceae*

Other names: kara-matsu (Japan); red larch (UK).

Distribution: Japan and introduced into Europe and the UK.

General description: The reddish-brown heartwood has clearly marked annual rings with well defined latewood bands. It is resinous with straight grain and a medium fine texture. Weight 530 kg/m³ (33 lb/ft³); specific gravity .53.

Mechanical properties: Seasoned timber is similar in most strength categories to European larch, except that it is 20% less stiff and resistant to radial splitting, and 30 % softer.

Seasoning: The material dries fairly rapidly with a tendency to warp, check and split. Best results are obtained by kilning slowly. There is only small movement. Very poor wood bending classfication.

Working properties: Works fairly easily with hand and machine tools except that the hard knots may be troublesome. Being milder than European larch the soft earlywood zones are liable to tear or crumble when planed and very sharp cutting edges are required. The wood tends to split when nailed so pre-boring is necessary. It can be painted or varnished without difficulty and gives good results.

Durability: The timber is moderately durable. It is subject to attack by pinhole borer beetle and *Sirex* is sometimes present. It is resistant to preservative treatment, and the sapwood is moderately resistant.

Uses: General construction purposes, furniture, flooring, bridge construction and boat building.

LATI (H)

Amphimas pterocarpoides, Harms,
A. ferrugineus, Harms,
A. klaineanus, Pierre,
Family: *Leguminosae*

Other names: bokanga (Congo); adzi (Cameroon); chickebati (Ivory Coast); vahnchu, salaki, m'futu (Gabon).

Distribution: Tropical West Africa.

General description: The heartwood is orange in colour darkening to orange-brown upon exposure. Has distinct growth rings and often ripple marks are present. The grain is straight and texture moderately coarse. Weight 740 kg/m³ (46 lb/ft³); specific gravity .74.

Mechanical properties: A compact, heavy and elastic hardwood with good strength properties in all categories and high resistance to abrasion.

Seasoning: Dries slowly but with tendency to warp and check. Best treatment is to kiln very slowly to avoid degrade. There is small movement.

Working properties: Difficult to work because of its very hard, tough structure; it has a moderately severe blunting effect on cutting edges. It is necessary to pre-bore for nailing or screwing to avoid splitting. The wood glues without difficulty and planed and sanded surfaces may be brought to a smooth finish; polishes well.

Durability: Moderately durable but liable to attack by powder post or common furniture beetle. It is extremely resistant to preservative treatment, and the sapwood is moderately resistant.

Uses: It is an ideal timber for flooring strips and blocks, and mosaic parquetry flooring as it has a high resistance to wear in normal conditions. Also for interior and exterior joinery and general construction.

LAUAN, WHITE (H)

Shorea contorta, Vid.
syn. *Pentacme contorta*, Vid. Merr. & Rolfe.
Family: *Dipterocarpaceae*

Distribution: Philippines.

General description: The heartwood colour is grey with a pinkish tinge. The grain is interlocked or crossed with a moderately coarse texture. Resin ducts in concentric arcs are filled with white resins. The weight is 540 kg/m^3 (33 lb/ft^3); specific gravity .54.

Mechanical properties: The wood has medium bending and crushing strength with low stiffness and shock resistance, and a good steam bending classification.

Seasoning: It seasons easily and well with little degrade.

Working properties: The wood works and machines well in most operations, especially turning and planing, but is rather poor in shaping, boring and mortising. It takes glue and stain well and polishes to a good finish.

Durability: The wood is moderately durable, and easily permeable to preservation treatment.

Uses: Furniture and cabinetmaking, interior joinery, veneer and plywood manufacture. Its waterproof properties make it particularly suitable for boat planking.

Note 1: White lauan proper, is often sold in conjunction with other white lauans, and also **apitong** or **bagac** (*Dipterocarpus grandiflorus*, Blco)

Note 2: White lauan is also a group name for light-weight species of *parashorea*, *pentacme*, and *shorea*.

Note 3: *Parashorea malaanonan*, (Blco) Merr, (*P. plicata* Brandis) and *P. tomentella*, (Sym) W. Meijer, (*P. malaanonan*, Merr. var. *tomentella*, Sym), produce **white seraya**, or **urat mata** in Sabah and **bagtikan** or **white lauan** in the Philippines.

Note 4: *Pentacme contorta* (Vidal) Merr. & Rolfe, and *P. mindanensis*, Foxw, produce **white lauan** and **lamao**, and **mindanao white lauan** is produced from *P. mindanensis*.

Note 5: *Shorea almon*, Foxw, produces **almon** and *Shorea squamata*, Dyer, produces **mayapis**.

LIGNUM VITAE (H)

Guaiacum officinale, L. principally,
and *G. sanctum*, L. and *G. guatemalense*, Planch.
Family: *Zygophyllaceae*

Other names: guayacan (Spanish); bois de gaiac (France); guayacan negro, palo santo (Cuba); ironwood (USA).

Distribution: The West Indies and Tropical America.

General description: One of the hardest and heaviest commercial timbers. The heartwood colour is dark greenish-brown to almost black. The grain is heavily interlocked and irregular, and the texture fine and uniform. The weight varies from 1150–1300 kg/m^3 (72–82 lb/ft^3) averages 1230 kg/m^3 (77 lb/ft^3); specific gravity 1.23. It has a characteristic oily feel due to its guaiac resin content that constitutes 25% of its air dry weight.

Mechanical properties: This exceptionally dense and heavy wood has very high crushing strength and resistance to shock loads and outstanding strength properties, particularly hardness. Straight grained material has a resistance to splitting in the radial plane but splits easily in the tangential plane. However as most material is severely interlocked and of irregular grain this is not usually a problem.

Seasoning: Refractory in drying; logs are liable to check and become ring shaken at the ends in strong sun. End coating is recommended to reduce this form of degrade. There is medium movement in service.

Working properties: It is difficult to work with hand tools and very hard to saw and machine, tending to ride over cutters in planing. There is a moderate blunting effect on cutting edges. The oily nature makes gluing difficult and surface treatment is required. It produces an excellent finish.

Durability: Logs liable to attack by forest longhorn beetle. Very durable and extremely resistant to preservative treatment.

Uses: Owing to the self-lubricating properties of the wood it is used for ship's propeller bushes and bearings, marine equipment, thrust bearings, pulley sheaves, wheels, guides, rollers and blocks, mallet heads, "woods" for bowls, cotton gins, dead eyes, die cutting and turning, and for any purpose where lubrication is impractical or unreliable.

LIME, EUROPEAN (H)

Tilia spp. principally *T. vulgaris*, Hayne., and *T. europaea*, Auct.

Family: *Tiliaceae*

Other names: tilleul (France); linden (Netherlands and Germany).

Distribution: Throughout Europe and the UK.

General description: Cream-yellow, maturing to yellow-brown to pale brown. The grain is straight and texture fine and uniform. Weighs about 540 kg/m³ (34 lb/ft³); specific gravity .54.

Mechanical properties: The wood is suitable for steam bending of a moderate radius of curvature, having medium bending and crushing strength, low stiffness and resistance to shock loads. Resistant to splitting.

Seasoning: Dries fairly rapidly with some tendency to distort with medium movement in service. May be kilned slowly with satisfactory results and little degrade.

Working properties: Lime works easily and readily with hand and machine tools but is inclined to be woolly and requires thin, sharp-edged tools for a smooth finish. A reduced cutting angle is ideal for planing and moulding due to the softness of the material and the slight blunting effect on cutting edges. Glues well and nails satisfactorily; can be brought to a good finish by staining and all finishing processes.

Durability: The sapwood is liable to attack by the common furniture beetle. The heartwood is perishable but permeable to preservative treatment.

Uses: The most important use is for wood carving since it has the ability to resist splitting in any cutting direction. Also as cutting boards for leather work, as it does not draw or bias the knife away from the desired direction of cut. Used for broom handles, bee-hive frames, hat blocks, sounding boards, piano keys, harps, oil cask bungs, toys, artificial limbs, clogs and soles, flat paint brushes, turnery, bobbins, etc. Selected stocks sliced into decorative veneers.

LOURO PRETO (H)

Nectandra mollis, Nees,
syn. *N. villosa*, Nees and Mart,
N. panamensis, Mez.
Family: *Lauraceae*

Other names: canela foreta, canella preta, canela preta, canela escura, canela ferrugem, canela parda. *See note.

Distribution: Brazil.

General description: The heartwood colour varies from light greyish-brown to dark grey-brown, with frequent long darker streaks. The grain is straight to irregular with medium texture and slight lustre. Weight is about 700 kg/m³ (43 lb/ft³); specific gravity .70.

Mechanical properties: This fairly hard and heavy wood has a very poor steam bending classification and medium strength in all categories, except stiffness, which is low. Mainly used for decorative purposes.

Seasoning: Drying should be carried out very slowly to avoid checking and degrade. There is small movement in service.

Working properties: The wood works well with both hand and machine tools with only slight resistance or blunting effect on tools. It finishes very smoothly when sanded. There is some tendency for the grain to pick up when planing or moulding irregular grain, and a reduced cutting angle of 20° is advised. It nails and holds screws well, has good gluing properties and takes stain and polish for an excellent finish.

Durability: Durable. Moderately resistant to attack by wood boring insects and to preservation treatment, but the sapwood is permeable.

Uses: Suitable for external joinery and construction work, ship building, and for furniture and cabinetmaking. Selected logs are sliced for decorative veneers.

*Note: Canela is a general trade name used, with qualifying adjectives, to describe a group of timbers mainly of the *Lauraceae* family, but from the *Ocotea*, *Aniba*, and *Phoebe* genera, in addition to *Nectandra*.

MACACAUBA (H)

Platymiscium pinnatum and allied spp.,
Family: *Leguminosae*

Other names: macacauba preta, macacauba vermelha, macacawood, macacahuba (Brazil); nambar (Nicaragua); vencola, roble colorado (Venezuela).

Distribution: Central and South America.

General description: The heartwood colour varies from rose-red to rich red-brown with darker variegated streaks and veins. The grain is irregular and interlocked, with a uniform, medium texture and a lustrous surface. Weight 960 kg/m³ (60 lb/ft³); specific gravity .96.

Mechanical properties: Macacauba has medium bending, crushing and impact strengths, with low stiffness, and a poor steam bending classification.

Seasoning: Requires care in drying to avoid checking and end splitting and with small movement in service.

Working properties: There are a number of species of *platymiscium* sold as macacauba, with varying working properties. Generally they are not difficult to work with hand or machine tools, except that the irregular or interlocked grain tends to pick up in planing and a reduced cutting angle is recommended. The wood nails and screws, glues and stains well and can be brought to a very good finish.

Durability: The wood is durable, and resistant to preservative treatment.

Uses: Cabinets and furniture making, high-class joinery, musical instruments, (marimba keys), flooring, bridge decking and heavy construction. Selected logs are sliced for decorative veneers.

MADRONA (H)

Arbutus menziesii, Pursh.
A. procera, Dough.
Family: *Ericaceae*

Other names: arbutus (Germany); jarrito (Mexico); madroño (Spain); Pacific madrone, manzanita (USA); strawberry tree (UK)*; also, madrona burr (UK).

Distribution: Canada and USA.

General description: The colour is pale reddish-brown with an irregular pattern of growth rings producing a very decorative effect. The material is straight grained to irregular with a smooth even texture. Weight varies according to growth conditions from 750–850 kg/m³ (46–53 lb/ft³) averaging about 770 kg/m³ (48 lb/ft³); specific gravity .77.

Mechanical properties: Compact and tough with high bending and crushing strength with medium stiffness and resistance to shock loads and a moderate steam bending classification.

Seasoning: Madrona is extremely difficult to season and warps and checks easily. It should be allowed to season very slowly by air drying before kilning. It is very stable after kilning with small movement in service.

Working properties: This hard timber has a moderately severe blunting effect on cutters but works satisfactorily with hand or machine tools, and sanded surfaces are particularly lustrous. Nailed and screwed and glued joints hold well, and it stains and polishes to a high finish.

Durability: Non-durable. Moderately resistant to attack by powder post and common furniture beetle. Resistant to preservative treatment, but the sapwood is permeable.

Uses: High-class furniture, interior fittings, all kinds of turned work such as bowls, novelties, souvenirs, lamp fittings, etc. Selected logs are sliced for very attractive decorative veneers suitable for panelling, cabinets and furniture. The burr (burl) of the tree is very popular for furniture work and marquetry. It is the best source of charcoal for making gunpowder.

*Note: *Arbutus unedo*, L. (strawberry madrone); *A. crispo*, Hoff; *A. salicifolia*, Hoff; *A. serratifolia*, Salisb; *A. vulgaris*, Bub., are other varieties of the same genus from Europe.

MAGNOLIA (H)

Magnolia grandiflora, L.,
M. virginiana, L., and allied spp.
Family: *Magnoliaceae*

Other names: southern magnolia, cucumber wood, black lin, mountain magnolia, sweet magnolia, bat tree, big laurel, bullbay (USA).

Distribution: USA.

General description: The heartwood is straw coloured to greenish-beige, often with dark purple streaks caused by mineral deposits, and fine, light coloured lines of terminal parenchyma. It is straight grained; the texture is fine and uniform with a satin-like lustre. Weight about 560 kg/m³ (35 lb/ft³); specific gravity .56.

Mechanical properties: This medium density timber has low bending strength and stiffness and medium crushing strength and a medium steam bending classification.

Seasoning: The wood is subject to a fairly high tangential shrinkage during air drying, but kilning may be carried out with almost no risk of checking or warping and it is extremely stable when seasoned. There is very small movement in service.

Working properties: The wood offers very little resistance and is easy to work with hand or machine tools. Planed surfaces are smooth and can be nailed, screwed, glued, stained and polished with excellent results.

Durability: The sapwood is liable to attack by the common furniture beetle and the timber is non-durable. The heartwood is moderately resistant to preservative treatment but the sapwood is permeable; it should not be used externally without treatment.

Uses: It is ideal for louvres, interior joinery, doors, boxes, crates, interior fittings, mouldings, foundry moulds, turnery and furniture. Selected logs are sliced for decorative veneers, especially those with variegated mineral stained streaks which are ideal for panelling. Also used for woodwool.

MAHOGANY, AFRICAN (H)
(1) *Khaya ivorensis*, A. Chév., W. Africa
(2) *K. anthotheca*, Welw. C.DC., W. and E. Africa
(3) *K. nyasica*, Stapf. ex Baker.f., E. Africa
Family: *Meliaceae*

Other names: (1) Nigerian, Benin, Lagos or Degema mahogany; (1) and (2) Ghana, Ivory Coast, Takoradi or Grand Bassam mahogany; (2) krala (Ivory Coast), mangona (Cameroon), munyama (Uganda); mbaua (Mozambique), mbawa (Malawi), mkangazi (Tanzania).

Distribution: Tropical West, Central and East Africa.

General description: Heartwood varies from light to deep reddish-brown. Grain straight to interlocked, moderately coarse textured to medium. Logs may have brittleheart or softheart and cross fractures or heartbreaks. Weight 540–590 kg/m³ (34–36 lb/ft³); s.g. .54 to .59.

Mechanical properties: *K. anthotheca* has moderately good wood bending properties, the other types cannot be bent without severe buckling or fibre rupture. The bending strength is low, stiffness and resistance to shock loads is very low and the crushing strength is medium.

Seasoning: Dries rapidly with little degrade except where tension wood occurs, causing serious distortion. Small movement in service.

Working properties: There is a moderate blunting effect on tools, and tension wood or brittleheart and interlocked grain can cause woolliness. To avoid tearing the grain a reduced cutting angle of from 15° to 20° is desirable. Nailing, screwing and gluing properties are good and it may be stained and polished to an excellent finish.

Durability: Liable to insect attack. The heartwood is moderately durable but extremely resistant to preservative treatment and the sapwood is moderately resistant.

Uses: Widely used for furniture and cabinetmaking, office, shop and bank fitting, interior joinery, boatbuilding and vehicle bodies. It is extensively used for laminations especially in cold moulded processes. Rotary cut logs are used for plywood and sliced veneers for decorative work.

Note: Related spp. include *K. grandifoliola*, C.DC., and *K. senegalensis*, (Desr) A. Juss, both sold as **heavy African mahogany** and sometimes mixed with shipments of lighter species.

MAHOGANY, AMERICAN (H)

Swietenia macrophylla, King
Family: *Meliaceae*

Commercial names: Central American mahogany, British Honduras mahogany, Costa Rican, Brazilian, Peruvian, Nicaraguan, etc. according to the country of origin (UK).

Other names: zopilote gateado (Mexico); araputanga, aguano, acajou, mogno (Brazil).

Distribution: Central and South America.

General description: The heartwood colour varies from light to dark reddish-brown to deep, rich red. The grain is straight to interlocked. Flat sliced or sawn timber shows a prominent growth ring figure. The texture is medium to coarse and uniform. Dark coloured gum or white deposits commonly occur in the pores, and sometimes ripple marks are seen. Weight varies from 540 kg/m^3 (34 lb/ft^3) Honduras, to 640 kg/m^3 (40lb/ft^3) Sth. American; s.g. .54 to .64.

Mechanical properties: The wood has low bending strength, medium crushing strength, very low stiffness and resistance to shock loads. It has moderately good steam bending properties.

Seasoning: Dries fairly rapidly and well, without distortion, but tension wood and the presence of glutinous fibres can result in a high rate of longitudinal shrinkage in kilning. There is small movement in service.

Working properties: Can be worked easily with hand or machine tools, if kept very sharp. It is easy to glue, takes nails and screws well, stains and polishes to an excellent finish.

Durability: Sapwood is liable to attack by powder post beetle and the common furniture beetle. The heartwood is durable and extremely resistant to preservative treatment.

Uses: High-class furniture and cabinetmaking, reproduction furniture, interior joinery, panelling, boat interiors, pianos, burial caskets, carving, pattern making, moulds and dies. Rotary cut veneers used for plywood manufacture and sliced veneers produce a wide variety of decorative figures such as fiddleback, blister, stripe, roe, curly, mottled, pommelle, etc. for decorative veneering.

Note: Related spp: Cuban or Spanish mahogany *Swietenia mahogani*, Jacq., which for 250 years was the most cherished cabinet wood in the world, has now become of more historical importance than commercial significance due to indiscriminate wastage. *S. candollei*, Pitt., Venezuelan mahogany.

MAKORÉ (H)

(1) *Tieghemella heckelii*, Pierre ex A. Chév.
syn. *Mimusops heckelii*, (A. Chév) Hutch & Dalz.,
and *Dumoria heckelii*, A. Chév.
(2) *Tieghemella africana*, Pierre.
Family: *Sapotaceae*

Commercial names: (1) makoré (Ivory Coast); baku, abaku (Ghana); agamokwe (Nigeria). (2) douka (Cameroon, Gabon); dumori (Ivory Coast).

Distribution: West Africa.

General description: The heartwood colour varies from pink-red to blood red and red-brown. The grain is often straight but many figured logs have a decorative moiré or watered silk appearance, or a chequered mottle, sometimes with streaks of a darker colour. The surface is lustrous and the texture uniform and fine. It weighs about 620 kg/m^3 (39 lb/ft^3); specific gravity .62. Liable to blue stain if in contact with iron compounds in moist conditions.

Mechanical properties: The wood has medium bending and crushing strengths but low stiffness and resistance to shock loads. Although the heartwood is suitable for steam bending of moderate curvature the sapwood will buckle or rupture.

Seasoning: Dries fairly rapidly but liable to twist a little or split around knots, otherwise little degrade. Small movement in service.

Working properties: Silica in the wood causes severe blunting of tools, and below 20% moisture content tungsten carbide tipped saws are essential. Tends to split in nailing, holds screws well, glues and stains satisfactorily and an excellent finish is obtained if filler is used.

Durability: Very durable. Sapwood is liable to attack by powder post beetle. Heartwood is extremely resistant to preservation treatment and the sapwood moderately resistant.

Uses: Furniture, cabinets, turnery, high-class joinery, interior fittings, laboratory benches, exterior joinery, framing for vehicles and carriages and in boat building large quantities of marine plywood are used. Selected logs are sliced for highly decorative veneers for coach and architectural panelling and for cabinetmaking and finished joinery.

MANGEAO (H)

Litsea calicaris, Kirk
syn. *Tetranthera calicaris*, Hook.f.
Family: *Lauraceae*

Other name: tangeao.
Distribution: New Zealand.
General description: The heartwood colour is creamy light brown with a dull lustre. Vessel lines are slightly darker in colour and visible on longitudinal surfaces; it is straight grained with a fine and even texture. Weight from 608–768 kg/m^3 (38–48 lb/ft^3), average about 640 kg/m^3 (40 lb/ft^3); specific gravity .64.
Mechanical properties: The timber has medium bending and crushing strengths, low stiffness and high resistance to shock loads. It has a very good steam bending classification.
Seasoning: Dries well without degrade. Small movement in service.
Working properties: Works easily with hand or machine tools, with a slight blunting effect on tools. Takes nails, screws, glue, stain and polish without problems and a good finish is obtainable.
Durability: Durable and immune from fungal and insect attack. Sapwood permeable for preservation treatment.
Uses: Suitable for a wide range of purposes requiring strength, toughness and elasticity in relation to its weight. Agricultural machinery working parts, ship's blocks, wheelwright's work, bullock yokes, cooperage, light framing, pick handles, jack stocks, sporting goods, motor bodies, bridge decking, stockyard gates, caravan ribs, exterior joinery, plywood manufacture, dowels, poles, scaffolding, mining timber, sleepers, mauls, boat building, rifle stocks, flooring for buses, dance halls, factories. Decorative veneers for furniture and panelling.

MANSONIA (H)

Mansonia altissima, A. Chév.
Family: *Triplochitonaceae*

Other names: aprono (Ghana); ofun (Nigeria); bété (Ivory Coast, Cameroon).

Distribution: West Africa.

General description: Grey-brown to light mauve, often purplish with lighter or darker bands. Wide variation in colour. Straight grained and fine smooth texture. Weight about 590 kg/m³ (37 lb/ft³); specific gravity .59.

Mechanical properties: Steam bending strength is high, also high crushing strength, medium resistance to shock loads and low stiffness. The bending classification is good but variable. It is not tolerant of knots. Buckling and fracture is avoided if bent in green condition.

Seasoning: Dries fairly rapidly and well except for splitting of knots and a tendency to warp. Kiln dries rapidly and well; shakes tend to extend and a little distortion in the length may occur. Shrinkage is small and there is medium movement in service.

Working properties: Mansonia is easy to work with hand and machine tools with only a moderate blunting effect on tools. It nails, screws and glues well, and stains and polishes to a good finish. The fine dust produced by machining and sanding operations can cause dermatitis and irritation of the nose, eyes and throat.

Durability: It is highly resistant to insect attack and moderately durable to marine borers. The heartwood is very durable and extremely resistant to preservative treatment although the sapwood is permeable.

Uses: Mansonia is often used as a substitute for American black walnut. High-quality cabinet work, chairs, radio and television cabinets, fancy turnery, window and door capping for luxury cars, dashboards, interior joinery, pianos, musical instruments, shop fittings. Also used for plywood. Slices well for decorative veneering and used in marquetry.

MAPLE, EUROPEAN (H)

Acer campestre, L.
A. platanoides, L.
Family: *Aceraceae*

Commercial names: *A. campestre*: field maple (UK); érable (France); ahorn (Germany). *A. platanoides*: Norway maple, European maple, Bosnian maple (UK).

Distribution: Throughout Europe including the UK, Asia Minor and Russia.

General description: Creamy white when fresh felled with a natural lustre on quartered surfaces. Tends to weather and mature into a light tan colour. The grain is generally straight but often curly or wavy grain is present. Fine textured. The weight of *A. campestre* is 690 kg/m³ (43 lb/ft³) and *A. platanoides* 660 kg/m³ (41 lb/ft³); specific gravity .69 and .66.

Mechanical properties: The timber has medium bending and crushing strengths, with low stiffness and resistance to shock loads. It is a good steam bending material.

Seasoning: Dries slowly without undue degrade, but is inclined to stain. If the original white colour is to be preserved it needs to be kiln dried fairly rapidly and carefully. There is small movement in service.

Working properties: It is easy to work with both hand and machine tools but with a moderate blunting effect on cutting edges. The cutting angle should be reduced to 15° for planing curly or wavy grained stock. Nailing may need pre-boring; the wood glues and stains well and can be brought to an excellent finish.

Durability: The heartwood is non-durable. The sapwood is subject to attack by common furniture beetle and is permeable for preservation treatment. The heartwood is resistant.

Uses: Maple is an excellent turnery wood. Also for brushbacks, domestic woodware, furniture and joinery work. Selected stocks are sliced for highly decorative veneers for panelling. Maple is also treated chemically to produce harewood with an attractive silver-grey colour and in which the veins appear tan coloured.

MAPLE, JAPANESE (H)

Acer mono, Maxim et al.,
principally, including
A. palmatum.
Family: *Aceraceae*

Distribution: Japan.

General description: The wood is creamy-tan to pinkish-brown in colour. The growth rings produce fine brown lines on longitudinal surfaces. Usually straight grained but sometimes wavy or curly. The texture is fine and even. The weight varies upon growth conditions between 610–710 kg/m³ (38–44 lb/ft³), with a fair average 670 kg/m³ (41 lb/ft³); specific gravity .67.

Mechanical properties: This timber has a good steam bending classification and is medium in all strength categories.

Seasoning: The wood dries slowly with no undue degrade and there is medium movement in service.

Working properties: Maple gives a moderate blunting effect on tools, and there is some tendency for tooth vibration in sawing. In machining there is a tendency to ride on cutters or burn on end grain working, and a reduction to 20° in the cutting angle should be used in planing. Nailing requires pre-boring, but gluing, staining and polishing give excellent results.

Durability: Non-durable and liable to attack by common furniture beetle. The heartwood is resistant to preservative treatment but the sapwood is permeable.

Uses: The timber has a high resistance to abrasion and makes an excellent flooring material suitable for heavy industrial traffic, roller skating rinks, dance halls, squash courts, bowling alleys etc. Also for rollers in textile mills, shoe lasts, piano actions and sports goods. Used as an alternative to rock maple for furniture, cabinetmaking, panelling, interior joinery, etc. Selected logs sliced for decorative veneers for panelling; rotary cut veneers for plywood manufacture.

MAPLE, ROCK (H)

Acer saccharum, Marsh. (principally),
and *A. nigrum*, Michx.f.
Family: *Aceraceae*

Commercial names: hard maple (UK, Canada and USA); white maple (sapwood) USA; sugar maple (*A. saccharum*) or black maple (*A. nigrum*) USA.

Distribution: Canada and Eastern USA.

General description: Cream-white with a reddish tinge. Large trees may have dark brown heart. Usually straight grained but sometimes curly or wavy. Fine brown lines give an attractive growth ring figure on plain sawn surfaces. Texture is fine and even. Weight average about 720 kg/m^3 (45 lb/ft^3); specific gravity .72.

Mechanical properties: High in all strength properties except stiffness which is medium. It has a very good steam bending classification.

Seasoning: The timber dries slowly without undue difficulty. There is medium movement in service.

Working properties: A difficult wood to work with a moderate blunting of cutting edges. A reduced cutting angle is required with wavy or curly grained material. Pre-bore for nailing or screwing; takes glue, stain and polish satisfactorily.

Durability: The heartwood is non-durable and the sapwood is liable to attack by furniture beetle. Growth defects caused by insects (pith flecks) are sometimes found. The heartwood is resistant to preservative treatment but the sapwood is permeable.

Uses: Has a high resistance to abrasion and wear and is used for all heavy-duty flooring. Also used for furniture and panelling, textile machinery rollers, shoe lasts, parts of piano actions, musical instruments, sports goods, butcher's blocks, dairy and laundry equipment and plywood. It is excellent for turnery. Selected stocks are rotary cut to produce **bird's eye maple** veneer, while others are sliced for highly decorative veneers for panelling etc.

MAPLE, SOFT (H)

(1) *Acer rubrum*, L.,
(2) *A. saccharinum* L.,
(3) *A. negundo*, L.,
(4) *A. macrophyllum*, Pursh.
Family: *Aceraceae*

Commercial names: (1) red maple (Canada and USA). (2) silver maple (Canada and USA). (3) Manitoba maple, ash-leafed maple (Canada) is often included in shipments but is actually box elder and weaker than maple. (4) Pacific maple (UK); Oregon maple (USA); big leaf maple (Canada).

Other names: (1–3) soft maple (UK). (4) Pacific maple (UK).

Distribution: Canada and Eastern USA.

General description: Creamy white and straight grained. It is less lustrous than rock maple and the growth rings are comparatively indistinct. The rays are narrower and less conspicuous but pith flecks more frequently present. Weight (1) 630 kg/m³ (39 lb/ft³); (2) 550 kg/m³ (34 lb/ft³); (3) 490 kg/m³ (30 lb/ft³) and (4) 560 kg/m³ (35 lb/ft³); specific gravity: (1) .63; (2–4) .54 average.

Mechanical properties: Medium bending and crushing strengths, low stiffness and resistance to shock loads. It is good for steam bending.

Seasoning: Dries slowly with little degrade or problems. There is small movement in service.

Working properties: Soft maple can be worked satisfactorily with hand and machine tools although it has a moderate dulling effect on cutters. Nailing is satisfactory with care; gluing results may be variable. May be stained and polished to an excellent finish.

Durability: The heartwood is non-durable and liable to attack by insects. It is moderately resistant to preservative treatment but the sapwood is permeable.

Uses: Soft maple is used for domestic flooring, furniture, interior joinery, piano actions, dairy and laundry equipment, sports goods, turnery, panelling, etc. Selected logs are rotary cut for plywood manufacture in Canada and USA, and sliced for highly figured decorative veneering.

'MARACAIBO BOXWOOD' (H)

Gossypiospermum praecox, P. Wils.
(Casearia praecox, Griseb.)
Family: *Flacourtiaceae*

Other names: Venezuelan boxwood, Columbian boxwood, West Indian boxwood, zapatero* (UK); palo blanco (Dominican Republic); pau branco, castelo, zapateiro (Brazil).

Distribution: Venezuela, Columbia and the West Indies.

General description: There is little difference between sapwood and heartwood which varies from almost white to lemon-yellow. It is usually straight grained, with a compact, fine uniform texture and high lustre. It is subject to blue stain in humid conditions. Weight from 800–900 kg/m³ (50–56 lb/ft³); specific gravity .85.

Mechanical properties: Because of the small dimensions of the timber and end-uses, the strength properties are not available. It is reported to have good steam bending properties where discolouration is unimportant.

Seasoning: The timber dries very slowly with tendency to split and surface check, and logs are often halved or cut into dimension stock before stacking. Very small movement in service.

Working properties: There is a high resistance in cutting and a moderate blunting effect on cutters. The wood carves and turns easily, and can be brought to a very smooth, highly polished finish.

Durability: Sapwood is liable to attack by common furniture beetle. The heartwood is durable, and resistant to preservative treatment.

Uses: Carving and turnery, shuttles, spindles, knife handles, piano keys, precision rulers and measuring instruments, mallet heads, engraver's blocks, inlay lines, stringings and bandings. Also dyed black in imitation of ebony for inlay purposes, and sliced or sawn for decorative veneers for cabinet work and reproduction furniture.

Note 1: Not a true boxwood (*Buxus sempervirens*). Other botanically unrelated species include *Phyllostylon brasiliensis* as **San Domingo Boxwood**; and *Gonioma kamassi* as **Kamassi boxwood** (UK). **Note 2:** The name zapatero is the name given to **purpleheart** (*Peltogyne spp.*) in Trinidad, and to **surudan** (*Hyeronima spp.*) in Panama.

MARBLEWOOD (H)

(1) *Diospyros marmorata*, Park.
(2) *Marmaroxylon racemosum*
Family: *Ebenaceae*

Other names: zebrawood (UK)

Distribution: (1) The Andaman Islands (2) Guyana

General description: The heartwood colour is grey-brown with darker brown or black bands, which alternate on quartered surfaces to provide a zebra-striped appearance. On end grain surfaces a pattern of irregular brown-black spots appear and give the wood a marble-like appearance. The wood is smooth and has a fine, even texture, and is usually straight grained. It weighs 1030 kg/m^3 (64 lb/ft^3); specific gravity 1.03.

Seasoning: The wood requires care in drying, and should be converted into the smallest sizes possible and allowed to dry slowly, well protected, to avoid the tendency to warp and for end and surface checking. There is small movement in service.

Mechanical properties: Although this timber is very strong and tough in bending, crushing, stiffness and impact properties, it is not used for its strength but for its highly decorative qualities.

Working properties: It is a difficult wood to work with hand and machine tools upon which it has a severe blunting effect. A very hard, smooth finish is obtainable, especially in turnery. The wood glues well and if care is taken not to use materials which affect the colour contrasts, a beautiful finish can be obtained.

Durability: This is a very durable wood, very resistant to preservative treatment.

Uses: Used for cabinet work, inlay and small decorative trinkets, brushbacks, carving, turnery. Selected logs are sliced for decorative veneers.

MERANTI, DARK RED;
SERAYA, DARK RED;
and LAUAN, RED (H)

Shorea spp. (1) *S. pauciflora*, King.
(2) *S. acuminata*, Dyer (in part)
(3) *S. curtisii*, Dyer ex King (in part)
(4) *S. negrosensis*, Foxw. (5) *S. polysperma*, Merr.
(6) *S. squamata*, Dyer
(*S. palosapis*, Merr.) (in part)
(7) *S. agsaboensis*, Stern
Family: *Dipterocarpaceae*

Commercial names: dark red meranti (Nos. 1, 2 & 3) West Malaysia, (No. 1) Sarawak and Brunei; red lauan (No. 4) Philippines; dark red seraya (No. 1) Sabah.

Other names: nemesu (No. 1 only) Malaysia; dark red lauan (Nos. 4 to 7) UK and Philippines; red lauan (No. 4) Philippines; tangile and bataan (No. 5 only) Philippines; mayapis (No. 6 and part No. 5) and tiaong (No. 7) Philippines; oba suluk (No. 1) Sabah.

General description: The heartwood colour is medium to dark red brown with conspicuous white dammar or resin streaks. Grain is interlocked; texture rather coarse. Brittleheart can be present. Weight from 580–770 kg/m^3 (36–48 lb/ft^3) average 670 kg/m^3 (42 lb/ft^3); s.g. .67.

Mechanical properties: The wood has medium bending and crushing strengths, but the stiffness factor is low and also low resistance to shock loads. Severe buckling occurs in steam bending and distortion during drying. The steam bending classification is poor.

Seasoning: Slower drying than light meranti, with tendency to distort and risk of splitting and checking in thicker material. There is small movement in service.

Working properties: Works well with hand and machine tools with only slight blunting effect on tools; sawn surfaces are fibrous. Nailing and screwing properties are good and the wood glues, stains and polishes well.

Durability: Sapwood liable to attack by powder post beetle. All species are moderately durable to durable, and from moderately resistant to extremely resistant to preservative treatment.

Uses: Exterior and interior joinery, shopfitting, boatbuilding and flooring. When treated, for exterior cladding and for use in exposed situations. Otherwise same uses as for light red meranti. Rotary cut for plywood manufacture and sliced for decorative veneers.

MERANTI, LIGHT RED;   *Shorea spp.* (1) *S. acuminata*, Dyer (in part)
SERAYA, LIGHT RED;   (2) *S. leprosula*, Miq. (3) *S. parvifolia*, Dyer
AND LAUAN WHITE (H)   (4) *S. ovalis*, Bl. (5) *S. macroptera*, Dyer
(6) *S. albida*, Sym (part) (7) *S. quadrinervis*, V.Sl.
(8) *S. leptoclados*, Sym. (9) *S. smithiana*, Sym. (10) *S. almon*, Foxw.
(11) *S. eximia*, Foxw. (12) *S. squamata*, Dyer (in part) (13) *S. palosapis*, Merr.
Family: *Dipterocarpaceae*

Commercial names: meranti (Malaysia, Sarawak, Brunei, Indonesia); seraya (Sabah); white lauan (in part) Philippines.

Other names: red meranti (Nos. 1 to 5) Malaysia, Sarawak, Indonesia and UK; perawan, meranti bunga and alan bunga (Nos. 3, 6 & 7) Sarawak; lanan (Nos. 2, 3 & 4) Kalimantan; red seraya and seraya merah (Nos. 2, 3, 8 & 9) Sabah; light red lauan (Nos. 10 & 11) UK; almon (Nos. 10 & 11) and mayapis (Nos. 12 & 13) Philippines.

General description: The heartwood varies in colour from very pale pink to light red-brown. The grain is interlocked and wavy and the texture coarse but even. The wood is lustrous. End grain surfaces may show tangential lines of white resin. The weight varies from 400 kg/m^3 (25 lb/ft^3) to 705 kg/m^3 (44 lb/ft^3), but the general average is 550 kg/m^3 (34 lb/ft^3); s.g. .55.

Mechanical properties: Bending and crushing strengths are medium but stiffness and resistance to shock loads is low. The steam bending class is very poor as severe buckling occurs.

Seasoning: Dries fairly rapidly with little distortion but liable to cup. Thicker material dries slowly with tendency to surface checking. There is small movement in service.

Working properties: Works well with hand and machine tools with only slight blunting effect on cutting edges. Takes nails and screws satisfactorily and glues well. Produces a good finish when filler is used.

Durability: Sapwood is liable to attack by powder post beetle. The heartwood varies from moderately durable to non-durable. All species vary from moderately resistant to extremely resistant to preservation treatment.

Uses: Interior joinery, light structural work, joinery, carpentry, domestic flooring, panelling, cheap-grade furniture, interior framing, and drawer sides and backs. Extensively used for plywood manufacture. Selected logs are sliced for decorative veneering.

MERANTI, WHITE (H)

*Shorea spp. (*section *Anthoshorea) principally:*
S. bracteolata, Dyer; *S. hypochra,* Dyer; *S. assamica,* Dyer
Family: *Dipterocarpaceae*

Commercial names: white meranti (West Malaysia, Sarawak, Brunei, Sabah).
Other names: lun and lun puteh (Sarawak); melapi (Sabah).
General description: The heartwood matures from almost white when freshly cut to a pale orange-brown, to deep gold-brown. The grain is interlocked and the texture moderately coarse but even. Minute grains of silica in the wood are a feature of these species. The surface is lustrous with a ribbon figure on radial surfaces. Weight about 660 kg/m^3 (41 lb/ft^3); s.g. .66.
Mechanical properties: This species has medium strength in all categories, but has a very poor steam bending classification.
Seasoning: The wood dries well without serious degrade. Small movement in service.
Working properties: Severe blunting effect on tools due to the high silica content in the ray cells. For sawing, tungsten carbide tipped saws and an increased tooth pitch are recommended. The wood nails and screws well, and glues without difficulty. The wood stains easily and can be brought to a good finish when filled.
Durability: The heartwood is moderately durable, and varies from resistant to extremely resistant to preservative treatment.
Uses: Furniture, joinery, ship and boat planking, shop fitting and carriage framing. Rotary cut into veneer for plywood; (the silica content does not affect the peeling process). Selected logs sliced for decorative veneering.
Note: White meranti is NOT the equivalent of Sabah **white seraya** or Philippines **white lauan**. **White seraya** is *Parashorea malaanonan,* Blco. Merr. from Sabah and the Philippines; other names: urat mata (Sabah), bagtikan (Philippines). Also *P. tomentella,* (Sym) W. Meijer, **white lauan** is a group name for species of *parashorea, pentacme* and *shorea.* Therefore white lauan from Sabah and the Philippines is (in part) *parashorea malaanonan,* and *P. tomentella,* but also *pentacme contorta* (Vidal) Merr. & Rolfe, from the Philippines, and also *pentacme mindanensis,* Foxw., known in the Philippines as **Mindanao white lauan**.

**MERANTI, YELLOW; and
SERAYA, YELLOW (H)**

Shorea spp: (Richetia group) principally:
(1) *S. faguetiana*, Heim (2) *S. multiflora*, Sym.
(3) *S. resina-nigra*, Foxw. (4) *S. hopeifolia*, Sym.
(5) *S. acuminatissima*, Sym. (6) *S.gibbosa*, Brandis.
Family: *Dipterocarpaceae*

Commercial names: yellow meranti (West Malaysia, Sarawak, and Brunei); yellow seraya (Sabah); meranti damar hitam (Malaya).

Other names: lun and lun kuning (1, 2 & 4) Sarawak; seraya kuning (1, 5 & 6) Sabah.

General description: Dull yellow or yellow-brown, maturing to dull brown. The grain is shallowly interlocked, texture moderately coarse but finer than red meranti. Brittleheart is sometimes present. Liable to develop blue mineral stain when in contact with iron compounds in moist conditions. Weight from 480–740 kg/m^3 (30–46 lb/ft^3), average weight about 660 kg/m^3 (41 lb/ft^3); specific gravity .66.

Mechanical properties: Bending strength and resistance to shock loads is low; crushing strength medium but stiffness very low with a moderate steam bending classification.

Seasoning: The wood dries slowly but well, with a slight tendency to cup. There is some risk of honeycombing in thick sizes and for existing shakes to extend. Small movement in service.

Working properties: Works satisfactorily with a moderate blunting effect on tools. Nailing and screwing properties are good. Gluing holds well, and the surface can be brought to a good finish when filled.

Durability: Sapwood is liable to attack by powder post beetle. The heartwood is moderately durable. The sapwood is moderately resistant to preservative treatment and the heartwood is extremely resistant.

Uses: This non-resinous wood is suitable for light building construction, interior joinery and fittings, furniture and flooring. Rotary cut for plywood manufacture in Malaya.

MENGKULANG (H)

Heritiera javanica, (Bl.) Kosterm.,
H. simplicifolia, (Mast.) Kosterm.,
H. borneensis, etc. (formerly Tarrietia spp.)
Family: *Sterculiaceae*

Other names: kembang (Sabah); chumprak, chumprag (Thailand); lumbayan (Philippines).
Distribution: Malaysia and South East Asia.
General description: The heartwood colour varies from medium to dark red-brown, sometimes with dark streaks on longitudinal surfaces, and fairly large rays appear as conspicuous red flecks on quartered surfaces. The wood is lustrous, the grain interlocked and irregular, and the texture moderately coarse and fairly even. It has a greasy feel, and ripple marks are commonly present. Weight range from 640–720 kg/m³ (40–45 lb/ft³) average 720 kg/m³ (45 lb/ft³), with kembang from Sabah in the lower weight range; specific gravity .72.
Mechanical properties: This heavy density wood has medium bending strength and medium stiffness, with high crushing strength and medium resistance to shock loads. It is not a steam bending wood.
Seasoning: The timber dries rapidly and well with some tendency to surface checking and some logs may warp or twist. There is small movement in service.
Working properties: There is severe blunting of tools, especially saws, but works with moderate ease. Tungsten carbide tipped saws are advised. Splits when nailed unless pre-bored. Gluing is satisfactory, and when filled, can be painted, stained or polished to a good finish.
Durability: The wood is non-durable and resistant to preservative treatment. The sapwood is moderately resistant. Liable to powder post beetle attack.
Uses: General construction, carpentry, interior joinery, panelling, cabinet and furniture fitments, wheelwrighting, domestic flooring. The wood is peeled for plywood manufacture in South East Asia. Selected logs are sliced for decorative veneers for panelling and cabinet work, marquetry, etc.

MERBAU (H)

(1) Intsia bijuga (Colebr) O. Ktze.
(2) *Intsia palembanica*, Miq.
Family: *Leguminosae*

Other names: (1) hintzy (Madagascar); ipil (Philippines); mirabow (Sabah). (2) merbau (Malaysia).

Distribution: Madagascar, Philippines, Malaysia and Indonesia.

General description: The yellowish-brown colour of the heartwood darkens to dark red-brown upon exposure. Lighter coloured parenchyma markings provide an attractive figure on tangential surfaces. The grain is interlocked, sometimes wavy, providing a ribbon striped figure on radial surfaces. The texture is coarse but even. Liable to stain if in contact with iron compounds in damp conditions and to corrode ferrous metals. Vessel cavities are often filled with sulphur yellow and dark deposits. (1) Weighs 900 kg/m^3 (56lb/ft^3); (2) Weighs about 800 kg/m^3 (50lb/ft^3); s.g. .90 and .80.

Mechanical properties: The timber has medium bending strength, stiffness and resistance to shock loads, and a high crushing strength. It has only a moderate steam bending classification due to gum exudation.

Seasoning: Dries well and without much degrade, and low shrinkage; if hurried there is a tendency for end splitting and surface checking to occur. There is small movement in service.

Working properties: The wood has a moderate blunting effect on cutters, and the gum tends to collect on saws. The grain may tear out on quartered material when planing or moulding unless a reduced cutting angle of 20° is used. The wood tends to split in nailing and pre-boring is necessary. It holds screws well and can be glued, stained and polished satisfactorily but requires considerable filling. The yellow deposits are water soluble and the dye has a lasting effect on textiles.

Durability: Durable and resistant to preservative treatment.

Uses: General and heavy constructional work, flooring, panelling, high-class joinery, furniture making, agricultural implements, axe and tool handles, and when treated, for railway sleepers, etc. Selected logs sliced for decorative veneering.

MERSAWA AND KRABAK (H)

Anisoptera spp.
Mersawa comprises principally: *A. costata*, Korth.,
A. laevis, Ridl., *A. scaphula*, Pierre, *A. curtisii*, Dyer, *A. marginata*, Korth.
Krabak comprises: *A. curtisii*, Dyer, *A. oblonga*, Dyer, *A. scaphula*, Pierre.
Palosapis comprises: *A. thurifera*, Bl.
Kaunghmu comprises: *A. scaphula*, Pierre.
Family: *Dipterocarpaceae*

Other names: pengiran (Sabah); kaunghmu (Burma); palosapis (Philippines).

Distribution: Malaysia and S.E. Asia.

General description: The colour of the heartwood is yellowish-brown with a pink tinge, maturing to a straw-brown on exposure. The grain is interlocked slightly; the texture moderately coarse but even. The prominent rays provide a silver grain figure and a slight stripe on quartered surfaces. This moderately hard wood varies in weight from 510–740 kg/m^3 (32–46 lb/ft^3), average about 640 kg/m^3 (40 lb/ft^3); specific gravity .64. Burmese supplies are lighter, weighing 560 kg/m^3 (35 lb/ft^3); specific gravity .56.

Mechanical properties: Low bending strength, medium crushing strength, low resistance to shock loads and very low stiffness; steam bending classification is poor.

Seasoning: The wood dries very slowly and there is some difficulty in extracting moisture from the centre of thick stock. Degrade is confined to slight distortion, and care is needed in accurately measuring initial moisture content for kilning.

Working properties: Relatively easy to work but the interlocked grain and silica content causes severe blunting of saw teeth and cutting edges. It nails and screws well, glues easily and stains and polishes satisfactorily.

Durability: Moderately durable; sapwood liable to attack by powder post beetle. Moderately resistant to preservative treatment.

Uses: General construction, interior joinery, vehicle bodies, flooring, boat planking. Used locally for furniture. Suitable for utility plywood but is not recommended for concrete shuttering as it retards the setting of cement. Selected logs sliced for veneering.

MESQUITE (H)

Prosopis juliflora, (Swartz) DC,
syn. *Neltuma juliflora*, (H)
Family: *Mimosaceae*

Other names: honey locust, ironwood, algaroba.

Distribution: North and South America.

General description: Rich dark brown heartwood with wavy darker lines, not lustrous but fragrant. Grain straight to wavy; texture medium to coarse. Distinct growth rings. Weight 800 kg/m³ (50 lb/ft³); specific gravity .80.

Mechanical properties: This is a hard, heavy, tough and strong timber, with high bending and crushing strengths, medium stiffness and resistance to shock loads. Moderate steam bending classification.

Seasoning: Tends to develop small checks when air dried with little other forms of degrade. Small movement in service.

Working properties: Works easily with most hand and machine tools with slight resistance or blunting effect, and finishes smoothly. Pre-bore for nailing. Glues well, but is difficult to stain and produce a good polish.

Durability: Durable, but moderately prone to termite attack, and susceptible to pinhole borers when freshly felled. Heartwood resistant to preservation treatment but sapwood permeable.

Uses: Heavy structural timber, heavy duty flooring, vehicle bodies, furniture and cabinet work, joinery, railway sleepers, poles, piles, turnery. Also sliced for decorative veneers.

Note: **Honey locust** (*Gleditsia triacanthus* (H)) from the USA is often confused with the above species. It has a light red to reddish-brown heartwood; is heavy, very hard, strong and fissile. Weight 700 kg/m³ (43 lb/ft³); specific gravity .70. Durable and stable with gum deposits and distinct rays and growth rings. Used for furniture, joinery, vehicles, etc.

MOABI (H)

Baillonella toxisperma, Pierre,
syn. *Mimusops djave*, Engl., and
M. toxisperma, (Pierre) A. Chév.
Family: *Sapotaceae*

Commercial names: moabi (France and Gabon).
Other names: djave (Nigeria).
Distribution: Southern Nigeria and Gabon in West Africa.
General description: The colour of the heartwood varies from light reddish-brown to rich red, sometimes with a greyish tinge. The texture is fine with a silken lustre and the wood is straight grained. Weight is 800 kg/m³ (50 lb/ft³); specific gravity .80.
Mechanical properties: It is reported to be extremely tough and resistant to compression, high bending strength, stiffness and to impact loads, but with a very poor steam bending classification.
Seasoning: Dries at a moderate rate with some tendency for twisting and distortion to occur and slight splitting around knots; generally the timber dries without excessive degrade. There is small movement in service.
Working properties: Works fairly easily with most hand and machine tools but with a moderate to severe blunting of cutting edges. Sawdust can be an irritant to mucous membranes and the eyes. A reduced angle of 20° is recommended for planing to avoid grain lifting. The wood nails and screws satisfactorily and glues well. It can be stained and polished to a good finish.
Durability: The timber is durable and resistant to fungal and wood borer insect attacks. It is extremely resistant to preservative treatment.
Uses: Suitable for exterior joinery and construction, furniture, cabinetmaking, flooring for medium to heavy industrial traffic, and selected logs are sliced for decorative veneers.

MUHIMBI (H)

Cynometra alexandri, C. H. Wright
Family: *Leguminosae*

Other name: muhindi (Uganda).

Distribution: Uganda, Tanzania and Zaire, Central and East Africa.

General description: The heartwood is a reddish-brown colour with irregular darker markings. The grain is interlocked and variable, with a very fine texture. Sometimes the wood has scar tissue along the grain and may also have white chalk-line deposits in the grain. The weight varies from 830–1020 kg/m³ (52–64 lb/ft³) but averages about 900 kg/m³ (56 lb/ft³); specific gravity .90.

Mechanical properties: The timber has high bending and crushing strengths, with medium stiffness and resistance to shock loads. It can be bent to a moderate radius of curvature if supported with a strap and end pressure device. The steam bending classification is moderate.

Seasoning: The wood dries out slowly with a marked tendency to end splitting and surface checking. There is medium movement in service.

Working properties: The interlocked grain affects machining properties and there is a high resistance to cutting, with a severe blunting effect on cutting edges. For planing, a reduction of the cutting angle to 15° is recommended to avoid the timber riding on the cutters. Pre-boring is necessary for nailing. Gluing can be a problem caused by gumminess. Staining and polishing are satisfactory if a suitable filler is used.

Durability: Highly resistant to termites in East Africa and durable. Moderately resistant to preservative treatment.

Uses: The timber has excellent resistance to abrasion and is extensively used for industrial and heavy-duty flooring in strip and block form. It is used locally for heavy construction work, bridge building, mine shaft guides, railway sleepers, etc. It is considered to be too heavy for general joinery or carpentry. Sliced decorative veneers are sometimes sliced from selected stocks.

MUHUHU (H)

Brachylaena hutchinsii, Hutch.
Family: *Compositae*

Other name: muhugwe (Tanzania).

Distribution: East Africa.

General description: The heartwood is orange-brown to medium brown with a greenish hue and a fragrant scent. The grain is closely interlocked and sometimes wavy or irregular with a very fine and even texture. Weight about 930 kg/m³ (58 lb/ft³); specific gravity .93.

Mechanical properties: Muhuhu has a high resistance to indentation and abrasion, with a high crushing strength, medium bending strength, low stiffness and very low resistance to shock loads. It has a mdoerate steam bending classification unless pin knots are present.

Seasoning: Dries fairly rapidly, with a tendency for surface checking and end splitting to develop. Thick material needs to be dried very slowly to avoid serious surface checking. There is small movement in service.

Working properties: The interlocked or irregular grain causes difficulty in machining, with a moderate blunting effect on cutters. Gum tends to build up on tools. Pre-boring necessary for nailing. Glues, stains and polishes well, and provides a good finish.

Durability: The wood is moderately resistant to termites in East Africa, but the heartwood is very durable and extremely resistant to preservative treatment.

Uses: Excellent heavy-duty floorng timber. Used locally for turnery, and provides an excellent finish. It is a good carving wood although exported only in short lengths or as flooring blocks or strips. In the countries of origin it is used for heavy construction, bridge decking and girders and railway sleepers. It is exported to India where it is used in crematoriums as a substitute for sandalwood.

MUNINGA (H)

Pterocarpus angolensis DC.
Family: *Leguminosae*

Other names: mninga (Tanzania); ambila (Mozambique); mukwa (Zambia); kiaat, kajat, kajathout (South Africa).

Distribution: Tanzania, Zambia, Angola, Mozambique, Zimbabwe and South Africa.

General description: Golden-brown to chocolate-brown with irregular darker reddish streaks. The grain is rarely straight, mostly irregularly interlocked, with medium to fairly coarse texture and uneven. Sometimes small white spots occur in the wood and these are a natural feature. The weight varies from 480–780 kg/m^3 (30–49 lb/ft^3), average about 620 kg/m^3 (39 lb/ft^3); specific gravity .62. Timber from Zimbabwe is softer and lighter, weighing 540 kg/m^3 (34 lb/ft^3).

Mechanical properties: This timber has medium bending strength, high crushing strength, low resistance to shock loads and very low stiffness. It has only a moderate steam bending classification as some buckling and fibre rupturing is liable, even when supported.

Seasoning: The wood has excellent drying properties in both air and kilning, although it dries slowly especially in thicker sizes. There is little tendency for splitting or distortion and knots split only slightly. There is small movement in service.

Working properties: Works well with hand and machine tools, but the interlocked grain affects machining operations with a moderate blunting effect on cutting edges. Care should be taken when nailing. It glues well and can be stained and polished to a very good finish.

Durability: The sapwood is liable to attack by powder post beetle. The heartwood is very durable and resistant to preservative treatment. The sapwood is moderately resistant.

Uses: Furniture, panelling and high-class joinery and domestic flooring. Selected logs are sliced for architectural veneers and for decorative veneering purposes. It is an excellent turnery wood.

MUTENYE (H)

Guibourtia arnoldiana, (De Wild. & Th.Dur) J. Léon,
syn. *Copaifera arnoldiana*, Wild & Durana
Family: *Leguminosae*

Other names: benge, libenge (Zaire).

Distribution: Tropical West Central Africa, Guinea, Congo, Cameroon, Cabinda and Zaire.

General description: The heartwood is light yellow-brown to medium olive-brown in colour, with a faint reddish tinge, marked by grey to almost black veining. The grain is interlocked and sometimes wavy producing a very attractive figure. Texture is fine and compact. Weight averages about 880 kg/m^3 (55 lb/ft^3); specific gravity .88.

Mechanical properties: Mutenye has medium strength properties except in stiffness which is low. The steam bending classification is moderate as the material is not tolerant of pin knots and inclined to distort during steaming and with a risk of resin exudation.

Seasoning: Care must be taken in drying as occasional gum pockets may exude gum at high temperatures; it has a high shrinkage rate and slow kilning is recommended. There is medium movement in service.

Working properties: The timber works well with both hand and machine tools although some difficulty may be experienced with interlocked and wavy grain. The wood nails, screws, glues and stains well and can be brought to an excellent finish with care.

Durability: The heartwood is moderately durable. Also moderately resistant to termites in West Africa.

Uses: Excellent for turnery; also for heavy duty flooring, joinery, furniture and cabinet parts (as a substitute for walnut), and musical instruments. It is extensively used as a highly decorative veneer for furniture, and selected logs sliced for architectural panelling.

Note: Also known as **olive walnut** in the UK – a name liable to cause confusion.

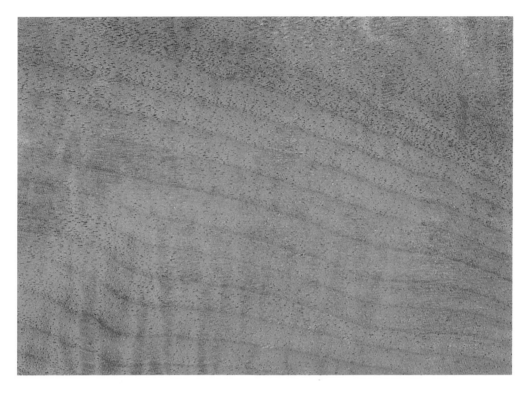

MYRTLE (H)

Umbellularia californica
Family: *Myrtaceae*

Commercial names: acacia, Californian laurel, Californian olive, mountain laurel, baytree.
Other names: pepperwood, spice-tree, Pacific myrtle.
Distribution: USA (Oregon and California).
General description: The heartwood colour is rich golden brown to yellowish-green, ranging in hue from light to dark with a large proportion of paler sapwood. It is straight grained, but often with irregular or wavy grain which is smooth, close and compact, with a firm texture and distinct rays. Weight 850 kg/m³ (53 lb/ft³); specific gravity .85.
Mechanical properties: The timber is heavy, very hard wearing and resilient.
Seasoning: Great care is necessary in seasoning as it has a marked tendency to check and warp.
Working properties: It is fairly difficult to work and has a rapid blunting effect on tools, and a reduced cutting angle to 20° for planing or moulding is recommended. It takes an excellent polish.
Durability: Moderately durable and resistant to insect attack.
Uses: An excellent wood for turnery, especially for bowls, candlesticks etc. Also for superior joinery, cabinetmaking and furniture, medium to heavy-duty flooring and wall panelling. The wood produces excellent mottled and swirling stumpwood, clusters or burrs (burls), a great favourite of cabinetmakers and marquetry craftsmen.

NARGUSTA (H)

Terminalia amazonia, (J.F. Gmel.) Exell.
syn. *T. obovata*, (H)
Family: *Combretaceae*

Other names: fukadi, coffee mortar (Guyana); almendro (Belize) cochun (Mexico); white oliver (Trinidad); guayabo (Venezuela); aromilla, nacastillo (W. Indies).

Distribution: Central and South America

General description: The heartwood has a variegated yellow-brown to olive-brown colour, with prominent reddish stripes and streaked markings. The grain is irregular or interlocked, medium texture with a high lustre. Weight 800 kg/m³ (50 lb/ft³); specific gravity .80.

Mechanical properties: Nargusta has medium bending and crushing strengths, and resistance to shock loads, with low stiffness. It has a moderate steam bending classification.

Seasoning: It is a difficult wood to dry with a strong tendency to split or check and it is difficult to dry out the centre of thicker material. There is medium movement in service.

Working properties: Rather difficult to work with severe blunting effect on cutting edges. The grain is liable to pluck or tear out in planing, which requires a reduced cutting angle. Also requires pre-boring for nailing but holds screws well. Glues, stains and polishes to a good finish.

Durability: Durable, and resistant to preservative treatment.

Uses: Cabinetmaking, furniture, flooring, interior joinery, planking and decking in boat building, turnery, and as a substitute for white oak. Used for plywood manufacture, and selected logs for sliced decorative veneers.

'NEW GUINEA WALNUT' (H)

Dracontomelum mangiferum, B.1.,
Family: *Anacardiaceae*

Other names: Pacific walnut, Papuan walnut (UK); loup, lup (Papua New Guinea).

Distribution: Papua New Guinea and neighbouring islands.

General description: The timber has a grey-brown background colour with an orange cast. The grain is moderately interlocked with wavy grain present producing a broken striped figure on quartered surfaces. The surface shows irregular dark brown to black bandings. The texture is medium and even. Weight 740 kg/m^3 (46 lb/ft^3); specific gravity .74.

Mechanical properties: This material has medium bending strength and resistance to shock loads, high crushing strength and low stiffness, and a moderate steam bending classification.

Seasoning: Dries readily with a slight tendency to warp in the thinner sizes and to check or distort if the drying is hurried. Dried slowly, there is minimum degrade. There is medium movement in service.

Working properties: Although this wood works readily and easily with hand and machine tools there is a moderate blunting effect on cutters, which should be kept sharp to produce a smooth finish. The wood nails and screws well; glues, stains and polishes satisfactorily.

Durability: Moderately durable. It is non-durable to marine borers but resistant to termites. The wood is resistant to preservative treatment.

Uses: Furniture and cabinetmaking, shop and office fitting, panelling, construction work, exterior cladding, interior and exterior joinery, and flooring for domestic purposes. It is an excellent turnery wood. Sliced for plywood faces and for decorative veneers suitable for panelling, doors, cabinets and marquetry.

Note: Not a true walnut.

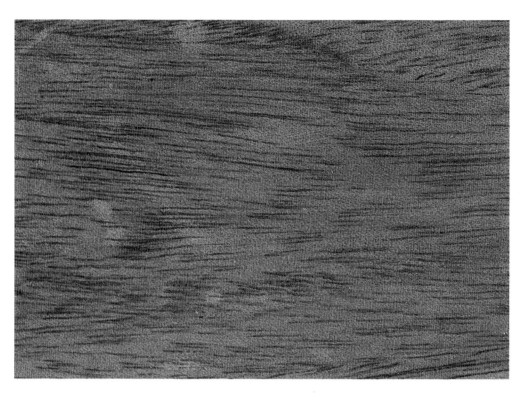

NIANGON (H)

(1) *Tarrietia utilis*, (Sprauge),
(2) *T. densiflora*, (Pellgr) Aubrev and Normand
Family: *Sterculiaceae*

Commercial names: (1) nyankom (Ghana); wishmore (Liberia); (2) ogoué (Gabon).

Distribution: West Africa.

General description: The heartwood colour varies from pale pink to reddish-brown. The grain is interlocked, wavy or irregular, producing an irregular striped figure when quarter sawn. The texture is rather coarse with a conspicuous ray figure. The wood feels greasy due to the presence of resin. The weight varies from 510 to 620 kg/m^3 (32–39 lb/ft^3), and 750–770 kg/m^3 (46–48 lb/ft^3); specific gravity .56 and .76 respectively.

Mechanical properties: A hard, strong wood with medium bending and crushing strength, very low stiffness and resistance to shock loads. It has a moderate steam bending classification.

Seasoning: The timber dries fairly rapidly and well and distortion is not appreciable, although a small proportion may twist; slight end-splitting and surface checking may develop and very slight collapse may also occur in a few boards. There is medium movement in service.

Working properties: The steeply interlocked grain affects machining and there is moderate blunting effect on tools. Tends to split in nailing. May need surface treatment prior to gluing (with a solution of caustic soda or ammonia) to overcome resinous nature of wood. Requires a fair amount of filler to produce a good finish.

Durability: Sapwood liable to attack by powder post beetle. The heartwood is durable. Extremely resistant to preservative treatment.

Uses: Furniture, general purpose carpentry and joinery, heavy joinery and construction, heavy-duty flooring, boatbuilding, and shop fitting. Recommended for use in exposed conditions such as external doors, frames, greenhouses, etc. Rotary cut for plywood manufacture; sliced for attractive decorative veneers.

NIOVÉ (H)

Staudtia stipitata, Warb.
S. gabonensis, Warb.
S. niohue, Pierre.
Family: *Myristicaceae*

Other names: Kamashi, n'kafi (Zaire); m'boun, mogoubi (Gabon); Oropa (Nigeria); m'bonda, ekop (Cameroon); menga-menga (Angola).

Distribution: Tropical West Africa, Cameroon, Gabon and Zaire.

General description: The heartwood is red-brown to orange with darker brown streaks. The grain is straight with a very fine texture. The surface is slightly lustrous and occasionally oily and with a peppery scent. Weight 830 kg/m³ (51 lb/ft³); specific gravity .83.

Mechanical properties: This tough, compact and heavy wood has good strength properties in all categories but is too heavy to work in the solid for general purposes; it has no steam bending properties.

Seasoning: Kiln seasoning is advised and to be carried out with care and very slowly to avoid checking and shakes. There is small movement in service.

Working properties: Despite its hardness, niové is fairly easy to work with either hand or machine tools. It should be quarter sawn, and it can be brought to a smooth finish with most operations. Takes and holds nails and screws fairly well, but pre-boring is advised to avoid a tendency to split. Gluing can be a problem due to the natural oiliness and requires pre-treatment. It can be brought to an excellent polish, especially a wax finish.

Durability: The timber is resistant to decay and insect attack. It is durable and extremely resistant to preservative treatment.

Uses: Externally in exposed conditions, such as door and window frames, external structural work, interior and exterior joinery, some cabinetwork, heavy duty flooring, gunstocks, and used in Africa for canoe paddles. Rotary cut for plywood manufacture, and sliced into very decorative veneers for panelling and cabinet and furniture veneering.

NYATOH (H)

Palaquium maingayi, P. rostratum,
P. xanthochymum, and *Payena maingayii*
Family: *Sapotaceae*

Other names: njatuh (Indonesia); padang (UK).

Distribution: Malaya and S.E. Asia.

General description: The heartwood colour varies according to the species, but generally from pale pink to reddish-brown, sometimes with darker streaks. The grain is straight or shallowly interlocked or wavy and the texture moderately fine. Has a resemblance to makore with a moiré or watered silk figure. Weight variable but averaging between 620–720 kg/m³ (38–45 lb/ft³); at 12% moisture content; specific gravity .62 to .72.

Mechanical properties: The wood has medium bending and crushing strength, with low stiffness and resistance to shock loads. It has a moderate steam bending classification.

Seasoning: Dries rather slowly with some tendency to end split, distort and surface check. There is medium movement in service.

Working properties: Some species are siliceous and can cause severe blunting of cutting edges. Non-siliceous wood planes easily to a smooth finish. It tends to split when nailed, but screws and glues well, and stains and polishes to an excellent finish.

Durability: Moderately durable. The sapwood is liable to attack by powder post beetle. It is very resistant to preservative treatment.

Uses: Furniture and cabinetmaking, high-class joinery, pattern making, and interior building construction. Rotary cut veneer used for plywood manufacture or corestock; selected logs produce very decorative veneers for panelling, cabinets, marquetry, etc.

Note: The trade names of **njatuh** and **padang** are given to various species of the *Sapotaceae* family which produces light to medium weight timbers of similar colour, density and other properties, chiefly from the *Palaquium* and *Payena* species. Timber up to 880 kg/m³ (55 lb/ft³) at 15% moisture content is known as **nyatoh**. Timber exceeding that weight is sold as **bitis** (*Palaquium ridleyi* and *P. stellatum*, with *Madhuca utilis*) in Malaya, and as **nyatoh batu** in Sabah.

OAK, AMERICAN RED (H)   *Quercus spp.*, principally:
(1) *Q. rubra*, L. emend. Du Roi *(Q. borealis*, Michx.f.*)*,
(2) *Q. falcata*, Michx.f. var. *falcata (Q.rubra*, L. in part, not of Du Roi*)*,
(3) *Q. falcata*, Michx.f. var. *pagodaefolia* Ell. (4) *Q. shumardii*, Buckl.
Family: *Fagaceae*

Other names: (1) northern red oak (Canada and USA); (2) southern red oak, Spanish oak (USA); (3) swamp red oak, cherrybark oak (USA); (4) shumard red oak (USA).

Distribution: Eastern Canada and USA.

General description: The heartwood resembles other oaks with a biscuit to pink colour, but has a reddish tinge. Mostly straight grained and coarse textured, with a less attractive figure than white oak due to smaller rays. Southern red oak has a more rapid growth than northern red oak and is harder, heavier and coarser textured. Weight about 770 kg/m³ (48 lb/ft³); specific gravity .77.

Mechanical properties: This timber has medium bending strength and stiffness with high crushing strength and is classified as a very good steam bending wood.

Seasoning: Natural tendency to dry slowly, with liability to split, check or honeycomb, and needs care in both air drying and kilning. There is medium movement in service.

Working properties: Varies according to the density of the wood and growth conditions. There is a moderate blunting effect on cutters which should be kept sharp. Nailing may require pre-boring and gluing properties are variable. Can be stained and polished to a good finish.

Durability: The heartwood is non-durable and liable to insect attack but is moderately resistant to preservative treatment; the sapwood is permeable.

Uses: Flooring, furniture, vehicle construction, interior joinery. Plywood manufacture and sliced for decorative veneers. It is unsuitable for exterior work.

OAK, AMERICAN WHITE (H)

Quercus spp., principally:
(1) Q. alba, L. (2) *Q. prinus*, L. (*Q. montana*, Willd.)
(3) *Q. lyrata*, Walt. (4) *Q. michauxii*, Nutt (*Q. prinus*, L. in part)
Family: *Fagaceae*

Commercial names: (1) white oak (USA); (2) chestnut oak (USA); (3) overcup oak (USA); (4) swamp chestnut oak (USA). Also marketed with regional names, e.g. Appalachian oak, northern or southern oak.

Distribution: Eastern USA and South Eastern Canada.

General description: Varies in colour from pale yellow-brown to biscuit with a pinkish tint, similar to European oak. Straight grain, with the characteristic silver grain on quartered material. Appalachian oak is slow grown producing light weight, mild wood, but southern states produce fast grown oak with wide growth rings, and a harder, tougher timber. Medium to coarse textured. Weight averages 760 kg/m^3 (47 lb/ft^3); specific gravity .76.

Mechanical properties: The wood has medium bending and crushing strengths with low stiffness which makes it an excellent steam bending material.

Seasoning: Dries relatively slowly with a tendency to check, split and honeycomb, and requires careful handling for air drying and kilning. There is medium movement in service.

Working properties: Vary according to rate of growth. Slow grown oak being much easier to work with hand and machine tools. The timber takes nails and screws well, although pre-boring is advised; its gluing properties are variable; stains and polishes to a good finish.

Durability: Logs are liable to severe insect attack. The heartwood is durable and extremely resistant to preservative treatment, and the sapwood is moderately resistant.

Uses: Milder than European oak to work and suitable for furniture and cabinetmaking, joinery, heavy construction, parquet and strip flooring, pews and pulpits, boat-building, ladder rungs, agricultural implements, waggon bottoms, tight cooperage and coffins. Rotary cut for plywood and sliced for highly ornamental veneers for panelling and decorative veneering.

OAK, EUROPEAN (H)

(1) *Quercus petraea* (Matt.) Liebl.
(*Q. sessiliflora*, Salisb.)
(2) *Quercus robur*, L.
(*Q. pendunculata*, Ehrh)
Family: *Fagaceae*

Commercial names: English, French, Polish oak, etc., according to country of origin. (1) sessile or durmast oak (2) pedunculate oak.

Other names: rovere, quercia (Italy); chêne (France); eiche (Germany); eik (Netherlands).

Distribution: UK and Europe, Asia Minor and North Africa.

General description: The heartwood is light tan to biscuit coloured, usually straight grained, but irregular or cross-grained material can occur depending on growth conditions. Characteristic silver grain figure on quartered surfaces due to broad rays. British and Baltic oaks are tough and hard, weighing 720 kg/m^3 (45 lb/ft^3), but the Volhynian oak of south east Poland, and even milder oak from Yugoslavia known as Slavonian oak weighs 670 kg/m^3 (42 lb/ft^3); specific gravity from .67 to .72, according to type.

Mechanical properties: Oak has a very good steam bending classification, but is liable to blue stain if in contact with iron compounds.

Seasoning: It dries very slowly with a tendency to split and check. Medium movement in service.

Working properties: There is a moderate to severe blunting effect on cutters, which should be kept sharp. Quartered stock requires a 20° planing or moulding angle. The wood takes waxing, liming, fuming and polishing treatments very well.

Durability: The heartwood is durable, extremely resistant to preservative treatment, but the sapwood is permeable. The acidic nature of oak will affect metals in indirect contact and cause corrosion. Non-ferrous or galvanised metals should be used.

Uses: The preponderance of tyloses in the pores of "white oaks" resists the passage of liquids and renders the wood ideal for tight cooperage for cognac, wine and beers. For furniture and cabinetmaking, Slavonian, Volhynian and Spessart (German) oaks are preferred. English oak is best for boat building, dock and harbour work, sea defences, railway waggons, ladder rungs, sills, thresholds, and for all purposes of exposure in contact with the ground. High-class joinery, coffins, ecclesiastical work such as pews, rood screens, pulpits, and carving. Flooring, vehicle body bearers and floors in trucks. Oak is rotary cut for plywood manufacture and sliced for very attractive "silver grain" and "raindrop" figured oak veneers for panels and cabinets.

Brown oak results from fungal attack in the growing tree, (*Fistulina hepatica*), causing the heartwood to turn a rich deep brown.

Bog oak: Brought about by chemical changes due to being buried for centuries in peat bogs. Both brown oak and bog oak are highly valued for furniture, although bog oak is usually saw cut.

Note: Golden oak – a yellow stain caused by a mould fungus *polyporous dryadeus* is only surface mould and harmless, and removed in processing.

Related spp. *Q. ilex*, L., **Holm oak** (common name: evergreen oak); *Q. castancaefolia*, C. A. Mey, **Persian oak**; *Q. cerris*, L., **Turkey oak**.

Illustrated above: Brown oak (left), Bog oak (right).

OAK, JAPANESE (H)

Quercus spp., principally,
Q. mongolica, Fisch. ex Turcz
var. *grosseserrata*, Rehd. & Wils.
(*Q. crispula* Bl., *Q. grosseserrata* Bl)
Family: *Fagaceae*

Other names: ohnara (*Q. mongolica*), konara (*Q. glandulifera*), kashiwa (*Q. dentata*), shira-kashi (*Q. myrsinaefolia*), ichii-gashi (*Q. gilva*), aka-gashi (*Q. acuta*), ubame-gashi (*Q. phillyraeoides*).

Distribution: Timber from Hokkaido, the north island of Japan is milder and preferred to the oaks from the main island of Honshu.

General description: The timber is paler and much milder than European or American white oak, due to slow, even growth. It is pale biscuit colour, but those grown on the main island have a pinkish shade. It is usually straight grained and free from knots; weight about 660 kg/m^3 (41 lb/ft^3); specific gravity .66.

Mechanical properties: The timber has medium wood bending and crushing strength, with low stiffness and resistance to shock loads, making it a very good steam bending wood.

Seasoning: Dries slowly without undue degrade. There is medium movement in service.

Working properties: Japanese oak is milder and much easier to work with hand or machine tools than other white oaks, due to its lower density, with only a slight blunting effect on tools. It nails and screws well, and also glues, stains and polishes to an excellent finish.

Durability: The timber may contain a high proportion of sapwood, and be liable to beetle attack, but the heartwood is durable, and the sapwood permeable for preservation treatment.

Uses: Furniture and cabinetmaking, interior fittings, joinery, panelling, flooring blocks, boat building, charcoal manufacture. Rotary cut for plywood manufacture, and sliced for decorative veneers.

OBECHE (H)

Triplochiton scleroxylon, K. Schum.
Family: *Triplochitonaceae*

Commercial names: obeche (Nigeria); wawa (Ghana).
Other names: arere (Nigeria); ayous (Cameroon & Zaire); samba (Ivory Coast).
Distribution: Tropical West Africa.
General description: Creamy-white to pale yellow in colour, with a moderately fine and even texture. Brittleheart is present in large logs. The grain is usually interlocked, giving a faint stripe on quartered surfaces but otherwise featureless. Weight about 380 kg/m^3 (24 lb/ft^3); s.g. .38.
Mechanical properties: The bending and crushing strengths are low, stiffness and resistance to shock loads very low. Steam bending classification moderate to poor due to slight wrinkling at edges of bends, even with supporting strap.
Seasoning: Dries very rapidly and well with very little tendency to warp or shake; slight distortion may occur and knots split a little. Liable to attack by staining fungi and should be piled in stick immediately after conversion. There is small movement in service.
Working properties: Very easy to work with hand or machine tools, with only a slight blunting effect on cutters. Nails easily but has poor holding qualities; gluing is good. Requires light filling to obtain a high grade finish.
Durability: The timber is non-durable. Sapwood liable to attack by powder post beetle. Non-resistant to termites in West Africa. The heartwood is resistant to preservative treatment but the sapwood is permeable. Liable to blue stain if exposed to iron compounds in moist conditions.
Uses: Extensively used where durability and strength are unimportant, such as for interior rails, drawer sides and linings, cabinet framing, interior joinery, sliderless soundboards for organs, model making, etc. Rotary cut into constructional veneer for plywood corestock purposes and as a backing veneer. Selected logs sliced for decorative veneers. Veneer with a scattered blue stain is valued for marquetry work.

OGEA (H)

Daniellia ogea, (Harms) Rolfe ex Holl.
D. thurifera, Bennett
Family: *Leguminosae*

Other names: daniellia, oziya (Nigeria); incenso (Portuguese Guinea); faro (France and the Ivory Coast); gum copal, copal (Liberia); hyedua (Ghana).

Distribution: West Africa.

General description: The heartwood colour varies from light golden-brown or pale pink, to reddish-brown marked with darker-streaks. It also has a very wide sapwood which is straw coloured. The grain is straight to shallowly interlocked; the texture is moderately coarse and inclined to be woolly. It is sometimes found to be gummy, and contains brittleheart near the centre. Weight varies from 420–580 kg/m^3 (26–36 lb/ft^3), average 500 kg/m^3 (31 lb/ft^3); specific gravity .50. Compression failures, thundershakes, etc., are prominent near the heart.

Mechanical properties: This medium density wood has low bending strength, very low stiffness and resistance to shock loads, and medium crushing strength. It has a very poor steam bending classification.

Seasoning: Ogea dries quite rapidly with little degrade. Slight distortion may take place and collapse may occur on thick material but not severely. There is medium movement in service.

Working properties: Easy to work with machine and hand tools, with only slight blunting effect on tools, unless interlocked grain or woolly texture is present. Nailing and screwing properties are good and gluing is satisfactory. It can be stained and polished, provided that the surface is filled, to a good finish.

Durability: Perishable. Sapwood is liable to attack by powder post beetle; the heartwood is moderately resistant to preservative treatment, but the sapwood is permeable.

Uses: Excellent for light joinery work, interior fitments for cabinets, boxes and crates and core veneer for plywood. Selected material is sliced for decorative veneers for cabinets and panelling.

OKWEN (H)

(1) *Brachystegia nigerica*, Hoyle & A.P.D. Jones,
(2) *B. kennedyi*, H. (3) *B. eurycoma*, Harms,
(4) *B. leonensis*, Hutch & Burtt Davy.
Family: *Leguminosae*

Other names: brachystegia (Nigeria); meblo (Ivory Coast); naga (Cameroon).

Distribution: West Africa.

General description: Pale fawn to dark brown heartwood, with deeply interlocked grain and medium to coarse texture. *B. leonensis* has prominent light and dark stripes, and *B. kennedyi* and *B. nigerica* also have in addition, a roe figure on radial surfaces. Weight (1) 700 kg/m^3 (44 lb/ft^3), (2) 540 kg/m^3 (34 lb/ft^3), (3) 640 kg/m^3 (40 lb/ft^3) and (4) 705 kg/m^3 (44 lb/ft^3); specific gravity .70, .54, .64 and .70 respectively.

Mechanical properties: Strength properties vary between the species: the strongest is *B. nigerica*. It has medium bending and crushing strength, with low stiffness and resistance to shock loads. It has a moderate steam bending classification.

Seasoning: Generally dries slowly but well, with distortion a main cause of degrade. (*B. kennedyi* dries rapidly with little degrade) There is medium movement in service.

Working properties: Difficult to work with hand tools, and there is a moderate blunting effect on cutting edges in machining; sawing and planing are difficult due to steeply interlocked grain. Pre-boring required for nailing. *B. kennedyi* has satisfactory machining properties and can be brought to a very good finish after the grain is filled. *B. nigerica* is not suitable for finishing treatments owing to the difficulty in obtaining a smooth surface.

Durability: Sapwood liable to attack by powder post beetle. The heartwood is moderately durable and extremely resistant to preservative treatment. The sapwood is permeable.

Uses: *B. nigerica*: vechicle building, general cosntruction, parquet flooring, interior joinery. *B. kennedyi* and others: joinery, domestic flooring, etc. Straight grained, selected logs are peeled for construction veneers and plywood. Selected logs sliced for decorative veneering.

OLIVE, EAST AFRICAN (H)

(1) *Olea hochstetteri*, Bak.
(2) *O. welwitschii*, (Knobl.) Gilg & Schellenb.
Family: *Oleaceae*

Commercial names: (1) East African olive; (2) loliondo; (1–2) olivewood.

Other names: (1) musheragi, Elgon olive (Kenya). **Distribution:** East Africa.

General description: Pale to mid-brown, attractively marked with irregular grey, brown and black streaks giving the wood a marbled appearance. The grain is shallowly interlocked and the texture is fine and even. Weight about 890 kg/m^3 (55 lb/ft^3); specific gravity .89.

Mechanical properties: High strength properties in bending, stiffness, crushing strength and resistance to shock loads. The sapwood can be steam bent to a smaller radius of curvature than the heartwood which has only a moderate classification. Resin exudation accompanies steaming. Has a good resistance to abrasion and has all round excellent strength.

Seasoning: Dries slowly with a tendency to check and split. If dried too quickly, thick material tends to check internally or honeycomb. There is large movement in service. Can be kilned successfully at a slow rate.

Working properties: The interlocked grain makes this a difficult timber to work, affecting machining properties. There is a moderate blunting effect on tools. Nailing requires pre-boring. Stains and polishes to an excellent smooth finish.

Durability: Logs are liable to attack by pinhole borer. Heartwood moderately durable and resistant to preservative treatment. The sapwood is permeable.

Uses: Olive makes high-grade, decorative flooring, with excellent resistance to abrasion, suitable for public buildings. It is an excellent turnery wood. Also suitable for furniture, panelling, and shop fitting. Plainer wood used for tool handles and vehicle building. Too heavy for plywood manufacture but sliced for highly attractive decorative veneers for panelling.

Note: Related spp. include: *Olea europae*, Linn, (Mediterranean countries), small billets only. *O. laurifolia*, Moench, from Africa produces **black ironwood**; *O. verrucosa* and *O. capensis* from South Africa produce **cape olive**. All are similar in appearance and general properties.

OMU (H)

Entandrophragma candollei, Harms.
Family: *Meliaceae*

Other names: kosipo (Ivory Coast); atom-assié (Cameroon); esaka (Zaire); lifuco (Angola).
Distribution: Tropical West Africa.
General description: The timber resembles sapele but is much darker reddish-brown in colour, with a purplish tinge. The grain is straight to interlocked and the texture is coarse. The rays may contain silica granules. Weight 640 kg/m³ (40 lb/ft³); specific gravity .64.
Mechanical properties: The timber has high crushing strength; medium bending strength and resistance to shock loads; low stiffness; and a poor steam bending classification, with severe rupturing and buckling when bent to a large radius of curvature.
Seasoning: Dries rather slowly with a great possibility of distortion, and careful kilning is the best way to season this material. There is medium movement in service.
Working properties: Omu has a moderate blunting effect on cutting edges but works readily with hand or machine tools. Interlocked grain will prove more troublesome. It nails, screws and glues well, stains readily, and when filled polishes to a good finish.
Durability: Sapwood is liable to attack by powder post beetle. The heartwood is moderately durable and resistant to preservative treatment.
Uses: Used for similar purposes as sapele and utile, although not as attractive as sapele, and not as durable as utile. High-class joinery, boat building, general utility work, furniture, shop fitting, domestic flooring. Rotary cut for plywood manufacture, and selected logs are sliced for attractive decorative veneers, with striped or sometimes moiré figure.
Note: In Nigeria this is also called **heavy sapele** and is misleading as it refers only to the fact that when green, the logs sink in water.

OPEPE (H)   *Nauclea diderrichii*, (De Wild & Th.Dur) Merr
                              syn. *Sarcocephalus diderrichii*, De Wild & Th.Dur.
                                                        Family: *Rubiaceae*

Commercial names: kusia (Ghana); badi, sibo (Ivory Coast); bilinga (Gabon).
Other names: n'gulu, maza, bonkangu (Zaire); kusiabo (Ghana); akondoe (Cameroon).
Distribution: West Africa.
General description: The heartwood is an orange-brown colour with a copper coloured lustre. The grain is mostly interlocked producing a striped or roll figure when quartered; sometimes with irregular grain. The texture is fairly coarse due to large pores. A reasonable proportion of straight grained material is obtained by grading. Weighs 740 kg-m^3 (46 lb/ft^3); s.g. .74.
Mechanical properties: An exceptionally strong timber with medium bending strength and stiffness; it has high crushing strength and low resistance to shock loads and a poor steam bending classification.
Seasoning: Quartered material dries fairly rapidly with very little checking or distortion; flat sawn timber is more refractory and checking and splitting and distortion may occur. In large sizes it dries very slowly. There is small movement in service.
Working properties: Works moderately well with hand or machine tools but there is a blunting effect on cutting edges due to the interlocked grain and coarse texture. Pre-boring is necessary for nailing, glues well, and a high finish is obtainable once filled.
Durability: The sapwood is liable to attack by powder post beetle. Moderately resistant to termites in West Africa. The heartwood is very durable, moderately resistant to preservative treatment but the sapwood is permeable. Opepe has a high resistance to marine borers.
Uses: Piling and decking in wharves and docks, jetty and marine work, boat building (except for bent parts), general construction work, exterior and interior joinery, domestic flooring, waggon bottoms, furniture, cabinet work and decorative turnery. Selected logs are sliced for very attractive veneers for panelling and decorative veneering.

OVANGKOL (H)

Guibourtia ehie, (A.Chév) J. Léon.
Family: *Leguminosae*

Other names: amazakoué (Ivory Coast); anokye, hyeduanini (Ghana).

Distribution: Ivory Coast, Ghana, southern Nigeria and Gabon.

General description: Mid-yellow to chocolate brown coloured, with greyish black stripes. The grain is interlocked and the texture moderately coarse. The average weight is about 800 kg/m³ (50 lb/ft³); specific gravity .80.

Mechanical properties: Has medium strength properties in each category but only a poor steam bending classification, as shallow bends only are possible.

Seasoning: The timber dries rapidly and reasonably well with only a slight tendency to distort; extra care is needed in kiln drying thick stock to avoid collapse. Medium movement in service.

Working properties: There is a moderate blunting effect on tools due to the silica content of the wood, and cutting edges must be kept thin and sharp. The wood saws slowly but well. The cutting angle should be reduced to 20° when planing to obtain a good finish due to the interlocked grain. The wood nails, screws well, glues without difficulty and can be stained and brought to an excellent finish.

Durability: Reported to be highly resistant to termites in West Africa. The heartwood is moderately durable and resistant to preservative treatment, and the sapwood is permeable.

Uses: Suitable for superior furniture making and high-class joinery, cabinetmaking, domestic flooring, turnery, shop fitting and interior decorative fittings. Sliced for attractive decorative veneers for architectural panelling and doors.

PADAUK, AFRICAN (H)

Pterocarpus soyauxii, Taub.,
P. osun, Craib.
Family: *Leguminosae*

Other names: camwood, barwood (UK); corail (Belgium).

Distribution: Central and West Tropical Africa.

General description: The heartwood is a vivid blood red, toning down to dark purple-brown with red streaks upon exposure. The grain is straight to interlocked with a moderately coarse texture. Weight varies from 640–800 kg/m^3 (40–50 lb/ft^3), average 720 kg/m^3 (45 lb/ft^3); specific gravity .72.

Mechanical properties: The timber has excellent strength properties especially in bending and crushing strengths, with medium resistance to shock loads and stiffness.

Seasoning: Dries fairly rapidly and very well with a minimum of degrade. The movement is exceptionally small in service.

Working properties: Despite its weight, the wood has only a slight blunting effect on tools, and machines very easily. It nails, screws, glues and polishes very well and an excellent finish is obtainable.

Durability: The heartwood is very durable and moderately resistant to preservative treatment.

Uses: This attractive wood has high strength properties, durability and outstanding stability and is ideal for high-class joinery, furniture and cabinetmaking. Also for fancy turnery and carvings, tool and knife handles, spirit levels, paddles and oars, and agricultural implements. It has a high resistance to abrasion and makes an excellent heavy-duty flooring timber, also suitable for floors where under-floor heating has been installed because of dimensional stability. Selected logs are sliced to form very attractive decorative veneers. Renowned as a dye wood.

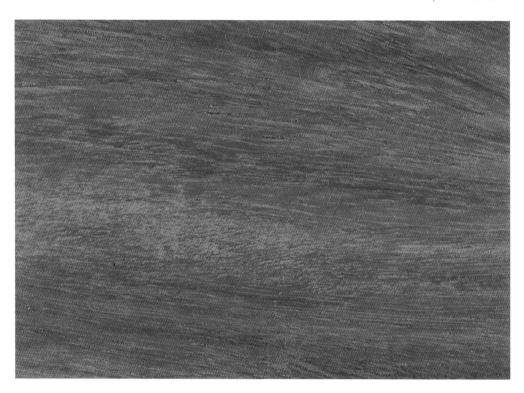

PADAUK, ANDAMAN (H)

Pterocarpus dalbergiodes, Roxb.
Family: *Leguminosae*

Other names: paduak (UK); Andaman redwood, vermillion wood (USA).

Distribution: The Andaman Islands.

General description: A most attractive wood, varying in heartwood colour from a rich crimson or brick red, sometimes having darker red to purplish streaks, gradually darkening upon exposure, to dark reddish-brown. The broadly interlocked grain produces a beatiful roe or striped figure on quartered surfaces, often with a curly figure. Some logs produce a yellowish-pink colour with darker red lines or streaks, but these are exceptional. The texture is medium to coarse. Weight about 770 kg/m^3 (48 lb/ft^3); specific gravity .77.

Mechanical properties: The timber has medium bending strength, low stiffness and resistance to shock loads and a high crushing strength. It is not suitable for steam bending.

Seasoning: Green timber can develop fine surface splits, but this can be overcome if the trees are girdled before felling, when the timber air dries well without undue degrade. Kiln drying is very satisfactory without checking or distortion. There is small movement in service.

Working properties: There is a moderate blunting effect on tools and machining is affected by the interlocked grain. It is an excellent turnery timber. Pre-boring is required for nailing, glues well, but requires filling to produce a good finish.

Durability: Moderately resistant to termites in India. The heartwood is very durable, and moderately resistant to preservative treatment, although the sapwood is permeable.

Uses: High-class joinery, furniture, bank counters, billiard tables, balustrades, decorative flooring, exterior joinery, boat building except for steam bent parts. It is used in India for vehicle framing, building and furniture. Selected logs are sliced for use as highly decorative veneers.

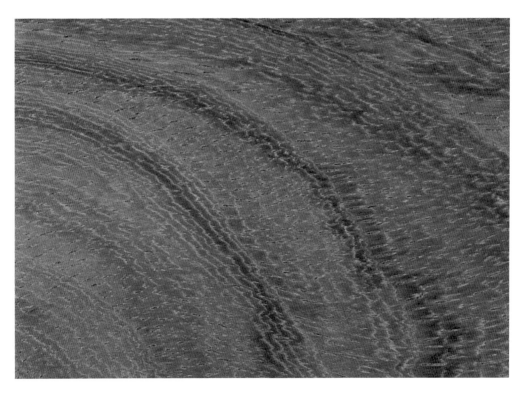

PADAUK, BURMA (H)

Pterocarpus macrocarpus, Kurz.
Family: *Leguminosae*

Other names: pradoo, mai pradoo (Thailand).

Distribution: Burma and Thailand.

General description: The heartwood varies from orange-red to dark brick-red streaked with darker lines, but matures to a golden red-brown. The grain is interlocked in narrow bands, producing a ribbon striped figure on quartered surfaces. The texture is fairly coarse. Weight 850 kg/m^3 (53 lb/ft^3); specific gravity .85. A heavy, hard, strong timber.

Mechanical properties: Compared to Andaman padauk, this timber is 40% stronger in bending and resistance to shock loads, 30% stronger in compression along the grain and 20% stiffer. The value of the timber is due to its strength and durability.

Seasoning: Air dries reasonably well without much distortion or splitting. May develop surface checks if converted green. Stored logs should have end protection against rapid drying. Kiln dries rather slowly with little degrade. Small movement in service.

Working properties: There is a moderate blunting effect on tools and is considered difficult to saw when dry. The wood turns very well. Pre-boring advised for nailing; screws hold well. The timber glues well, and can produce an excellent finish when the grain is properly filled.

Durability: The heartwood is very durable. The sapwood is liable to attack by powder post beetle. The heartwood is extremely resistant to preservative treatment.

Uses: Suitable for billiard table frames, high-class joinery, bank counters, domestic flooring, shop fitting, counters, and constructional purposes. It is used in India for the bottoms of railway trucks, waggons, shafts, wheel hubs and oil presses. It is sliced to produce excellent quartered decorative veneers.

PALDAO (H)

Dracontomelum dao, Merr & Rolfe.
Family: *Anacardiaceae*

Other name: dao (Philippines).
Distribution: Philippines.
General description: An attractive wood with heartwood that is grey-brown in colour with a faint greenish tinge and irregular dark brown to black streaks. The grain may be straight, interlocked or wavy with a medium texture, producing a broken ribbon stripe on quartered surfaces. Weight about 740 kg/m³ (46 lb/ft³); specific gravity .74.
Mechanical properties: This is a moderately strong timber with medium bending strength, crushing strength and resistance to shock loads, with low stiffness. It is not suitable for steam bending.
Seasoning: Dries well with great care but with a marked tendency for the timber to warp in thinner sizes or to check if the drying is hurried. There is medium movement in service.
Working properties: The wood works easily with both hand or machine tools with a moderate blunting effect on cutting edges. Straight grained material finishes smoothly but interlocked grain tends to pick up on quartered surfaces. Nails and screws well, glues satisfactorily, and can be stained and polished to a high finish. It is an excellent turnery wood.
Durability: The heartwood is moderately durable and resistant to termites in the Philippines. The wood is resistant to preservative treatment and non-durable to marine borers.
Uses: Furniture and cabinetmaking, carpentry and flooring for domestic use. Interior joinery, shopfitting and panelling, turnery. In the Philippines, the buttress timber is used to create decorative table tops. Principally used for highly decorative veneers for best grade furniture, architectural panelling, flush doors, etc.

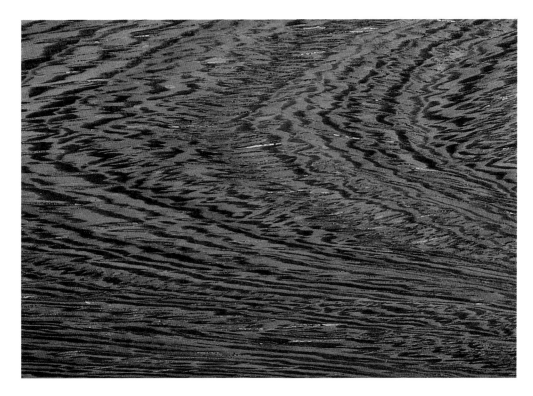

PANGA PANGA (H)

Millettia stuhlmannii, Taub
Family: *Leguminosae*

Distribution: East Africa.

General description: The heartwood colour is dark chocolate-brown with alternate bands of light and dark coloured parenchyma bands which provide a distinctive decorative figure. Fairly straight grained, with a coarse texture which is not uniform. Weight from 830–1,000 kg/m^3 (52–62 lb/ft^3); specific gravity .91.

Mechanical properties: This very heavy, dense wood, has high bending strength and resistance to shock loads, with medium crushing strength and stiffness. It has a low steam bending classification, and high resistance to abrasion.

Seasoning: The wood seasons slowly and requires careful drying to minimise surface checking tendencies. There is small movement in service.

Working properties: The wood has a moderate blunting effect on cutting edges, and needs a reduced cutting angle for planing or moulding. Resin cells in the wood may interfere with gluing. Nailing requires pre-boring. It is an excellent turnery wood. The grain requires filling and then can be brought to a good finish. It is unsuitable for plywood manufacture because it is too heavy.

Durability: Durable and extremely resistant to preservative treatment.

Uses: It is ideal for flooring strips or blocks, for normal pedestrian traffic in public buildings, hotels, showrooms, boardrooms etc. Interior and exterior joinery, general construction work. Sliced for decorative veneers for panelling and furniture.

'PARANA PINE' (S)

Araucaria angustifolia, (Bert) O. Ktze.

Family: *Araucariaceae*

Other name: Brazilian pine (USA).

Distribution: Brazil, Paraguay and Argentina.

General description: The heartwood is pale brown with a dark brown inner core, sometimes streaked with a bright red colour. The grain is mostly straight with a close, uniform texture and very inconspicuous growth rings. It contains little resin, and varies in density from light and soft to hard and heavy. Weight range 480–640 kg/m^3 (30–40 lb/ft^3) but averages 540 kg/m^3 (33 lb/ft^3); specific gravity .54.

Mechanical properties: The timber has medium bending and crushing strength, low stiffness, very low resistance to shock loads; lacks toughness. It has a poor steam bending classification.

Seasoning: Parana pine is more difficult to dry than most other softwoods. The darker coloured material is very prone to split, distort and dry slowly. The load should be weighted to minimise distortion and a prolonged conditioning period and repeated moisture content checks made to ensure uniformity of drying. There is medium movement in service.

Working properties: Works easily with hand and machine tools with very little blunting effect on cutters; planes and moulds to a clean, smooth finish. It can be glued, stained, painted or polished to a good finish.

Durability: Non-durable. Liable to insect attack. It is moderately resistant to preservative treatment but the sapwood is permeable.

Uses: Only the higher grades are exported for use in internal joinery, including doors and staircases, but its lack of toughness renders it unsuitable for long ladder stringers or scaffold boards for example. It is used locally for joinery, furniture and turnery, sleepers, general construction work, and in the round for telegraph poles, piles (when treated), and pitprops. Logs are peeled for plywood manufacture, and selected logs sliced for decorative veneers.

Note: Not a true pine.

PAU MARFIM (H)

Balfourodendron riedelianum, Engl.
Family: *Rutaceae*

Other names: moroti, guatambu moroti (Argentina); farinha seca, quatamba, guatambu, pau liso (Brazil); kyrandy (Paraguay); quillo bordon (Peru); yomo de huero (Columbia); ivorywood (USA).

Distribution: South America, principally in Brazil and Argentina.

General description: The wood is cream to lemon coloured, sometimes with darker streaks. The grain is straight or irregular, sometimes interlocked and the texture very fine and uniform with a medium lustre. The weight is about 800 kg/m³ (50 lb/ft³); specific gravity .80.

Mechanical properties: This tough, hard wood is high in all strength categories and too strong for steam bending purposes.

Seasoning: The timber dries readily with little degrade and small movement in service.

Working properties: The wood works well with both hand and machine tools, with a moderate to severe blunting effect on cutting edges. Straight grained material planes very smoothly, but irregular or interlocked surfaces tend to pick up or tear out in planing or moulding. It nails and screws well, glues easily and can be stained and polished to a high smooth finish.

Durability: The timber is liable to insect attack and is not durable. The heartwood is resistant to preservative treatment but the sapwood is permeable.

Uses: This compact, fine textured wood, is excellent for turnery. Also suitable for shoe lasts, textile rollers and domestic flooring. Used in Brazil for oars, implements etc., and for cabinet work. Selected logs are sliced for decorative veneers for panelling and cabinets.

Note: The name pau marfim is also used in South America for other fine textured, creamy coloured woods especially for species of *Aspidosperma*.

PEAR (H)

Pyrus communis, L.
Family: *Rosaceae*

Other names: wild pear, choke pear (UK).

Distribution: Europe, including the UK, and Western Asia.

General description: The heartwood is pinkish-brown in colour with very fine rays and pores, straight grained and a very fine and even texture. Weight about 700 kg/m³ (44 lb/ft³); specific gravity .70.

Mechanical properties: Because pear is only available in fairly small sizes its strength is relatively unimportant for the uses to which it is applied. It is a fairly tough, very stable wood, but not used for steam bending purposes.

Seasoning: The wood dries slowly with a marked tendency to warp and distort. It is best to kiln dry the wood for best results. There is very small movement in service.

Working properties: It is a hard wood to saw with a moderate blunting effect on cutting edges. It is an excellent turnery wood. Nailing and screw holding are good, it glues well, and is particularly good for staining and polishing to a high finish. It is often dyed black to resemble ebony.

Durability: The heartwood is non-durable and liable to insect attack, but the wood is permeable for preservative treatment.

Uses: Widely used for fancy turnery and excellent for carving. Also for brushbacks, umbrella handles, measuring instruments such as set squares and T-squares. In Europe it is used for recorders, and when dyed black, for violin and guitar fingerboards and piano keys. Selected logs of suitable diameter and clean bole are sliced for decorative veneering, the quartered surfaces often displaying a large mottled figure.

PECAN (H)

(1) *Carya illinoensis*, K. Koch
(*C. pecan*, Engl. & Graebn. *Hicoria pecan*, Brit)
(2) *Carya aquatica*, Nutt (*Hicoria aquatica*, Brit)
Family: *Juglandaceae*

Other names: (1) pecan hickory, sweet pecan; (2) water hickory, bitter pecan (USA).

Distribution: South Eastern USA and Mexico.

General description: The wide sapwood is preferred to the heartwood, and is sold as "white hickory", while the heartwood, which is reddish brown is sold as "red hickory" – a distinction by colour which has no relation to strength. Mostly straight grained, but sometimes wavy or irregular, with a coarse texture. Weight 750 kg/m³ (46 lb/ft³); specific gravity .75. Pecan may be separated from true hickory by weight, and also by the narrow bands of parenchyma, which appear between the rays and between the large earlywood pores; in hickory the band occurs after the first row of earlywood pores.

Mechanical properties: Pecan and the true hickories exceed most other American hardwoods where high strength is required. It has high bending strength and crushing strength, high stiffness and very high shock resistance, with an excellent steam bending classification.

Seasoning: The timber seasons rapidly with little degrade but shrinkage is fairly high. There is small movement in service.

Working properties: There is moderate to severe blunting effect on cutters and a reduction to 20° is required for planing or moulding irregular grain. Pre-bore for nailing, gluing is satisfactory; it can be stained and polished to a good finish.

Durability: Non-durable; liable to insect attack. Moderately resistant to preservative treatment.

Uses: Wheelwrights work, chairmaking, ladder rungs, tool handles, sports goods and turnery, shunting poles, vehicle bodies, drum sticks, etc. Selected logs are sliced for decorative veneers.

Note: Closely related species: *Carya glabra*, **pignut hickory**; *C. tomentosa*, Nutt., **mockernut hickory**; *C. laciniosa*, Loud., **shellbark hickory**; *C. ovata*, K. Koch., **shagbark hickory**.

PEROBA, ROSA (H)

Aspidosperma peroba, Fr.All.,
(*A. polyneuron*, Muell. Arg.)
Family: *Apocynaceae*

Other names: red peroba, rosa peroba (UK). **Distribution:** Brazil.

General description: Variegated pink to rose red with yellow or orange and purple streaks and patches. The grain varies from straight to very irregular with a fine, uniform texture. The weight varies from 700–850 kg/m³ (44–53 lb/ft³), average about 750 kg/m³ (47 lb/ft³); s.g. .75.

Mechanical properties: Rosa peroba is comparable to European beech in compressive strength; has medium bending strength and resistance to shock loads, high crushing strength and low stiffness. Due to its considerable variation in strength, it is not usually used for steam bending purposes.

Seasoning: Requires care in drying to avoid splitting; some distortion may develop. Medium movement in service.

Working properties: The timber works well with hand and machine tools with only minor blunting effect on tools. May require pre-boring for nailing; glues well, and can be brought to an excellent finish when stained and polished.

Durability: The heartwood is durable and extremely resistant to preservative treatment; the sapwood is permeable.

Uses: Suitable for construction work where strength and durability are required, exterior joinery, and shipbuilding. Also for superior furniture and cabinetmaking, panelling, strip and parquet flooring, turnery, and selected logs are sliced for highly ornamental decorative veneers for panelling and marquetry.

Note: Various colour types of peroba are given different names, peroba preta, rose red with black streaks; peroba muida, red with darker patches; peroba poca, almost white; peroba rajada, light pinkish red with large black patches; peroba tremida, yellow with golden patches; and peroba revesa, with bird's eye figuring.

PEROBA, WHITE (H)

Paratecoma peroba, Kuhlm.
Family: *Bignoniaceae*

Other names: peroba de campos, ipé clare, ipé peroba, peroba amarella, peroba branca (Brazil); white peroba, golden peroba (UK).

Distribution: Brazil.

General description: The heartwood is variable in colour, basically light olive-brown with yellow, green or reddish shading, in the form of variegated stripes or streaks. The grain is commonly interlocked or wavy, producing a narrow striped or roe figure on quartered surfaces. The texture is fine and uniform. The weight varies from 690–830 kg/m³ (43–52 lb/ft³), averaging about 750 kg/m³ (47 lb/ft³); specific gravity .75.

Mechanical properties: It has medium bending strength, high crushing strength and low stiffness and resistance to shock loads, with a moderate steam bending classification.

Seasoning: Dries fairly rapidly and well with very slight splitting, but variable grain can lead to severe twisting in a few pieces. Generally, the distortion is not serious. Medium movement in service.

Working properties: Fine dust produced by machining operations may cause skin irritation and splinters are poisonous. There is only slight blunting effect on tools, and planed surfaces can be quite silken, except when interlocked or wavy grain is present on quartered material. Nailed and screwed joints hold well, it glues easily and can be stained and polished to a very high finish.

Durability: The timber is very durable, resists insect and fungal attacks, and is resistant to preservative treatment.

Uses: Because of its excellent durability it is used for civil and naval construction, decking, exterior construction and joinery work, and heavy duty flooring. Also for vehicle bodies and for vats to contain foodstuffs and chemicals. Selected logs are sliced for highly decorative veneers for cabinet work, panelling, marquetry, etc.

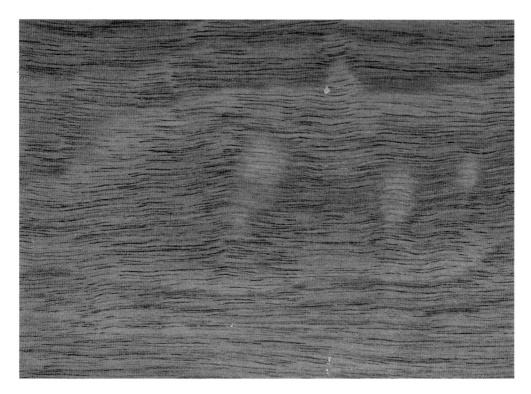

PERSIMMON (H)

Diospyros virginiana, L.
Family: *Ebenaceae*

Other names: bara-bara, boa wood, butter wood, possum wood, Virginian date palm.
Distribution: Central and southern USA.
General description: Belongs to the ebony family. The tree consists almost entirely of straw coloured sapwood, the heartwood being a small central core of dark brown or black. The commercial timber is the sapwood in this case although there are selected logs with variegated heartwood streaks of orange-brown, dark brown and black which are used for decorative items. The grain is straight and the texture, fine and even. Average weight 830 kg/m^3 (52 lb/ft^3); specific gravity .83.
Mechanical properties: The bending and crushing strengths are high with medium stiffness. The wood is tough, hard, elastic, resistant to wear, and moderate bends can be obtained.
Seasoning: Dries fairly rapidly with a liability to check; there is large movement in service.
Working properties: The timber has a moderate blunting effect on cutting edges which must be kept sharp. A reduced cutting angle for planing greatly helps achieve the very smooth surface attainable. Nailing requires pre-boring; gluing is difficult. It is capable of producing an exceptionally smooth, excellent finish.
Durability: The sapwood is liable to attack by powder post beetle. The heartwood is durable and resistant to preservative treatment.
Uses: Persimmon is used for the manufacture of textile shuttles, and it is claimed that the shuttle can be used for more than 1,000 hours without replacement. Also for shoe lasts, turnery, and golf club heads. Suitable for any purpose which requires a very heavy, close, compact wood with outstanding ability to wear very smoothly. Selected logs with wavy grain are sliced for ornamental veneers with variegated or roey figure and used for cabinets and panelling. Generally, the timber is only available in small sizes and is too heavy for plywood manufacture.

PINE, AMERICAN PITCH (S)

(1) *Pinus palustris*, Mill, principally,
(2) *P. elliottii*, Engelm.
Family: *Pinaceae*

Commercial names: (1) Florida longleaf or yellow pine, Georgia yellow pine; (2) slash pine.
Other names: Gulf coast pitch pine, longleaf pitch pine (UK); longleaf yellow pine, longleaf (USA); southern yellow pine*, southern pine*.
Distribution: Southern USA.
General description: The heartwood is orange to reddish-brown in colour and resinous. The growth rings are clearly marked by the contrast between the light earlywood and darker, more dense latewood, giving a coarse texture, especially in rapid grown timber. The weight varies between 660 and 690 kg/m^3 (41–43 lb/ft^3); specific gravity .67.
Mechanical properties: American pitch pine has identical strength properties to Douglas fir. Not suitable for steam bending due to its resin content.
Seasoning: Dries well with little degrade, and small movement in service.
Working properties: The timber has a moderate resistance to cutting edges with machine and hand tools and finishes cleanly. However, the resin can be troublesome in clogging cutters and sawteeth. Saws with a long pitch reduces this effect. The timber holds nails and screws firmly and it can be glued without difficulty. Paint and other finishing treatments are fairly satisfactory.
Durability: The timber is moderately durable, and it is susceptible to insect damage. The heartwood is resistant to preservation treatment, but the sapwood is permeable.
Uses: Heavy construction work, lorry and railway waggons, shipbuilding, spars, masts, exterior finish, flooring, dock work, decking etc. Lower density grades are used for joinery, light construction, boxes, crates, pallets etc. A large percentage of the resin and turpentine of the world is produced from these species.
***Note:** Southern yellow pine and southern pine, also includes two closely related species *P. echinata*, Mill, **shortleaf pine** and *P. taeda*, L., **loblolly pine**. Also related is *P. caribaea*, Morelet, and *P. oocarpa*, Schiede, producing **Caribbean pitch pine** (Central America).

PINE, PONDEROSA (S)

Pinus ponderosa, Douglas
Family: *Pinaceae*

Other names: western yellow pine (USA and Australia); bird's eye pine, knotty pine, British Columbia soft pine (Canada); Californian white pine (USA).

Distribution: Western Canada and Western USA.

General description: The tree has a wide, pale yellow sapwood, with a much darker heartwood varying from deep yellow to reddish-brown in colour. The resin ducts appear as fine dark brown lines on longitudinal surfaces, and the heartwood is considerably heavier than the softwood which is soft, uniform in texture and non-resinous. The weight is 510 kg/m^3 (32 lb/ft^3); specific gravity .51.

Mechanical properties: The timber has low stiffness and resistance to shock loads with medium bending and crushing strengths. It has a poor steam bending classification. There is medium movement in service.

Seasoning: The timber dries easily and well, but the wide sapwood is susceptible to fungal staining, requiring care in stacking during air drying.

Working properties: The wood works easily and well with little blunting effect on cutters. The plentiful knots are usually sound. Resin exudation is the chief problem, as this is the most resinous of Canadian pines. It can be glued satisfactorily, takes nails and screws, stains and gives reasonable results in painting and varnishing if treated for gumminess.

Durability: The timber is non-durable and subject to insect attack; moderately resistant to preservative treatment, but the sapwood is permeable.

Uses: The valuable sapwood is used for pattern making and similar purposes where stability is important, kitchen furniture and doors, turnery and carving, building construction, window frames, interior trim, boxes and packing cases, general carpentry. When treated, it is used for sleepers, poles and posts. It is occasionally found with bird's eye figure, and extensively used as "knotty pine" for interior decoration. Selected logs are sliced for veneers suitable for panelling.

Note: Closely related species *P. jeffreyi*, A. Murr, known as **Jeffrey pine** is marketed with ponderosa pine and sold under that name.

PINE, RADIATA (S)

Pinus radiata, D.Don.
(*P. insignis*, Dougl. ex Loud.)
Family: *Pinaceae*

Other names: Monterey pine (USA and Australia); insignis pine.

Distribution: USA (southern Californian) and introduced into New Zealand, Australia and South Africa.

General description: The tree has a large, wide pale-coloured sapwood, which is distinct from the pinkish-brown heartwood. The growth rings show rather less contrast than in other pines, such as Scots or Corsican, with the result that the texture is relatively uniform. Resin ducts appear on longitudinal surfaces as fine brown lines. Weighs 480 kg/m³ (30 lb/ft³); specific gravity .48. Spiral grain may be present.

Mechanical properties: The bending strength and stiffness qualities are low, crushing strength and resistance to shock loads is medium. It is not suitable for steam bending purposes.

Seasoning: With care, this timber seasons with little degrade. In timber from immature trees, spiral grain may cause warping. Steaming under weight for several hours reduces the distortion. There is medium movement in service.

Working properties: Works more easily than Corsican pine, with little dulling effect on cutters, which must have thin, very sharp edges. These will provide a clean finish except around knots which tend to tear. Nail holding is good, gluing is satisfactory, and the surfaces will provide a satisfactory finish.

Durability: Non-durable. Liable to insect damage. The bulk of commercially available timber comprises young rapidly grown plantation trees almost entirely of deeply permeable sapwood and ideal for preservation treatment.

Uses: Building and general construction, crates and boxes. Dressing grades are used for joinery. In New Zealand it is used for kraft and newsprint paper pulp. Selected logs are sliced for attractive decorative veneers for panelling.

PINE, SIBERIAN YELLOW (S)

Pinus sibirica, Du Tour
(P. cembra, L. var. *sibirica*, Loud)
P. koraiensis, Sieb. & Zucc.
Family: *Pinaceae*

Other names: Siberian pine, Korean pine, Manchurian pine (UK).
Distribution: Principally Siberia and Manchuria, also N. Korea.
General description: This is a soft, yellow-brown timber with only a little resin, seen on longitudinal surfaces as thin dark lines due to resin canals. Straight grained, and with a fine, even texture. Commercially it is available in narrow widths and much of the timber is knotty. Weight 420 kg/m^3 (26 lb/ft^3); specific gravity .42.
Mechanical properties: The timber has medium compression strength, but is low in bending strength, stiffness and resistance to shock loads and to splitting. It has a poor steam bending classification.
Seasoning: The timber seasons easily and uniformly without degrade. There is small movement in service.
Working properties: The timber works easily with hand and machine tools with little dulling effect on cutting edges. If the cutters are kept sharp it finishes cleanly in most operations, both with and across the grain. Being soft, it tends to crumble under dull cutters. It has good nailing and screwing properties and takes glue, stain, paint, and polish easily and well.
Durability: Non-durable; susceptible to attack by common furniture beetle. Moderately resistant to preservative treatment. The sapwood is permeable.
Uses: This material is extensively used for carvings, pattern making, and for panelling when selected with a suitable complement of decorative knots. It is also used for construction purposes, doors, high-class joinery, farmhouse furniture; selected logs are sliced for attractive decorative veneers.

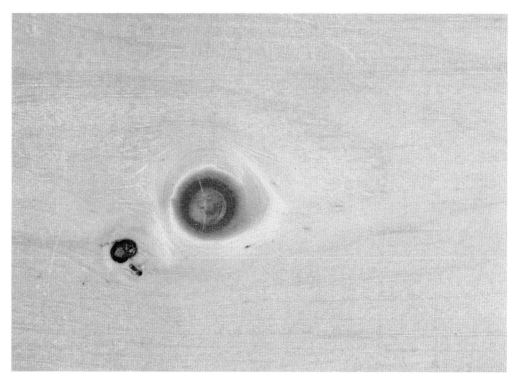

PINE, WESTERN WHITE (S)

Pinus monticola, Dougl.ex D.Don
Family: *Pinaceae*

Other name: Idaho white pine.

Distribution: Western Canada and Western USA.

General description: The heartwood is a pale straw colour, only slightly darker than the wide sapwood, and the colour tone varying from straw to reddish-brown with fine brown lines of the resin ducts on longitudinal surfaces. There is hardly any contrast between early and latewood zones. It is straight grained with an even and uniform texture. Weight about 420 kg/m^3 (26 lb/ft^3); specific gravity .42.

Mechanical properties: Although yellow pine (*P. strobus*) is known as "white pine" in Canada and the USA, western white pine is 30% harder, 25% stronger in compression along the grain, 15% stronger in bending and 25% more resistant to shock loads. It is not suitable for steam bending.

Seasoning: The timber dries readily with little checking or warping. There is small movement in service.

Working properties: The wood is very easy to work with all tools, and if cutting edges are kept sharpened, an excellent finish is obtained. Takes nails and screws without difficulty; glues, stains and takes paint and varnish well.

Durability: It is non-durable and liable to insect attack. The heartwood is moderately resistant but the sapwood is permeable to preservation treatment.

Uses: Joinery, doors and windows, interior trim, fitments, shelving, light and medium construction, pattern making, drawing boards, furniture making, boat and ship building, match splints, wooden-ware, and plywood manufacture. Selected logs are sliced for decorative veneers.

Note: Closely related species is *P. contorta*, Dougl. which produces **lodgepole pine** or **contorta pine** (UK).

PINE, YELLOW (S)

Pinus strobus
Family: *Pinaceae*

Other names: white pine, spruce pine (Canada and USA); eastern white pine, northern white pine, northern pine (USA); Quebec pine, soft pine, Weymouth pine (UK).

Distribution: Eastern Canada and USA.

General description: The heartwood colour varies from pale straw to light reddish-brown. Although not very resinous, resin ducts appear on longitudinal surfaces as fine brown lines. It is a soft, straight grained and very even textured wood with inconspicuous growth rings. The average weight is 390 kg/m³ (24 lb/ft³); specific gravity .39.

Mechanical properties: This is a light, soft and weak wood in all strength properties and not suitable for steam bending.

Seasoning: The wood dries readily and well, and an important characteristic is its low shrinkage. There is very small movement in service.

Working properties: The wood works very easily with hand or machine tools and has very little dulling effect on the cutters. It finishes cleanly in most operations, and has good nailing and screwing properties, glues well, and takes stain, paint, polish, etc., very well.

Durability: Non-durable. Insect damage may be present. Moderately resistant to preservation treatment but the sapwood is permeable.

Uses: This species produces the most valuable softwood timber in North America. It is well suited to pattern making, carving, drawing boards, high-class joinery and general carpentry work. Also for furniture making, musical instruments, ship and boat building, light and medium construction and domestic woodware. Selected logs for veneering.

Note: Second growth timber is much coarser in texture and prone to knots and crossgrain. Related spp. include: *P. banksiana*, Lamb, **jack pine**, also known as **princess pine** and **banksian pine**. *P. contorta*, Dougl., **lodge pole pine**, also known as **contorta pine**. *P. resinosa*, Ait, produces **Canadian red pine** (Canada) **Norway pine** (USA).

PINE, JAPANESE RED (S)

Pinus densiflora
Family: *Pinaceae*

Other name: aka matsu.
Distribution: Japan.
General description: The heartwood colour is light reddish-brown to orange, generally straight grained, medium to fine texture, and inclined to be knotty and slighly resinous. Weight about 400 kg/m³ (25 lb/ft³); specific gravity .40.
Mechanical properties: The wood has medium bending and crushing strength, with low stiffness and resistance to shock loads. It has a very poor steam bending classification due to knots and resin.
Seasoning: Dries easily and uniformly with little checking or distortion; kilning improves its finishing qualities by setting the resin content. It has medium shrinkage and movement in service.
Working properties: It works easily with hand or machine tools and finishes cleanly and smoothly in most operations. The knots cause little trouble in machining, although cutters should be kept thin edged and sharp. Takes nails and screws well, glues satisfactorily, and takes stain, paint, varnish or polish to a good finish.
Durability: Non-durable. Damage by longhorn beetle and pinhole borer may be present. Moderately resistant to preservative treatment, but the sapwood is permeable.
Uses: Used locally for building construction, joinery, panelling, boat building, masts and spars, and building interiors.

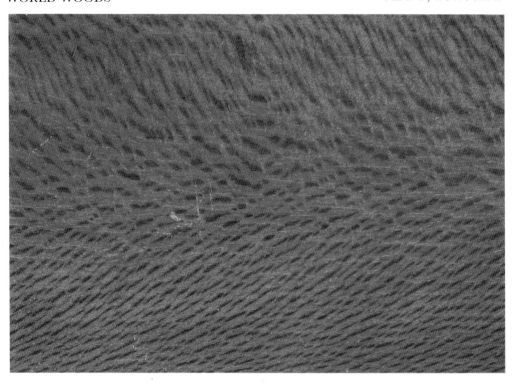

PLANE, EUROPEAN (H)   *Platanus hybrida*, Mill (*P. acerifolia*, Willd)
Family: *Platanaceae*

Other names: London plane, English plane, French plane, etc., according to origin (UK); quartered wood known in the trade as **lacewood** (UK). See also footnote.

Distribution: Europe including the UK (**oriental plane**, *platanus orientalis*, L.) S.E. Europe and West Asia.

General description: The heartwood is light reddish-brown with very conspicuous and numerous broad rays present on quartered material, which show against the light coloured background as a decorative fleck figure. The wood is straight grained with a fine to medium texture. Some logs are much lighter in colour, pale pinkish-brown, with a small, irregular, darker coloured core. Weight about 620 kg/m^3 (39 lb/ft^3); specific gravity .62.

Mechanical properties: Plane has medium strength in most categories and low stiffness making it a very good steam bending wood.

Seasoning: Dries fairly rapidly without much splitting but with a tendency to distort. There is small movement in service.

Working properties: Works well with hand and machine tools, but there is a moderate blunting effect on cutters, and a tendency to bind on saws. The wood glues well and stains and polishes, with care, to an excellent finish.

Durability: Perishable. The sapwood is liable to attack by the common furniture beetle, but is permeable for preservation treatment.

Uses: Furniture and cabinetmaking, joinery, carriage interiors, light construction and panelling; and ornamental inlay work on boxes and furniture. It is an excellent turnery wood for fancy and decorative items. Selected logs are cut to produce **lacewood**, the highly decorative flecked surface ideal for panelling and cabinet interiors, desks, etc. Plane and lacewood are treated chemically to produce a form of harewood, in whch the background colour becomes silver grey but the flecked rays retain their original colour. Used for marquetry work.

Note: Related spp. *platanus occidentalis* is known as **sycamore** in America.

PODO (S)

Podocarpus spp., principally
P. gracilior, Pilg., *P. milanjianus*, Rendle,
P. usambarensis, Pilg.
Family: *Podocarpaceae*

Other names: yellow-wood (South Africa); musengera wood (West Africa).

Distribution: East and South Africa.

General description: Podo differs from European softwoods in that it has no clearly defined growth rings, giving it a more uniform texture. It is straight grained, non-resinous and odourless. The heartwood colour is light yellowish-brown and weighs 510 kg/m³ (32 lb/ft³); specific gravity .51.

Mechanical properties: Medium bending and crushing strength, very low stiffness and low resistance to shock loads. It has a moderate steam bending classification.

Seasoning: The material dries quite rapidly with a risk of distortion and should be heavily weighted or mechanically restrained to reduce this. It may split or check, and where compression wood is present, longitudinal shrinkage may result. Medium movement in service.

Working properties: Works easily with hand and machine tools with little dulling effect on cutters. The timber is brittle and occasionally some logs have hard abrasive patches. With cutters kept sharpened, the wood saws, planes and moulds to a good finish and turns well. It may split when nailed unless thin gauge nails are used. Holds screws well and glues satisfactorily. It does not always stain uniformly but takes varnish, paint and polish well.

Durability: Subject to attack by pinhole borer and longhorn beetle. Non-durable, but permeable to preservative treatment.

Uses: *P. gracilior* is suitable for good grades of plywood; *P. milanjianus* only for lower grade plywood and plywood corestock. Selected material used for joinery and interior fittings and as a general utility softwood where durability is unimportant. It is also sliced for decorative veneers and used for panelling and cheaper grades of furniture.

POPLAR (H)

Populus spp: (1) *P. nigra*, L.,
(2) *P. canadensis*, Moench, var. *serotina*, Rehd.,
(3) *P. robusta*, Schneid., *(4) P. tremula*, L.
Family: *Salicaceae*

Commercial names: (1) European black poplar; (2) black Italian poplar (UK); (3) robusta (UK); (4) Finnish aspen, Swedish, French aspen, etc. according to origin; European aspen.

Distribution: Europe including the UK.

General description: The heartwood is usually creamy-white to grey in colour, sometimes very pale brown or pinkish-brown. Straight grained and inclined to be woolly; texture fine and even. (4) is generally whiter, and finer in texture and quality. Weight ranges from 380–530 kg/m³ (23–33 lb/ft³) averaging 450 kg/m³ (28 lb/ft³); specific gravity .45.

Mechanical properties: Very low stiffness and resistance to shock loads, medium crushing strength and a low bending strength. It has a very poor steam bending classification.

Seasoning: Dries rapidly and fairly well, but local pockets of moisture sometimes remain in the wood and knots are inclined to split. There is medium movement in service.

Working properties: Poplars have only a slight blunting effect on tools. Very sharp, thin cutting edges are required to overcome the woolly texture and produce a good finish. Nailing is satisfactory and gluing is easy, but staining can produce patchy results. The surface will take paint, varnish and polish satisfactorily.

Durability: The wood is perishable and liable to insect attack, but the sapwood, which constitutes a large proportion of the tree, is permeable for preservative treatment. The heartwood of (1) and (2) is moderately resistant to preservative treatment.

Uses: The tough, non-splintering, woolly nature of poplar is suitable for rough usage such as the bottoms of trucks, waggons and carts. Also for furniture framing, drawers, interior joinery, toys, flooring, boxes and crates. As a veneer for plywood, chip-baskets, match splints, etc. Selected logs of European aspen are sliced for attractive decorative veneers often with pink and orange streaks, and a lustrous surface.

Note: *P. alba*, L., produces **white poplar** or **abele**; *P. canescens*, Sm., **grey poplar** (UK).

'PORT ORFORD CEDAR' (S)   *Chamaecyparis lawsoniana*, (A.Murr.) Parl.
(Cupressus lawsoniana, Murray)
Family: *Cupressaceae*

Other names: Lawson's cypress (UK); Oregon cedar (USA).
Distribution: Oregon and California, USA, and introduced into the UK.
General description: The heartwood colour is pale pinkish-brown. Typically non-resinous but occasionally exuding an orange-yellow resin. It has a characteristic spicy odour and a fine, even texture and is straight grained. Weight 485 kg/m^3 (30 lb/ft^3); specific gravity .48. UK grown material may have wavy grain.
Mechanical properties: The material has medium bending and crushing strength with low stiffness and resistance to shock loads. It has a very poor steam bending classification as severe buckling and fibre rupture occurs.
Seasoning: Dries readily with little degrade, and kilns directly from green.
Working properties: The wood works easily with hand or machine tools, with little blunting effect on cutting edges and finishes cleanly in most operations. Takes nails and screws well, glues satisfactorily and gives good results with stain, paints or polishes.
Durability: Moderately durable. Damage by longhorn beetle and *Sirex* is sometimes present. It is moderately resistant to preservative treatment by pressure but the sapwood is permeable by pressure with oil based preservatives or boron salts by diffusion process.
Uses: In America the wood is used for ship and boat building, oars, canoe paddles, furniture and cabinet work, and organ building. Selected logs are sometimes sliced for decorative veneers, especially the knotty wood which is used for decorative panelling.
Note: Not a true cedar.

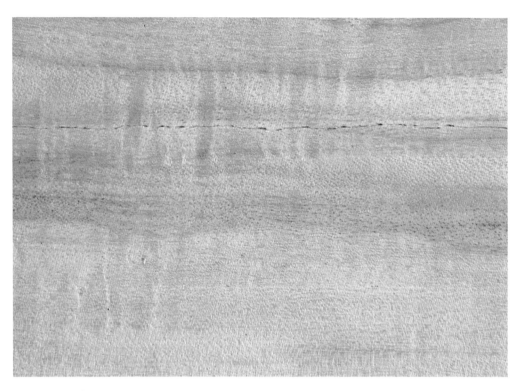

PRIMA VERA (H)

Tabebuia donnell-smithii, J.M. Rose
(*Cybistax donnell-smithii*, (J.M. Rose) Seibert)
Family: *Bignoniaceae*

Other names: durango, palo blanco (Mexico); san juan (Honduras); roble (USA).

Distribution: Central America, particularly in Mexico and Nicaragua.

General description: The timber is a light yellow-rose colour with streaks of red, orange and brown. The grain is straight to interlocked and wavy, and quartered surfaces can offer a roey, striped, or mottled figure. The texture is medium-coarse. Weight about 450 kg/m^3 (28 lb/ft^3); specific gravity .45.

Mechanical properties: Medium strength in bending, crushing and resistance to shock loads, and with low stiffness, making it a good timber for steam bending.

Seasoning: Dries well with little degrade; small movement in service.

Working properties: Works easily and well with both hand and machine tools, and finishes smoothly. Where irregular grain is present on quartered surfaces a reduced cutting angle is necessary. It has a medium blunting effect on cutters. Holds nails and screws well and glues without difficulty. Generally it can be brought to an excellent finish.

Durability: Non-durable. Liable to attack by common furniture beetle and pinhole borer. Moderately resistant to preservative treatment but the sapwood is permeable.

Uses: Suitable for furniture and cabinets and often used as a substitute for superior hardwoods as it is so easy to work. Also for panelling and high-class interior joinery. Selected logs are sliced to form highly decorative veneers for panelling and face veneers for cabinets.

Interesting note: The sap of these tropical trees rises and falls with the phases of the moon, and not in the spring and winter as in temperate zones. If felled in the "dark of the moon" when the sap is down, it minimises exudation of sap from the ends of the log which attracts the insects that cause damage to the timber.

PTERYGOTA, AFRICAN (H)

(1) *Pterygota bequaertii*, De Wild
(2) *P. macrocarpa*, K. Schum
Family: *Sterculiaceae*

Other names: (1) koto (Ivory Coast); ware, awari (Ghana); kefe, poroposo (Nigeria).

Distribution: Nigeria and Cameroon Republic.

General description: The heartwood is creamy-white in colour with a greyish tint. The grain is interlocked with small knot clusters present in some logs. The texture is moderately coarse. Quartered surfaces reveal a striking flecked figure due to the high rays. The weight is variable from 530–750 kg/m^3 (33–47 lb/ft^3) with the average for (1) 650 kg/m^3 (41 lb/ft^3) and (2) 560 kg/m^3 (35 lb/ft^3); specific gravity (1) .65 and (2) .56.

Mechanical properties: (1) Has medium bending strength and crushing strength, medium-low resistance to shock loads and low stiffness with a very poor steam bending classification; (2) is lower in all categories.

Seasoning: Dries fairly rapidly with a tendency for some surface checking, shakes, or moderate cupping to occur. It needs to be dried quickly to avoid staining. There is medium movement in service.

Working properties: Generally works well with hand and machine tools provided that cutters are kept sharp. Tends to split when nailed near the edges; glues satisfactorily. Requires grain filling to provide a good finish.

Durability: Perishable. Sapwood liable to attack by powder post beetle; non-resistant to termites in West Africa. Permeable to preservation treatment. Timber requires rapid extraction and conversion to be in a clean condition, free from stain and insect damage.

Uses: Core stock for plywood manufacture and as a backing veneer for plywood panels. Suitable as substitute for beech or ramin in furniture manufacture, interior joinery and carpentry, and general utility timber for interior work, boxes, crates etc. Selected logs sliced for decorative veneer.

PURPLEHEART (H)   *Peltogyne pubescens*, Benth., *P. porphyrocardia*, Griseb.,
P. venosa, (Vahl) Benth, var. *densiflora* (Spruce) Amsh.
also: *P. confertiflora, P. paniculata* and *P. purpurea*, Pitt.
Family: *Leguminosae*

Other names: amaranth, violetwood (USA); koroboreli, saka, sakavalli (Guyana); purperhart (Surinam); pau roxo, nazareno, morado (Venezuela); tananeo (Columbia).
Distribution: Central America and tropical South America.
General description: The heartwood is a deep purple-violet when freshly cut, maturing to a dark brown; the original colour is restored when re-cut. Straight grained, but often irregular, wavy, and sometimes interlocked, producing a pleasing striped figure on quartered surfaces. Texture moderate to fine. Weight varies from 800–1,000 kg/m³ (50–63 lb/ft³) averaging 860 kg/m³ (54 lb/ft³); specific gravity .86.
Mechanical properties: High strength in bending, stiffness and crushing categories and medium resistance to shock loads, with a moderate steam bending classification.
Distribution: Dries fairly rapidly with little degrade, but care is needed to dry out the centre of thick pieces. Air drying is slow, with some end and surface checking or case hardening. There is small movement in service.
Working properties: It is rather difficult to work with moderate to severe blunting effect on tools. It exudes gummy resin when heated by dull cutters and the material is best run slowly through machines equipped with high speed steel knives. The wood turns well and smoothly. Pre-bore for nailing; glues without difficulty and stains and wax polishes easily. Spirit finishes remove the purple colour; lacquer finishes preserve the colour.
Durability: Very durable. Sapwood liable to attack by powder post beetle. Extremely resistant to preservative treatment but the sapwood is permeable.
Uses: Although expensive, it is used for heavy outdoor constructional work, bridge building, fresh water piling, dock work, cladding, house construction and vats. Excellent for flooring, and suitable for gymnasium equipment, shafts, tool handles, boat building, turnery, furniture and billiard tables. Also as decorative veneers for inlaying and marquetry work, etc. Best colour from sawcut, as steaming affects the soluable *phonicoin* content.

QUANGDONG, WHITE (H)

Elaeocarpus grandis, F. Muell & others
Family: *Elaeocarpaceae*

Other names: caloon, aborig, blue fig, blueberry ash.

Distribution: Queensland, Australia.

General description: The colour varies from white to grey-brown. It is straight grained, light and very strong, porous and open grained. Weight from 448–560 kg/m^3 (28–35 lb/ft^3); specific gravity .50.

Seasoning: The timber dries readily with little degrade. There is small movement in service.

Working properties: The wood is easily wrought and cuts cleanly; it holds nails and screws well, and glues easily; stains and polishes to an excellent finish.

Durability: Non-durable. The wood has natural durability for interior work, but should not be used externally in contact with the ground.

Uses: Although detailed mechanical properties are not known, the wood is used in Australia and New Zealand for joinery, cabinetmaking, bentwood, turnery, and sliced into veneers for decorative panelling.

Note: Closely related spp. include *E. coorangoolou* and *E. ruminatus*, producing **brown quangdong**, which is also sold as **caloon**.

'QUEENSLAND MAPLE' (H)

(1) *Flindersia brayleyana*, F. Muell
(2) *F. pimenteliana*, F. Muell
(3) *F. laevicarpa* var. *heterophylla*
Family: *Rutaceae*

Commercial names: Australian maple (UK); maple silkwood (Australia); (2) and (3) scented maple.

Distribution: Australia and Papua New Guinea.

General description: The colour of the heartwood is light brown to flesh pink with a silken lustre, the grain often interlocked, wavy or curly, producing a wide range of figure. The texture is medium and uniform. (1) and (2) weigh about 550 kg/m³ (34 lb/ft³); (3) weighs 690 kg/m³ (43 lb/ft³); specific gravity .55 and .69.

Mechanical properties: Medium bending and crushing strengths; low stiffness and resistance to shock loads. This is a poor steam bending wood.

Seasoning: This timber requires much care as there is a great tendency for distortion to occur, and for wide boards to cup or collapse. Also has medium to high shrinkage during drying. All three species should have reconditioning treatment in the kiln. Medium movement in service.

Working properties: Works fairly readily with only a moderate blunting effect on cutters. A reduced cutting angle to 20° is required in planing or moulding quarter sawn surfaces due to interlocked grain. Nails and screws satisfactorily, and can be stained and polished to an excellent finish; it also fumes well.

Durability: The heartwood is moderately durable and resistant to preservative treatment.

Uses: Cabinet work, furniture, high-class joinery, vehicle bodies, rifle stocks, printing blocks, interior fittings, mouldings, boat fittings, oars, superstructures, turnery, and in Australia for plywood. Selected logs are sliced to produce very attractive decorative veneers, including butts, moiré and ripple figure, block mottle, fiddleback, striped and bird's eye figure.

Note: Not a true maple.

'QUEENSLAND WALNUT' (H)

Endiandra palmerstonii, (F.M. Bail)
C.T. White and W.D. Francis.
Family: *Lauraceae*

Other names: Australian walnut (UK); oriental wood (USA); walnut bean (Australia).

Distribution: Australia.

General description: Varies in colour from light to dark brown streaked with pinkish, grey, green or black stripes on quartered surfaces. The grain is irregular and interlocked, sometimes wavy, producing a checkered or broken striped figure. The texture is medium and even and the surface is fairly lustrous. The disagreeable odour rapidly disperses in use. Weighs from 600–770 kg/m³ (37–48 lb/ft³), average about 680 kg/m³ (42 lb/ft³); specific gravity .68.

Mechanical properties: This heavy density wood has medium bending strength, high crushing strength, low resistance to shock loads and low stiffness; it has a moderate steam bending classification.

Seasoning: It kiln dries rapidly in thin sizes without checking but thick sizes tend to warp, cup and collapse if hurried. However, the timber responds well to re-conditioning treatment. There is medium movement in service.

Working properties: It is rather difficult to saw and machine due to silica, requiring the use of tungsten carbide tipped saws and high speed cutters. An increased tooth pitch to the saws is also recommended for bandsawing. Nailing, screwing and gluing is satisfactory and the timber takes an excellent polish.

Durability: Non-durable and the heartwood is resistant to preservative treatment.

Uses: This material has high insulation properties. It is used for high-class furniture and cabinetmaking, panelling, flooring, shop and office fitting, joinery and construction. It is also sliced for plywood face veneers, and attractive decorative veneers for panelling, cabinet work and marquetry.

Note: Not a true walnut.

RAMIN (H)

Gonystylus macrophyllum, (Miq.) Airy Shaw
Family: *Gonystylaceae*

Other names: ramin telur (Sarawak); melawis (West Malaysia) (see Note 2).

Distribution: Sarawak and West Malaysia, and South East Asia.

General description: The heartwood is a uniform pale straw colour, the grain straight to shallowly interlocked and texture moderately fine and even. The weight varies from 640 to 720 kg/m³ (40–45 lb/ft³), average about 660 kg/m³ (41 lb/ft³); specific gravity .66.

Mechanical properties: Ramin has high bending and crushing strengths, medium stiffness and low resistance to shock loads. It cannot be steam bent satisfactorily without buckling and has a very poor classification.

Seasoning: The timber dries readily with little distortion, but with a tendency for end splitting or surface checking to occur. It is prone to mould growth staining and must be dipped immediately after conversion. Clean, air dry stock is easily kilned without undue degrade, but a strong, unpleasant odour evolves during kilning. There is a large movement in service.

Working properties: Works fairly well with hand and machine tools but with moderate blunting of cutting edges. There is a tendency to split in nailing. Gluing is good and staining and polishing is satisfactory if a small amount of filler is used.

Durability: Perishable. Sapwood is liable to attack by powder post beetle and subject to dry wood termites in Borneo. It is permeable to preservative treatment.

Uses: Furniture making, interior joinery, shop fittings, carving, turnery, panelling, flooring, toys, picture frame mouldings, and plywood manufacture. Also sliced for decorative veneering.

Note 1: Skin irritation can be caused when handling timber containing sharp pointed bark fibres.

Note 2: Related spp. include *G. affinis* and *G. confusus* which, collectively with *G. macrophyllum*, are marketed as **melawis**.

RATA (H)

Metrosideros robusta, A. Cunn.
M. lucinda,
Family: *Myrtaceae*

Other names: northern rata, New Zealand ironwood.

Distribution: New Zealand.

General description: The wood varies from reddish-brown to chocolate-brown colour, with a straight grain, sometimes wavy or interlocked, and a fine, even texture. It weighs from 720–880 kg/m³ (45–55 lb/ft³), average 800 kg/m³ (50 lb/ft³); specific gravity .80.

Mechanical properties: This very heavy wood has high bending and crushing strengths, and high stiffness with medium resistance to shock loads. It has a moderate wood bending classification.

Seasoning: Requires great care in drying as it possesses a very high shrinkage potential. Partial air drying before kilning is advised. Movement in service is large.

Working properties: There is a high resistance in cutting with a moderate blunting effect on cutting edges. In planing or moulding a cutting angle of 15° is required to avoid the grain from picking up. Nailing and screwing is difficult, but the wood takes glue easily and can be stained and polished satisfactorily.

Durability: Durable and extremely resistant to preservative treatment. The sapwood is immune from powder post beetle attack and is permeable for preservation treatment.

Uses: The wood has excellent strength properties and is very suitable for wheelwright's work, the framework of railway waggons and carriages, machine beds and bearings, shipbuilding, structural work, sports goods, etc. When treated it is used for railway sleepers. Sliced veneers are used for decorative veneering.

Note: *M. queenslandica* produces **pink myrtle** or **myrtle satinash**.

'RED BEECH' (H)

Nothofagus fusca, (Hook f.) Oerst.
Family: *Fagaceae*

Distribution: New Zealand.

General description: The heartwood is light reddish-brown in colour, straight grained and of fine, even texture. Weight varies according to location from 610–690 kg/m^3 (38–43 lb/ft^3); specific gravity .68.

Mechanical properties: The majority of red beech has medium bending and crushing strength, stiffness and resistance to shock loading, with a good steam bending classification. The timber from the Murchison Reef area of South Island is the lighter material with 30% lower strength values, i.e. low bending, crushing and stiffness, and resistance to shock loads. Moderate bending classification.

Seasoning: The wood seasons slowly and unevenly with a tendency to warp and check. If kilned from green there is a liability to collapse or honeycomb. Partial air drying before kilning is satisfactory. Small movement in service.

Working properties: The wood is easy to work with hand or machine tools; can be nailed, screwed, glued, stained and polished to a good finish. The lower density beech from South Island is even easier to process or machine, with only slight blunting effect.

Durability: Durable; the heartwood is liable to attack by pinhole borer, but these do not remain active or re-infest dried timber. It is permeable to preservation treatment.

Uses: Furniture and cabinetmaking, joinery, turnery, brushware, boat building, house building, flooring, bridge timber and wharf decking. It is sliced for decorative veneers for cabinets and panelling.

Note: Not a true beech (*Fagus* spp.)

'RED TULIP OAK' (H)

Tarrietia argyrodendron,
T. peralata,
Family: *Sterculiaceae*

Distribution: Queensland, Australia.

General description: The heartwood is variegated pale pink to reddish-brown. Straight, open grain, sometimes interlocked or wavy and irregular, producing some beautifully figured wood with a striking silver grain on quartered surfaces, and a mottled figure. It has a moderately fine to coarse texture. It is also fissile. Weight about 850 kg/m^3 (53 lb/ft^3); specific gravity .85.

Mechanical properties: A hard, heavy density wood with medium bending and crushing strengths, and low stiffness and resistance to shock loads. The steam bending classification is moderate, but the timber is elastic and strong.

Seasoning: Requires very careful seasoning and liable to serious degrade if hurried. Partial air drying before kilning at low temperatures is recommended. There is small movement in service.

Working properties: Rather difficult to work with hand tools but satisfactory with machine tools; there is moderately severe blunting effect on cutters. The cutting angle should be reduced to 20° when planing or moulding to avoid tearing the grain on quartered material. Nailing may require pre-boring and the wood does not glue readily. However, it can be stained, fumed or polished to a very good finish.

Durability: Non-durable. Liable to attack by powder post beetle. Heartwood is resistant to preservative treatment, and the sapwood permeable.

Uses: Suitable for furniture and cabinetmaking, superior joinery, plywood manufacture, bent work for boat or vehicle bodies, domestic flooring, electrical fittings and fishing rods. Selected logs are sliced for decorative veneers for panelling and cabinet work.

Note 1: Not a true oak (*Quercus* spp.)

Note 2: Closely related spp. include *Argyrodendron actinophyllum*, syn. *Heritiera actinophylla* and *Tarrietia actinophylla*, known as '**blush tulip oak**'.

RENGAS (H)

Melanorrhoea curtisii* and related spp.,
Family: *Anacardiaceae*

Other names: Borneo rosewood, Straights mahogany, black varnish tree (UK).

Distribution: Malaysia, Philippines and Papua New Guinea.

General description: The heartwood is a rich vivid red, with variegated streaks. The rays have horizontal canals which exude sap which forms black blotches on the wood surface; these disappear when the wood is planed. The grain is interlocked, with a rather coarse texture. The weight varies from 670–990 kg/m^3 (41–61 lb/ft^3); specific gravity .83 average.

Mechanical properties: This heavy, dense wood, has low bending and crushing strength, very low stiffness and resistance to shock loads. It is a poor steam bending wood due to resin exudation.

Seasoning: Dries easily and well with little degrade. There is very small movement in service.

Working properties: Rengas works reasonably well with hand and machine tools, but has a blunting effect on tools which need to be kept sharpened. The interlocked grain may tear in planing unless a reduced cutting angle is used. It nails, screws, glues and takes stain and polish well. The sanding dust can cause irritation to the skin.

Durability: The wood is moderately durable, and resistant to preservation treatment.

Uses: Cabinetmaking, furniture and superior joinery, ornamental work. Selected logs are sliced for veneers.

Note: The following species are sold under the group name of **rengas**:

Melanorrhoea torquata, King., *M. wallichii*, Hook.f., *M. aptera*, *M. malayana*, and *M. woodsiana*; *Gluta elegans*, *G. renghas*, and *G. wrayi*; *Melanochyla auriculata*, *M. bracteata*, *M. kunstleri*, *M. rugosa*.

REWAREWA (H)

Knightia excelsa, R. Br.
Family: *Proteaceae*

Other name: New Zealand honeysuckle.

Distribution: New Zealand.

General description: The heartwood colour is deep red, with a strong ray figure, quartered wood with dark red-brown rays has a very striking appearance. A more subdued figure appears on flat sawn material in the form of a ray speckled figure. The grain is irregular and the wood has a fine texture, is lustrous, hard and strong. Weight about 736 kg/m^3 (46 lb/ft^3); specific gravity .73. Blackheart is prevalent with heart shakes.

Mechanical properties: The timber has medium bending strength, but high stiffness, crushing strength and resistance to shock loads. It has a poor steam bending classification.

Seasoning: It is difficult wood to dry. The distorted grain resulting from crooked logs, and presence of blackheart can cause collapse. Tangential (flat-sawn) shrinkage is about three times as great as the radial shrinkage, therefore any timber not sawn accurately, true to the flat or quarter, will seriously distort. Collapse can be restored by reconditioning. There is large movement in service.

Working properties: The wood works well with hand or machine tools and there is medium bluntness to cutting edges. Nailing can be difficult, but it holds screws well and glues satisfactorily. Oily substances should be avoided when finishing as they are absorbed to the detriment of the fine grain. Varnishing is also a disadvantage.

Durability: Non-durable. Will not stand exposure to variations of weather if used externally, but the sapwood is permeable to preservative treatment.

Uses: Furniture and cabinetmaking, flooring, interior finishing and building construction, machine beds, inlay work, ornamental turnery, plywood corestock, and sliced for decorative panelling veneers. Treated wood is suitable for decking, gates, rails, stair treads, piling and railway sleepers.

RIMU (S)

Dacrydium cupressinum, Soland.
Family: *Podocarpeceae*

Other name: red pine.
Distribution: New Zealand.
General description: Rimu is a fine, even textured, medium density softwood. The seasoned heartwood is reddish-brown, sometimes yellowish-brown, and has a pigmented figure which fades upon exposure to light. The intermediate zone has an even, light-brown colour and sapwood a lighter brown tone. It is straight grained. Weight 530 kg/m^3 (33 lb/ft^3); specific gravity .53.
Mechanical properties: Medium crushing strength, low bending strength and resistance to shock loads, and a very low stiffness category. It also has a very poor steam bending classification.
Seasoning: Dries moderately easily with only a slight tendency for surface checking and can be kiln dried from green with few problems. There is medium movement in service.
Working properties: There is a slight dulling effect on cutters, and the material works readily with hand or machine tools. Glues well and holds screws satisfactorily but tends to split in nailing. The material has good staining or painting and finishing properties.
Durability: Moderately durable. The sapwood and intermediate zones are susceptible to insect attack and are non-durable. The heartwood is difficult to treat under pressure.
Uses: The better grades are used for furniture manufacture, interior panelling, weatherboards, flooring, interior trim and rotary cut for plywood manufacture. Building grades are used for framing and structural purposes. Selected logs are sliced for architectural veneers. The pigmented figure is highly decorative and can be used with a natural finish.
Note: See also **huon pine**.

ROBINIA (H)

Robinia pseudoacacia, L.
Family: *Leguminosae*

Other names: false acacia (UK); black locust (USA).

Distribution: North America, and planted in Europe, Asia, North Africa, and New Zealand.

General description: Greenish when freshly cut turning to golden brown. Straight grained, coarse textured due to contrast between large pored earlywood and dense latewood. Weight varies from 540–860 kg/m^3 (34–54 lb/ft^3) but averages at about 720 kg/m^3 (45 lb/ft^3); specific gravity .72.

Mechanical properties: Medium strength in bending and crushing; low resistance to shock loads and stiffness, which provide very good steam bending properties, equal to beech or ash. The steamed material tends to stain if in contact with iron or steel.

Seasoning: The timber dries slowly with a marked tendency to distort or warp badly. There is medium movement in service.

Working properties: It is fairly difficult to machine due to the texture and there is moderate blunting of tools which should be thin edged and sharp. It is difficult to nail and should be pre-bored. Gluing is easy, and the material stains and polishes satisfactorily.

Durability: Durable. The sapwood is liable to attack by powder post beetle and the common furniture beetle. Reported to be highly resistant to termites in Central America. It is extremely resistant to preservative treatment. Older trees often have a rotten heart and are liable to windbreak. Young trees of rapid growth are preferred.

Uses: This tough, durable wood is used externally for wheels, barrows, waggon bottoms, stakes, posts, gates, boat planking, vehicle bodies, weatherboards, fencing, etc. Selected material is used for joinery and cabinetwork, and sliced for decorative veneering.

ROSEWOOD, BRAZILIAN (H)

Dalbergia nigra, Fr.All.
Family: *Leguminosae*

Commercial names: Bahia rosewood, Rio rosewood (UK).
Other names: jacaranda, jacaranda da Bahia, jacaranda preto (Brazil); palissander, palissandre du Brazil (France).
Distribution: Brazil.
General description: The heartwood colour varies from chocolate or violet-brown to violet streaked with black, often with variegated streaks of golden brown. The grain is mostly straight, sometimes wavy and the texture rather coarse. It is oily and gritty to the touch. The weight varies from 750–900 kg/m^3 (47–56 lb/ft^3) averaging 850 kg/m^3 (53 lb/ft^3); specific gravity .85.
Mechanical properties: This timber has high strength in all categories except stiffness, which is low and therefore has very good steam bending classification for straight grained material.
Seasoning: It air dries slowly with a tendency to check, but kilning shows little degrade. There is small movement in service.
Working properties: There is a severe blunting effect on cutting edges and tends to be difficult to work. Requires pre-boring for nailing; gluing can be troublesome and the oiliness can also make high polishing difficult. However, with care, a beautiful smooth finish can be obtained.
Durability: Very durable, the heartwood resists biodegradation.
Uses: This beautiful timber has been prized world-wide for centuries and is used in both solid and veneer form for highest quality furniture and cabinetmaking, piano cases, shop and bank fitting, superior joinery, parquet flooring, instrument making, tool and knife handles, wood sculpture, carving and turnery. Selected logs are sliced for panelling, doors, etc., and face veneers for all forms of decorative veneering.
Note: *D. spruceana*, Bth., produces **jacaranda do Para**, and is used locally for similar purposes. Also, *Machaerium scleroxylon* closely resembles Brazilian rosewood and is sold as a substitute for it. The machinery dust from this species can cause severe skin irritation.

ROSEWOOD, HONDURAS (H)

Dalbergia stevensonii, Standl.
Family: *Leguminosae*

Other name: nogaed (USA).

Distribution: Grows exclusively in Belize.

General description: The heartwood colour varies from pinkish to purple-brown with irregular black markings which are independent of the growth rings, and give the wood a very attractive appearance. The grain is straight to slightly roey or wavy, the texture is medium to fine. Weight from 930–1100 kg/m^3 (58–68 lb/ft^3) averages about 960 kg/m^3 (60 lb/ft^3); specific gravity .96.

Mechanical properties: Although this species is denser and tougher than Brazilian rosewood it is mainly used for purposes where strength properties are of minor importance. It is too heavy for bending.

Seasoning: The material dries slowly with a tendency to split, but can be kilned with care without undue degrade. There is small movement in service.

Working properties: It is rather difficult to work and has a moderate blunting effect on cutting edges and must be held firmly. It is satisfactory in sawing operations, but a reduced cutting angle of 20° should be used for planing when interlocked or wavy grain is present. It is excellent for turnery. Pre-boring for nailing is required. Some very oily specimens may cause gluing and finishing problems and the wood will not take a high natural polish, but generally a good finish is obtainable with care.

Durability: Very durable. Moderately resistant to termites in Belize.

Uses: Fingerboards for banjos, guitars and mandolins, percussion bars for xylophones, harp bodies, piano legs, mouldings, picture frames etc. Selected logs are sliced for very decorative veneers used for piano cases, furniture, cabinets, billiard tables, bank, shop and office fitting, panelling and doors, and decorative veneer faces. Widely used for turnery.

ROSEWOOD, INDIAN (H)

Dalbergia latifolia, Roxb., principally,
also: *D. javanica*, Miq., *S. marginata*, Roxb., *D. sissoo*, Roxb.
Family: *Leguminosae*

Commercial names: Bombay blackwood (India); East Indian rosewood, Bombay rosewood (UK). **Other names:** shisham, sissoo, biti, eravadi, kalaruk (India).

Distribution: India – especially southern India, and Java.

General description: From rose to dark purple-brown with darker purple-black lines terminating the growth zones. The grain is narrowly interlocked producing a ribbon grain figure; the texture uniform and moderately coarse, and the surface dull but with a fragrant scent. It weighs about 850 kg/m³ (53 lb/ft³); specific gravity .85.

Mechanical properties: The material has high bending and crushing strengths with low stiffness and medium resistance to shock loads.

Seasoning: The timber air dries fairly rapidly with no undue degrade but must be protected against too rapid drying to avoid surface checking and end splitting. Kiln dries well but slowly, and the colour improves during this process. There is small movement in service and it has remarkable dimensional stability.

Working properties: There is severe blunting of cutting edges, and is fairly hard to saw or machine due to calcareous deposits present in some of the vessels (the heart is usually boxed out in conversion). It is not suitable for nailing. Glues satisfactorily and requires grain filling for an excellent polished or waxed finish.

Durability: Very durable and moderately resistant to termites in India. Sapwood liable to attack by powder post beetle.

Uses: This very handsome timber is used for high-class furniture, cabinetmaking, shop, office and bank fitting, flooring, musical instruments, boatbuilding, brake blocks, posts, rafters and exterior joinery. It is an excellent turnery wood. Selected logs are converted into valuable decorative veneers for panelling, doors, cabinets and luxury interiors.

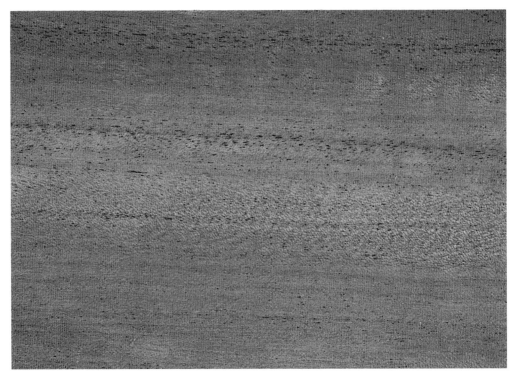

SAPELE (H)   *Entandrophragma cylindricum*, Sprague.
                                                    Family: *Meliaceae*

Commercial names: sapelewood (Nigeria); aboudikrou (Ivory Coast); sapelli (Cameroon).
Other names: Gold Coast cedar, penkwa.
Distribution: West and East Africa.
General description: The heartwood has a medium to dark reddish-brown colour, characterised by a well-defined ribbon striped figure on quartered surfaces. Sometimes, when wavy grain is present, a very attractive fiddleback figure, roe figure or occasionally, beautiful mottled figure is obtained. The grain is interlocked or wavy and the texture fairly fine. Has a cedar-like scent when freshly cut. The timber is liable to ring or cup shakes. Weight varies between 560–690 kg/m³ (35–43 lb/ft³) averages about 620 kg/m³ (39 lb/ft³); specific gravity .62.
Mechanical properties: Despite high crushing and medium bending strength and resistance to shock loads, with a low stiffness category, sapele has a poor steam bending classification as the wood buckles and ruptures severely.
Seasoning: Dries fairly rapidly with a marked tendency to distort. Quartered material is less liable to degrade. Medium movement in service.
Working properties: Works without difficulty with both hand and machine tools but the interlocked grain affects machining properties. It nails, screws and glues well; care is required when staining, but it provides an excellent polished finish.
Durability: Moderately durable. The sapwood is liable to attack by powder post beetle and moderately resistant to termites in Africa. The heartwood is resistant to preservative treatment and the sapwood moderately resistant.
Uses: Quality furniture and cabinetmaking, joinery, shop fitting, office furniture, solid doors, boat building, musical instruments, sports goods, counter tops and flooring. Extensively used as a constructional veneer for plywood and selected logs are sliced for panelling and decorative face veneers for cabinets and marquetry, etc.

SASSAFRAS (H)

Sassafras officinale, Nees & Eberm.
syn: *S. variifolium*, Kuntze.
Family: *Lauraceae*

Commercial names: cinnamon wood, red sassafras (USA).
Other name: black ash.
Distribution: Eastern USA, chiefly Arkansas and Missouri.
General description: The heartwood is pale to dark brown in colour with a straight grain and coarse texture. It is a soft, light, flexible wood weighing about 450 kg/m³ (28 lb/ft³); specific gravity .45.
Mechanical properties: Sassafras is lower in strength than ash, although of similar appearance. It has medium strength in all categories except stiffness which is low, and the wood is suitable for steam bending purposes.
Seasoning: Requires care in drying as it has a marked tendency to check. Small movement in service.
Working properties: Medium resistance to cutting edges and tools should be kept sharp; a good finish obtainable in planing or moulding. Pre-boring may be necessary to avoid splitting when nailing near edges; holds screws well and glues very well. It can be stained and brought to a good finish.
Durability: Moderately durable. Sapwood liable to attack by powder post beetle. Heartwood is moderately resistant to preservative treatment but the sapwood is permeable.
Uses: Large sizes are scarce but it is used locally for furniture; boat building for superstructures, cabins and interior fitments; boxes, crates and containers, fencing and for cooperage. Selected logs are sliced for decorative veneers.
Note: Sassafras oil is distilled from the roots and used for flavouring medicines and perfuming soap; also, sassafras tea comes from the flowers or root bark. This is from *Sassafras albidum* a closely related species, sold together with *S. officinale*.

SATINÉ (H)

Brosimum paraense, Hub.
Family: *Moraceae*

Other names: muirapiranga (Brazil); bois satiné (France); satiné rubané, cardinal wood, Brazil wood*, satinee (USA).

Distribution: Tropical America.

General description: The heartwood colour varies from grey-red to deep rich red, with a golden lustre and variegated yellow and red stripes. The grain varies from straight to variable, fine textured and smooth with distinct rays. Weight: 1010 kg/m³ (63 lb/ft³) when dry; specific gravity 1.01.

Mechanical properties: The wood has high bending and crushing strength, medium stiffness and resistance to shock loads, but tends to splinter and has a low steam bending classification.

Seasoning: Dries slowly without much degrade and there is small movement in service.

Working properties: This very hard, tough wood works fairly easily with hand and machine tools in all operations. It may need pre-boring for nailing, but it holds screws well; glues, stains and polishes to a very good finish.

Durability: The timber is durable and very resistant to preservative treatment.

Uses: Chiefly used for cabinetmaking and furniture, marquetry work, fancy boxes, turnery, and selected logs are sliced for highly decorative veneers.

*Note: Not to be confused with BRAZILWOOD (pau ferro) *Guilandina echinata*. There are several Brazilian woods marketed as 'Brazilwood'.

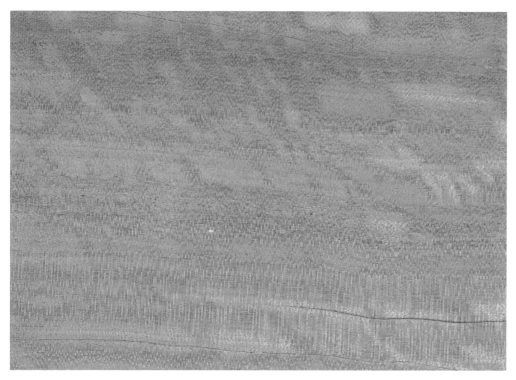

SATINWOOD, CEYLON (H)

Chloroxylon swietenia, DC.
Family: *Rutaceae*

Commercial name: East Indian satinwood.

Other names: burutu (Sri Lanka); bhera, behra, mutirai (India).

Distribution: Central and Southern India and Sri Lanka.

General description: The heartwood colour is golden yellow, maturing to golden brown with darker streaks. It is lustrous, fragrant and smooth. The grain is narrowly interlocked and variegated, producing mottle, roe and ribbon striped figure, broken stripe, and so called "bee's wing" cross mottled figure. Liable to gum veins and cup shakes. The texture is fine and even. Weight average 980 kg/m^3 (61 lb/ft^3); specific gravity .98.

Mechanical properties: The timber has high bending strength and crushing strength, medium stiffness and low resistance to shock loads, but strength is of little importance for the uses to which this species is put.

Seasoning: The timber has a tendency to surface cracking with some warping or twisting, and air drying of girdled trees seasoned in the log gives best results. It must be protected from too rapid drying. It kiln dries well with little degrade. There is small movement in service.

Working properties: Fairly difficult to work, even with machine tools, and having a moderate blunting effect on cutting edges. Nailing must be pre-bored. It is also difficult to glue. Stains and polishes extremely well if a little filler is used.

Durability: Durable. Non-resistant to termites in India. Extremely resistant to preservative treatment. Subject to marine borers but resists teredo.

Uses: High-quality cabinets, furniture making and interior joinery. Excellent for turnery, jute bobbins, and locally for structural work, piling, etc; office and bank fitting, and the manufacture of inlay bandings. Selected logs are sliced for extremely attractive veneers in a wide variety of figures for panelling, cabinets, marquetry, etc.

SEN (H)

Acanthopanax ricinofolius, Seem
Syn. *Kalopanax pictus*, Nakai
Family: *Araliaceae*

Other names: haragiri, sen-no-ki (Japan); nakada (Manchuria); tse tsin (Sri Lanka); castor arabia (USA).

Distribution: Japan, China and Sri Lanka.

General description: Heartwood colour is yellow to greenish-brown with a straight grain and moderately coarse texture. Weight about 560 kg/m^3 (35 lb/ft^3); specific gravity .56.

Mechanical properties: Sen is weaker in all categories compared to Japanese ash and has none of its valuable attributes, although strength is less important for the uses to which it is applied. It has a very poor steam bending classification.

Seasoning: Dries rapidly with a marked tendency to degrade. Care must be taken in air drying to avoid very high shrinkage, and is best finished in the kiln with a slow schedule. It is susceptible, after drying, to warping, shrinking or swelling according to changing atmospheric conditions. The movement in service is very large.

Working properties: It works easily and well with both hand and machine tools and planed surfaces are quite silky. It nails, screws, glues and stains well, and all finishing agents may be used on sanded surfaces.

Durability: Perishable and liable to attack by powder post and common furniture beetle. Moderate resistance to impregnation but the sapwood is permeable to preservation treatment.

Uses: In Japan it is extensively used for chests, furniture, passenger coaches, interior joinery, panelling, construction, naval furnishings, piano cases, sports bats, artistic joinery, carvings, turnery. Rotary peeled for plywood manufacture, and selected logs sliced for attractive decorative veneers for panelling, cabinets, marquetry, etc.

SEPETIR (H)

Sindora spp., principally
S. coriacea and *S. echinocalyx*
Family: *Leguminosae*

Other names: makata (Thailand); supa (Philippines); petir (Sarawak); gu (S. E. Asia).

Distribution: Khmer Republic, Thailand, Malaysia, Philippines.

General description: The heartwood colour varies from pinkish-brown to golden-brown to red-brown, darkening as it matures, with dark brown or black streaks producing handsomely figured wood. The grain is shallowly interlocked and variable in direction, and the texture moderately fine and even. A growth ring figure appears on tangential surfaces due to irregularly spaced terminal parenchyma bands, and quartered wood has a striped figure. The wood has a greasy feel and a characteristic odour. The weight is from 640–720 kg/m³ (40–45 lb/ft³); specific gravity .67.

Mechanical properties: It has medium bending and crushing strength, with low stiffness and resistance to shock loads. It has a poor steam bending classification due to resin exudation.

Seasoning: The wood dries out slowly with only slight distortion and a tendency for end splitting.

Working properties: It is difficult to saw and plane due to the resin content. Pre-boring for nailing is advised and screw holding is good. Gives a good finish in most operations and stains and polishes well despite the resin.

Durability: Heartwood is durable, and the sapwood perishable but permeable, and liable to attack by powder post beetle. The heartwood is extremely resistant to preservative treatment.

Uses: Furniture, cabinetmaking, joinery, panelling, musical instruments, sporting goods, light construction. Figured logs are sliced for very decorative veneers for furniture, cabinets and panelling.

Note: A closely related spp. *Pseudosindora palustris* occurs in Sarawak and Brunei in freshwater swamps and is known as **swamp sepetir**.

SEQUOIA (S)

Sequoia sempervirens, (D.Don) Endl.
Family: *Taxodiaceae*

Other names: Californian redwood (UK and USA); vavona burr.

Distribution: USA.

General description: The heartwood colour is dull reddish-brown with a distinct growth ring figure produced by contrasting earlywood and latewood zones. It it straight grained, and although much of the timber is of fine, even texture, some is coarser and heavier. The wood is non-resinous and non-tainting. The average weight is 420 kg/m³ (26 lb/ft³); specific gravity .42.

Mechanical properties: Strength tests reveal an extreme range of properties dependent on growth rates and latewood development. At its best rating, sequoia has low bending strength, crushing strength and resistance to shock loads and very low stiffness.

Seasoning: Kiln drying should be undertaken with care to avoid collapse, but air drying is rapid and with very little degrade. There is small movement in service.

Working properties: Works easily and well with both hand and machine tools with very little dulling effect on cutting edges but splinters and chip bruises easily during machining. It has poor nail-holding ability. Liable to stain with alkaline adhesives but can be glued easily otherwise. Gives good results with paint and usual finishing treatments.

Durability: Logs are subject to attack by longhorn beetle and pinhole borer. The wood is durable out of ground contact and moderately resistant to preservative treatment.

Uses: Exterior cladding, shingles, exterior joinery, wooden pipes etc. In America it is used for vat making, especially where resistance to decay is required. Interior joinery, organ building, especially for pipes, coffins, posts, panelling, and in the round for telegraph poles. Rotary cut for plywood manufacture, and selected logs sliced for decorative veneers. The bark is used for chipboard manufacture and filtering plant.

Note: Closely related to *Sequoiadendron giganteum*, (Lindl) Buch., **wellingtonia** (UK), and *Sequoia gigantea*, (Lindl.) Deene, the **giant redwood**, (the largest known trees in the world), the timbers of which are of little commercial value.

SCOTS PINE (REDWOOD) (S)

Pinus sylvestris, L.
Family: *Pinaceae*

Commercial names: red deal or 'red' if imported from Europe (northern UK); yellow deal or 'yellow' (southern UK). Timber grown in the UK is called Scots pine. Baltic, Finnish, Swedish, Polish, etc., redwood or yellow deal according to country of origin.

Other names: Norway fir, Scots fir (UK); red pine (Scotland).

Distribution: Europe, UK, Scandinavia and Russia.

General description: The wide geographical range of this species provides varying strength, texture, densities, number and size of knots, etc. When dry, the heartwood colour is pale reddish-brown, and resinous. The annual rings clearly marked by contrasting light earlywood and darker latewood zones. The weight is an average 510 kg/m^3 (32 lb/ft^3); specific gravity .51.

Mechanical properties: The species has low stiffness and resistance to shock loads, and medium crushing strength. UK timber has medium bending strength; European material has low bending strength. The UK material is 20% harder on the side grain and tougher, and from 15–30% more difficult to split. It has a very poor steam bending classification.

Seasoning: Seasons very rapidly and well, but with a tendency to blue sap stain. It should be anti-stain dipped or kilned immediately after conversion. There is medium movement in service.

Working properties: The timber works easily and well with both hand or machine tools; can be stained, painted, varnished or polished satisfactorily. Gluing can be troublesome in very resinous material.

Durability: Non-durable; susceptible to insect attack. The heartwood is moderately resistant to preservative treatment, but the sapwood is permeable.

Uses: The best grades are used for furniture, joinery and turnery, vehicle bodies; and generally for building construction, carcassing, railway sleepers, etc. In the round for telegraph poles, piles and pitprops. It is rotary cut for plywood manufacture, and selected material is sliced for decorative veneers.

'SILVER ASH' (H)

Flindersia schottiana, F. Muell.
Family: *Rutaceae*

Other names: southern silver ash, bumpy ash, cudgerie.

Distribution: Australia and Papua New Guinea.

General description: The heartwood colour is pale brown or slightly tawny. The grain is mainly straight, occasionally wavy or shallowly interlocked, with medium texture. The weight is 560 kg/m^3 (35 lb/ft^3); s.g. 56.

Mechanical properties: The timber has medium bending and crushing strength and low stiffness or resistance to shock loads. It has a very good steam bending classification. Tough, resilient and elastic.

Seasoning: The wood dries rather slowly and shows little tendency to warp. It can be air or kiln dried satisfactorily up to 50mm thicknesses. Small movement in service.

Working properties: Works easily with hand and machine tools with only a moderate blunting effect on cutting edges. Quartered surfaces tend to pick up when planing or moulding and a reduction of the cutting angle to 20° overcomes this problem. The material takes nails and screws well, glues easily, and if care is taken in filling and staining, the wood polishes to a good finish.

Durability: Moderately durable to very durable above ground; the heartwood is very resistant to impregnation of preservative treatment, but the sapwood is permeable.

Uses: Structural timber, flooring, ship and boat building, vehicle bodies, furniture and cabinet work, sporting goods, musical instruments, precision equipment, interior trim, joinery, carving, turnery, food containers, veneer and plywood.

Note 1: Not a true ash.

Note 2: Other spp. include *F. bourjotiana*, F. Muell, **Queensland silver ash**; and *F. pubescens*, F. M. Bail, **northern silver ash**.

'SILVER BEECH' (H)

(1) *Nothofagus menziesii*, (Oerst)
(2) *N. truncata*, (Col) Cockayne
Family: *Fagaceae*

Other names: (1) Southland beech (2) hard beech or clinker beech.

Distribution: New Zealand.

General description: The heartwood colour is salmon pink to pinkish-brown. There is an intermediate zone in addition to sapwood but for practical purposes this is regarded as sapwood. The grain is generally straight, sometimes curly, and the texture is fine and even. The weight of (1) varies between 475–550 kg/m³ (29–34 lb/ft³) and for (2) 690 kg/m³ (43 lb/ft³); specific gravity (1) .47 to .55 (2) .69.

Mechanical properties: These timbers are of medium density, bending and crushing strengths; they have low stiffness and resistance to shock loads. All have good steam bending classification, but slight buckling sometimes occurs on bends of large radii.

Seasoning: Boards up to 25mm thickness dry without difficulty but problems increase with thickness which retains moisture. End splitting can result if hurried but surface checking or distortion are slight. Partial air drying before kilning is recommended. There is small movement in service.

Working properties: The wood is easy to work with hand or machine tools with generally only a moderate blunting effect on cutting edges; the blunting effect with (2) hard beech, can be moderately severe due to the presence of silica in the ray cells. The material nails, screws and glues well, and can be stained and polished to an excellent finish.

Durability: Non-durable, and liable to attack by powder post beetle and common furniture beetle. Hard beech is durable. Both may be permeated for preservative treatment.

Uses: Furniture, joinery, turnery, brush ware, boat building, building construction, light flooring, bridge timbers, wharf decking, vehicle body work, tool handles, toys, food containers, etc. Sliced veneers used for plywood; decorative veneers for furniture and panelling.

Note: Not a true beech.

SIRIS, YELLOW (H)

Albizia xanthoxylon,
Family: *Leguminosae*

Other name: golden bean.

Distribution: Queensland, Australia.

General description: A lustrous, oily natured wood coloured old-gold with dark brown vessel lines on longitudinal surfaces. On the transverse end it has large pores thickly margined by parenchyma. It is a soft, light but tough wood with a straight grain and woolly texture. Weight 410 kg/m^3 (25 lb/ft^3); specific gravity .41.

Mechanical properties: In relation to its weight it has excellent strength properties, but in terms of bending and crushing strength and resistance to shock loads the category is low, with a poor steam bending classification.

Seasoning: The timber seasons quickly and should be carefully dried in well-ventilated stacks under cover; there is little degrade and small movement in service.

Working properties: It is very easy to cut and work with little blunting effect on cutting edges. Sanding dust can cause irritation to the eyes, nose and throat and has been the cause of nose bleeding in machine operatives. It holds nails and screws well, and takes glue, stain and polish.

Durability: Durable. Subject to attack by white ants. Some logs develop in-growing bark (bark-veins) and grub holes cause waste in conversion. Also some heart rot may be present. Although resistant to preservative treatment, the sapwood is permeable.

Uses: It does not absorb water to any extent when dry and never becomes waterlogged, therefore useful for boat-building floats, hulls, etc. Also for flooring, window sills, stair treads, external cladding, general building, studding, linings, ceilings, etc. Selected material is sliced for decorative veneers.

Note: see also **Albizia, West African.**

SNAKEWOOD (H)

Piratinera guianensis, Aubl.
and allied species
syn. *Brosimum aubletti*
Family: *Moraceae*

Other names: letterwood (UK); amourette (France); bourra courɽa (Guyana); letterhout (Surinam); polo do oro (Venezuela); leopard wood, speckled wood (USA).

Distribution: Central and Tropical South America.

General description: The appearance of snakewood is similar to that of snakeskin, sometimes also spotty like leopard spots, or speckled with peculiar markings. The timber is usually exported in small billets stripped of sapwood. The heartwood colour is basically red-brown with black speckles and also sometimes with black vertical stripes. It is very hard and heavy, weighing 1,300 kg/m^3 (81 lb/ft^3) when dry; specific gravity 1.30.

Mechanical properties: The timber is exceptionally tough and strong in all categories, but the gummy deposits which fill the cell cavities make a very poor steam bending classification due to exudation of the gum.

Seasoning: Difficult to season and with tendency to warp and degrade. Medium movement in service.

Working properties: It is a very difficult wood to work but will finish smoothly from the tool. There is a blunting effect on cutting edges; and care should be taken when gluing. The wood is capable of a beautiful finish.

Durability: Very durable and extremely resistant to preservative treatment.

Uses: Turned articles such as walking sticks, drum sticks, fishing rod butts, handles for cutlery, umbrella handles, violin bows, fancy trinkets and brushbacks. Also for archery bows. Selected flitches may be sliced into veneer for marquetry or decorative purposes.

SOPHORA (H)

(1) *Sophora japonica*, L.
(2) *S. tetraptera*,
syn. *Edwardsia microphylla*,
Family: *Leguminosae*

Other names: *S. japonica* is known as yen-ju, or en-ju in Japan and China, and *S. tetraptera* is called kowhai in New Zealand; pagoda tree (UK).

Distribution: (1) China and Japan (2) New Zealand.

General description: The heartwood is golden brown in colour with a greenish tint, resembling laburnum wood. It has a lustrous sheen and rather fine texture with a ray flecked figure. It is straight grained. Weighs 680 kg/m³ (42 lb/ft³); specific gravity .68.

Mechanical properties: This is a heavy, fairly hard timber with high bending and crushing strength and resistance to shock loads with low stiffness. It is resilient and elastic and should be suitable for steam bending.

Seasoning: Dries readily with little degrade. Medium movement in service.

Working properties: Works easily with hand or machine tools, with moderate blunting of cutting edges. Sharp tools will produce clean, smooth surfaces. It nails, screws, and glues without difficulty and can be stained and polished to a good finish.

Durability: Durable. Not subject to insect attack and is highly resistant to preservation treatment.

Uses: Used locally for house framing, shafts, tool handles, implements and also for cabinet work. It is not usually available in large dimensions.

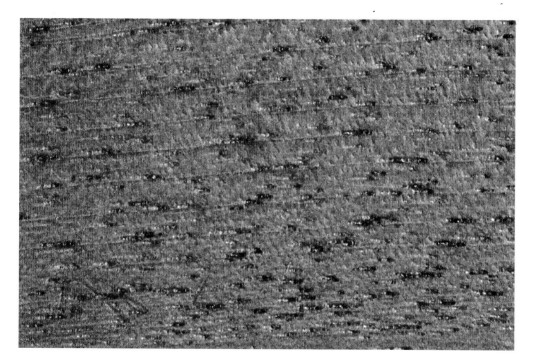

'SOUTH AMERICAN CEDAR' (H)   *Cedrela fissilis*, Vell., and allied spp.
Family: *Meliaceae*

Commercial names: Brazilian cedar, British Guiana cedar, Peruvian cedar, cigar-box cedar, cedar (UK). Usually named after the country of origin.

Other names: cedro, cedro batata, cedro rosa, cedro vermelho (Brazil).

Distribution: Central and South America except Chile.

General description: The colour varies according to growth conditions but is usually from pale pinkish-brown to dark reddish-brown. Straight grained or shallowly interlocked with a moderately coarse texture. Resinous with a fragrant scent due to a volatile oil which may exude and appear on the surface as a sticky resin. Weight varies from 370 to 750 kg/m^3 (25–46 lb/ft^3) but averages about 480 kg/m^3 (30 lb/ft^3); specific gravity .48.

Mechanical properties: Moderately good steam bending qualities, and is strong in relation to its weight.

Seasoning: It dries rapidly with very minor warping and slight checking and end splitting. Distortion or collapse of some pieces in kiln drying can be avoided with a low temperature schedule. There is very small movement in service.

Working properties: It is easy to work with hand or machine tools; edges must be kept sharp to avoid a tendency to woolliness. The presence of gum presents some dificulty in staining and polishing, but after suitable filling, can be brought to a good finish. It holds nails, screws well, and can be glued satisfactorily.

Durability: The wood is durable. Liable to attack by powder post beetle but resistant to termites. The heartwood is extremely resistant to preservative treatment but the sapwood is permeable.

Uses: Furniture, cabinets and panelling, high-class joinery, flooring, house construction, boat building, skins of racing boats, canoe decks, cigar boxes, sound boards for organs, clothing chests. Sliced for decorative veneers for panelling and as plywood and panel corestock.

Note 1: Related spp. includes *C. odorata*, L., **Central American cedar** (and according to origin, e.g. **Honduras cedar**). Also named as '**Spanish cedar**'. **Note 2:** Not a true cedar.

'SOUTHERN WHITE CEDAR' (S)

Chamaecyparis thyoides, (L) B.S.P.
syn. (*Cupressus thyoides*, L.)
Family: *Cupressaceae*

Other names: 'Atlantic white cedar', 'white cedar'.

Distribution: Southern states of America.

General description: This spicey, aromatic wood is pink in colour, and usually straight grained and fine textured. It is soft and light in weight, 370 kg/m^3 (23 lb/ft^3); specific gravity .37.

Mechanical properties: The timber is weak, having very low stiffness, medium bending strength, crushing strength and resistance to shock loads. The timber has a very poor steam bending classification.

Seasoning: Although care is needed to avoid internal honeycombing or collapse in thicker material, thin dimensions dry readily with little degrade, and there is small movement in service.

Working properties: Works easily with both hand and machine tools and provided that the tools are kept sharp, there is little blunting effect on cutting edges. The wood nails and screws well, and takes stain and finishing treatments satisfactorily.

Durability: Durable. Liable to insect attack. It is resistant to preservative impregnation treatment.

Uses: The timber is used for exterior work, and in work where it is in contact with the ground such as fence posts, rails, sleepers, shingles, boat building, and in timber framed houses for light construction.

Note: Not a true cedar.

SPRUCE, JAPANESE (S)

Picea jezoensis, Carr.
syn. *P. ajanensis*, Fisch.
Family: *Pinaceae*

Other names: yeddo spruce (UK); yezo matsu (Japan).

Distribution: Japan.

General description: The timber is non-resinous, without odour and non-tainting, whitish in colour with a pink cast. Mainly straight grained but with some spiral grain occasionally. It weighs about 430 kg/m³ (27 lb/ft³); specific gravity .43.

Mechanical properties: The strength properties are high in relation to its weight. It has medium bending and crushing strength, medium stiffness and low resistance to shock loads. The timber has the same hardness and resistance to splitting as Baltic redwood. It has a very poor steam bending classification.

Seasoning: It is not difficult to season and tends to dry rapidly and well, but some warping, splitting and loosening of knots must be expected. There is small movement in service.

Working properties: The wood works easily with all hand and machine tools with little dulling effect on cutters. A clean finish can be obtained in all operations if cutters are kept sharp. It takes nails and screws well; glues readily and produces a good finish if care is taken to prevent grain raising.

Durability: Non-durable. May be subject to attack by pinhole borers; resistant to preservative treatment.

Uses: The wood is used in Japan for building construction and joinery and sliced for special laminates for aircraft, glider construction, boat building and oars, racing sculls, etc.

SPRUCE, SITKA (S)

Picea sitchensis, (Borg) Carr.
Family: *Pinaceae*

Other names: silver spruce (UK, Canada and USA); tideland spruce (Canada and USA); Menzies spruce, coast spruce (Canada).

Distribution: Western Canada and USA coastal strip through Washington and into California. It is abundant in Queen Charlotte Islands.

General description: The wood is creamy-white with a pink tinge at the sapwood running into a light pink-brown heartwood. It is mostly very straight grained, but occasionally spiral grain is present. The texture is medium and even, depending on the growth rate. The wood is non-resinous, odourless and non-tainting. Weight 430 kg/m^3 (27 lb/ft^3); specific gravity .43.

Mechanical properties: The wood has medium bending and crushing strengths, and medium stiffness and resistance to shock loads; its strength to weight ratio is high, and it has a very good steam bending classification.

Seasoning: The timber dries fairly rapidly and well, although some warping, splitting and loosening of knots must be expected, care is needed in drying high value stock of larger sizes.

Working properties: The wood works easily with hand and machine tools with little dulling effect on cutters. It finishes cleanly, takes nails and screws well, stains readily and can give excellent results with various finishing treatments.

Durability: It is non-durable; liable to attack by pinhole borer beetle and to damage by jewel beetle. The heartwood is resistant to preservative treatment.

Uses: The timber is sliced into veneers for laminates for aircraft and glider construction, sail planes, oars and racing sculls. It is also widely used in boat building, soundboards in piano manufacture, interior joinery, building construction, cooperage, box-making, musical instruments, etc.

Note: Other spp. include *P. engelmannii*, Engelm., **Englemann spruce**; *P. glauca*, Moench, **western white spruce**.

STERCULIA, BROWN (H)

Sterculia rhinopetala, K. Schum.
Family: *Sterculiaceae*

Other names: wawabima (Ghana); aye (Nigeria); red sterculia (UK); lotofa (Ivory Coast); n'kananh, bojanga (Cameroon).

Distribution: West Africa.

General description: The heartwood varies from yellow-orange-red to deep red-brown. The deep colour of the high rays provides a very striking figure on quartered surfaces in contrast to the plain background material. Straight to interlocked grain; texture coarse and fibrous. Weight varies from 530 to 1020 kg/m^3 (33–64 lb/ft^3) but fair average is 820 kg/m^3 (51 lb/ft^3); s.g. .82.

Mechanical properties: The timber has high bending strength and crushing strength, with medium stiffness and resistance to shock loads. It has only a moderate steam bending classification as it is intolerant of pin knots.

Seasoning: Dries very slowly with severe cupping, but other forms of distortion are slight. There is large movement in service.

Working properties: Works with moderate ease with hand and machine tools with some blunting of the cutting edges. The cutters must be kept sharp to deal with the woolly texture and tendency to spring. The interlocked grain can cause tearing in planing and moulding. Pre-boring is required for nailing. It glues, and stains satisfactorily but requires grain filling for a good finish.

Durability: Heartwood moderately durable. Sapwood liable to attack by powder post beetle. Moderately resistant to termites in West Africa. Extremely resistant to preservative treatment, and the sapwood moderately resistant.

Uses: Constructional work, tool handles, interior joinery and flooring blocks. In Nigeria selected logs are peeled for plywood manufacture, corestock and facings for blockboard. Also sliced to provide striking decorative veneers for panelling and interior decoration.

Note: Related spp. include *S. oblonga*, Mast., **yellow sterculia** or **white sterculia** (UK).

STINKWOOD (H)

Ocotea bullata,
Family: *Lauraceae*

Other names: Cape olive, laurel.
Distribution: South Africa.
General description: The heartwood ranges in colour from light grey to black, from straw to brown mottled with yellow. The grain also varies from straight to spiral and many logs are crooked. The texture is moderately fine and surfaces nicely figured. The weight varies with colour, the lighter the colour the lighter the weight. It is malodourous before seasoning. Weight about 800 kg/m³ (50 lb/ft³); specific gravity .80.
Mechanical properties: This heavy density wood has medium bending and crushing strength and medium stiffness. It is hard and strong.
Seasoning: The timber is difficult to season with a tendency to honeycomb and uneven shrinkage in thick sizes. Light material has little degrade but darker coloured material shrinks twice as much and collapses badly. Best results are obtained by partial air drying before kilning. There is large movement in service.
Working properties: The ease of working varies with density but generally it is easily worked. Nailing and screwing may require pre-boring; glues well and can be stained and polished to a good finish.
Durability: Non-durable. Susceptible to attack by termites and teredo. Heartwood resistant to preservation treatment but sapwood permeable. The resistance varies with density. Large logs often have rotten hearts.
Uses: High-class cabinet work and furniture making, light structural work, light flooring, vehicle bodies, handles, ladders, sporting goods, wheelwrighting, agricultural implements, joinery, battery separators, toys, novelties, turnery. Selected logs sliced for decorative veneers.

SUCUPIRA (H)

Bowdichia nitida, Benth.
Family: *Leguminosae*

Other names: black sucupira (UK); sapupira (Brazil)* see footnote.

Distribution: South America, chiefly Brazil.

General description: The heartwood is a dull reddish-brown to dark chocolate-brown with light yellow paremchyma markings which are noticeable on quartered surfaces as a striped figure. The grain is interlocked, sometimes wavy or irregular and the texture is moderately coarse. The average weight is about 1,000 kg/m³ (62 lb/ft³); specific gravity 1.00. A hard, heavy, tough timber.

Mechanical properties: Sucupira has high strength in every category almost approaching the strength of greenheart. It is not a steam bending wood.

Seasoning: It is difficult to dry and is liable to check and cup in kilning unless great care and a slow drying schedule is adopted. There is medium movement in service.

Working properties: The timber is hard to work, with high resistance in cutting and blunting of cutting edges. Difficulties with irregular or interlocked grain will require a reduced cutting angle and considerable sanding. It turns well, has good nailing and screw holding power, and glues well. When filled, takes a good wax or polished finish.

Durability: Very durable; not subject to insect attack or decay.

Uses: Ideal for structural purposes and excellent for domestic flooring. Also used for furniture, turnery and boat building. It is too heavy for plywood manufacture but selected logs are sliced for strikingly attractive, decorative veneers, used for inlay in furniture, doors, and panelling.

*Note: The name sapupira is also applied in Brazil to *Diplotropis racemosa*, (Hoehna) Amsh., *Diplotropis purpurea*, (Rich) Amsh., and *Ferreirea spectabilis*, Fr., which is called **yellow sucupira**. *D. purpurea* also grows in Guyana and Surinam and is known as **tatabu**, where it is used for similar purposes.

SUGI (S)

Cryptomeria japonica, (L.f) D.Don.
Family: *Taxodiaceae*

Other name: Japanese cedar (UK).
Distribution: Japan and Taiwan.
General description: The colour is warm brown, with both yellow and dark brown streaks forming a wavy pattern. Another feature is the resin which occurs mainly in vertical parenchyma cells, black in colour and imparting a lustre to the wood. It is straight to wavy grained, with a coarse texture and distinct growth rings and fine rays. Weighs about 400 kg/m^3 (25 lb/ft^3); specific gravity .40.
Mechanical properties: This is a soft, light and weak timber with low strength properties in all categories. Poor steam bending classification.
Seasoning: The material requires care in drying, especially in thicker sizes, and there is a pronounced tendency for the wood to split and check; after partial air drying it may be kilned without degrade. There is medium movement in service.
Working properties: It can be worked with hand or machine tools with only a moderate blunting effect on cutting edges, due to the resin content. Knots can be troublesome in planing or moulding. Pre-boring is necessary for nailing, but it holds screws well; glues, stains and polishes satisfactorily.
Durability: Durable and resistant to preservative treatment.
Uses: Clear, selected timber is suitable for house framing, gate-ways, joinery and furniture framing. Selected logs are sliced for decorative veneers for furniture and panelling.

SYCAMORE (H)

Acer pseudoplatanus, L.
Family: *Aceraceae*

Other names: sycamore plane, great maple (UK); plane (Scotland). (In the USA the name sycamore refers to *Platanus occidentalis*, L., **American plane** or **buttonwood**; (see **Plane**).

Distribution: Central Europe and the UK. Also Western Asia.

General description: White to creamy-white in colour with a natural lustre. Straight grained, but often curly or wavy producing the attractive fiddleback figure on quartered surfaces. The texture is fine and even, and sometimes quartered stock has a beautiful lacey figure due to conspicuous rays. Average weight about 610 kg/m^3 (38 lb/ft^3); specific gravity .61.

Mechanical properties: This excellent wood of medium density has medium bending and crushing strengths, low resistance to shock loads and very low stiffness, and a very good steam bending classification.

Seasoning: It air dries well but is inclined to stain. Very rapid surface drying prevents this, and end-stacking of boards is the usual practice to allow this. For kiln drying a low temperature is the best treatment. Rapid drying preserves the white colour but slow drying causes the colour to mature into pink-brown "weathered" sycamore. There is medium movement in service.

Working properties: Works easily with hand or machine tools, and provides a fine, smooth finish. There is a moderate blunting effect on tools. Nails, glues, stains and polishes excellently.

Durability: Perishable. Sapwood is liable to insect attack but it is permeable to preservative treatment.

Uses: Turnery, bobbins, textile rollers, brush handles, furniture, flooring for domestic use, domestic and dairy utensils, laundry and butcher appliances, food containers, musical instruments, cooperage. Selected logs are sliced for highly decorative veneers for panelling, cabinets and marquetry. Fiddle-back is supplied for the backs of violins. When chemically treated into shades of silver grey it is sold commercially as **harewood**, and it is often steamed or treated to change colour into a pink or mid-brown and sold as **weathered sycamore**. It is also the best veneer for processing into dyed veneers in a range of colours including dyed black.

'TASMANIAN MYRTLE' (H)   *Nothofagus cunninghamii*, (Hook) Oerst.
                                            Family: *Fagaceae*

Other names: myrtle beech, myrtle, 'Tasmanian beech'.

Distribution: Tasmania and Victoria, Australia.

General description: Pink to reddish-brown coloured heartwood, paler sapwood separated from the heartwood by a zone of intermediate colour. The grain is straight to slightly interlocked, sometimes wavy. The texture is very fine and uniform. The weight averages at 720 kg/m^3 (45 lb/ft^3); specific gravity .72.

Mechanical properties: This heavy density timber has medium bending strength and stiffness, high crushing strength and low resistance to shock loads. It has a good steam bending classification.

Seasoning: The material is very variable in its drying characteristics. The outer zone, lighter timber, dries readily and gives little degrade. The darker red, true heartwood, requires very careful drying to avoid internal honeycombing and surface checking and collapse. It is recommended to air dry the timber to fibre saturation point (about 30% moisture content) prior to kilning at low temperatures. Small movement in service.

Working properties: The wood works readily with hand and machine tools with only a moderate blunting effect on cutting edges. It has a tendency to burn in cross cutting and boring. It holds nails and screws well, glues satisfactorily and can be stained and polished to a good finish.

Durability: Non-durable. The sapwood is liable to attack by powder post beetle.

Uses: The timber is used for similar purposes to European beech: for furniture, cabinetmaking, joinery, flooring, parquetry, shoe heels, brush backs, bobbins, tool handles, interior trim, panelling, bridge and wharf decking, food containers, and motor body work. Also for bent work of all kinds and plywood manufacture. Selected logs are sliced for decorative veneers for panelling and cabinets.

Note: Not a true myrtle.

'TASMANIAN OAK' (H)

(1) *Eucalyptus delegatensis*, R.T. Bak
(E. gigantea, Hook.f.*)*
(2) *E. obliqua*, L'Hérit (3) *E. regnans*, F. Muell
Family: *Myrtaceae*

Commercial names: (1) alpine ash (2) messmate stringybark (3) mountain ash, Victorian ash (1–3) Australian oak (Australia). **Other names:** (1) white-top or gum-top stringybark, woollybutt (2) brown-top stringybark (3) stringy gum, swamp gum.
Distribution: Australia and Tasmania.
General description: All similar in appearance being pale to light brown in colour with a pinkish tinge. Straight grained and open texture, with interlocked or wavy grain in (3) and fiddleback figure on quartered surfaces. Gum veins are also present. Weight averages (1) 640 kg/m³ (40 lb/ft³) (2) 780 kg/m³ (49 lb/ft³) and (3) 620 kg/m³ (39 lb/ft³); s.g. .64, .78 and .62.
Mechanical properties: All have medium bending strength and stiffness properties and high crushing strength. Steam bending classifications are (1) poor, (2) moderate, (3) poor. Some buckling and fracture of the fibres likely to occur.
Seasoning: Dries readily and fairly quickly, with tendency for surface checks and distortion and internal checking and collapse. Air drying followed by high temperature kilning in final stages is recommended to remove collapse and recondition. Medium movement in service.
Working properties: There is moderate blunting of cutting edges and tools must be kept sharp, but all machining operations are satisfactory. Pre-bore for nailing; screwing, gluing and finishing processes are good.
Durability: Sapwood is liable to attack by powder post beetle. The heartwood is moderately durable and resistant to preservative treatment but the sapwood is permeable.
Uses: Furniture, joinery, panelling, weatherboards, agricultural implements, handles, structural use, domestic flooring, cladding, boxes and crates, cooperage. Used in Australia for plywood manufacture. Usually exported in the form of highly decorative veneers for panelling etc.
Note 1: Not a true oak (*Quercus* spp.) or ash (*Fraxinus* spp.). **Note 2:** *E. fraxinoides*, Dean & Maiden, produces **white Australian ash** and is similar to 'Tasmanian oak'.

TATAJUBA (H)

Bagassa guianensis, Aubl.,
B. tiliaefolia, (Desv.) R. Ben.
Family: *Moraceae*

Other names: bagasse (Guyana); gele bagasse (Surinam).

Distribution: Guyana, French Guiana and the Amazon region of Brazil.

General description: The heartwood colour is a lustrous golden brown to russet when mature, often streaked. Straight, interlocked or irregular grain; the texture is medium to coarse, with distinct rays. This hard, heavy timber weighs 800 kg/m^3 (50 lb/ft^3); specific gravity .80.

Mechanical properties: It has medium strengths in bending and crushing and has a good steam bending classification.

Seasoning: It dries slowly but with little degrade. It is very stable in service.

Working properties: The wood is easy to work with both hand or machine tools with very slight blunting effect on tools; finishes cleanly, takes nails with difficulty unless pre-bored, as it splits easily, but screw holding properties are good. Glues, stains and polishes to a high lustrous finish.

Durability: Not subject to fungal or insect attack and is durable.

Uses: Heavy construction for civil and marine purposes, furniture manufacture, cabinetmaking and joinery, decking and framing in boat building. Sliced for decorative veneering.

TAUN (H)

Pometia pinnata, Forst
Family: *Sapindaceae*

Other names: kasai, awa, ako (Solomons); tava (Western Samoa); ahabu (Papua New Guinea); malagai (Philippines).

Distribution: Widely distributed throughout the South Pacific.

General description: The heartwood colour matures from pink-brown to a dull reddish-brown with age. The grain is usually straight but sometimes interlocked or with a regular wave. The timber from Papua New Guinea has a moderately coarse texture; it is non-siliceous and fissile. From the Philippines it is rather finer and smoother. The weight averages 680–750 kg/m³ (42–46 lb/ft³); specific gravity .70 average.

Mechanical properties: High bending and crushing strengths, medium stiffness and resistance to shock loads. It has a good steam bending classification.

Seasoning: Dries fairly well but needs care to avoid warping and splitting. Preliminary air drying under cover, adequately weighted, is advised. A small proportion of boards is subject to extreme collapse, but can be reconditioned satisfactorily. There is medium movement in service.

Working properties: Works well with hand and machine tools with only a moderate blunting effect on cutting edges. It nails and holds screws well, glues satisfactorily and can be stained, painted or polished to a very smooth, high finish.

Durability: Moderately durable. The timber is subject to attack by *Lyctus* wood borers, pinhole borers and marine borers. It is also liable to blue stain. The heartwood is extremely resistant to preservative treatment and the sapwood moderately resistant.

Uses: Locally for structural work for beams, joists, rafters, ceilings, flooring, joinery, furniture, cabinets, pianos and interior trim; boat planking and framing, wharf decking, levers, capstan bars, masts and spars; turnery, bobbins, mouldings and panelling. Taun peels excellently for plywood and slices into decorative veneers for panelling, cabinets, etc.

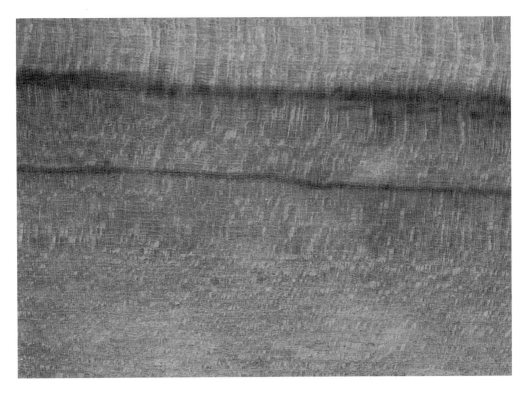

TAWA (H)

Beilschmiedia tawa, Benth. & Hook.f.
Family: *Lauraceae*

Other names: 'New Zealand chestnut', 'New Zealand oak'.* (See Note 2)

Distribution: New Zealand.

General description: A white to yellow coloured heartwood with a straight grain and fine texture, similar in appearance to sycamore. The logs sometimes contain portions of black heartwood and "black heart" is usually marketed separately. The rays produce a fine fleck figure on quartered surfaces. Weight 730 kg/m³ (45 lb/ft³); specific gravity .73.

Mechanical properties: Medium bending strength and stiffness, high crushing strength, with low resistance to shock loads. It has a poor steam bending classification.

Seasoning: Kiln dries readily with a little tendency to check; there is small movement in service.

Working properties: There is a medium resistance to tools and a moderate blunting effect on cutting edges. Tends to split in nailing. It glues, stains and finishes well.

Durability: The "black heart" wood is moderately durable, but normal heartwood is non-durable. Sapwood is liable to attack by powder post beetle and common furniture beetle. The heartwood is moderately resistant to preservative treatment but the sapwood is permeable.

Uses: Better grades for high-quality furniture, interior joinery and flooring. Also for turnery and dowelling. Lower grades are suitable for framing, dunnage and hardwood pulp. Used in New Zealand for plywood manufacture. Selected logs sliced for decorative veneers, suitable for panelling and cabinets.

Note 1: Related spp. include: *B. bancroftii*, (F.M. Bail) C.T. White, **yellow walnut, yellow nut** or **canary ash**. *B. obtusifolia*, (F. Muell.ex Meissn) F. Muell, **blush walnut, hard bollygum** or **tormenta**. *B. elliptica*, C.T. White and W.D. Frnacis, **grey walnut**.

Note 2: Not a true chestnut or oak.

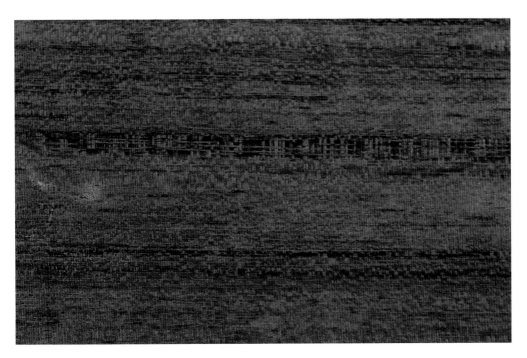

TCHITOLA (H)

Oxystigma oxyphyllum, (Harms) Léon,
syn. *Pterygopodium oxyphyllum*, Harms.
Family: *Leguminosae*

Other names: lolagbola (Nigeria); kitola (Zaire and Congo); m'babou (Gabon); tola mafuta, tola manfutu, tola chimfuta or tola (Angola and Portuguese territories).

Distribution: Tropical West Africa.

General description: Heartwood colour matures from pinkish-brown to reddish-brown, with a straight to shallowly interlocked grain with a medium to coarse, compact texture. The wood has three zones: the sap is very gummy and exudes a copal-like cedar scented gum and is pale yellow; the middle of the log is also gummy but a pale reddish colour and the richer coloured heart which is less gummy. Dark gum rings give a walnut-like appearance with striking black and yellowish variegated stripes. Weight about 610 kg/m^3 (38 lb/ft^3); specific gravity .61.

Mechanical properties: Tchitola has high crushing strength, medium bending strength, low stiffness and very low resistance to shock loads. It is resistant to splitting. Very poor steam bending classification due to gum exudation.

Seasoning: The timber air dries with little distortion or splitting, but great care must be taken as the high resin content causes surface spotting if it is seasoned too rapidly. Medium movement in service.

Working properties: The presence of gum is a problem with machining operations, accumulating in the teeth of saws, cutters, benches etc. It nails well and is satisfactory in gluing; it stains and polishes to a good finish.

Durability: The wood is non-durable. The heartwood is moderately resistant to termites in West Africa and is permeable for preservative treatment.

Uses: Furniture and cabinetmaking, shipbuilding, interior joinery and domestic flooring. Peels and slices very well for veneers and is used in Africa for plywood manufacture. The ornamental veneers are used for panelling, radio and television cabinets and marquetry, etc.

Note: This species should not be confused with **agba**, *Gossweilerodendron balsamiferum*, which is known as tola, tola branca, and white tola.

TEAK (H)

Tectona grandis, Linn.f.
Family: *Verbenaceae*

Other names: mai sak, pahi (Burma); sagwan, tekku, kyun, sagon, tegina, tadi (India); jati sak (Thailand); djati, gia thi (Indonesia).

Distribution: Indigenous to Burma and India, and S.E. Asia, and introduced into East and West Africa and the Carribean.

General description: The true teak of Burma is a uniform golden-brown colour without markings, but most other teak is rich brown with darker chocolate-brown markings. Indian teak is wavy grained and mottled, but generally straight to wavy grained, coarse textured, uneven, oily to the touch, and sometimes with a white glistening deposit. Weight varies from 610–690 kg/m^3 (38–43 lb/ft^3), average 650 kg/m^3 (40 lb/ft^3); specific gravity .65.

Mechanrcal properties: This hard, medium density wood has medium bending strength, high crushing strength combined with low stiffness and resistance to shock loads. It is fissile and brittle with great dimensional stability; it is fire and acid resistant. Teak can be steam bent to a moderate radius of curvature.

Seasoning: Dries well but rather slowly. Variations in drying rates can occur in individual pieces. Standing trees are girdled and left to dry out for three years before felling. There is small movement in service.

Working properties: Teak offers medium resistance to tools but a severe blunting effect on cutters. Tungsten carbide tipped saws are suitable. Pre-boring is necessary for nailing. Gluing is good on freshly planed or sanded surfaces. Fine machine dust is a skin irritant. Stains well and takes a satisfactory finish, especially an oil finish.

Durability: Very durable; liable to insect attack. It is extremely resistant to preservation treatment.

Uses: Extensively used for ship and boat building for decking, rails, hatches, etc. Furniture and cabinetmaking, interior and exterior joinery, flooring, exterior structural work and garden furniture. Also for acid resistant purposes such as chemical vats, fume ducts and laboratory benches. All grades of plywood, and sliced for decorative and face veneers.

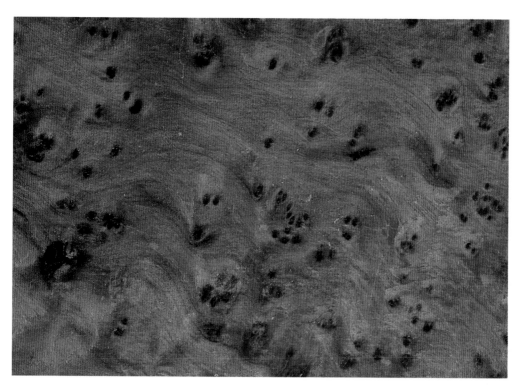

THUYA BURR (S)

Tetraclinis articulata, (Vahl) Mast.
syn. *Callitris quadrivalvis*.
Family: *Cupressaceae*

Other names: thyine wood, citron burl (USA).

Distribution: North Africa, principally Morocco and Algeria, and introduced into Malta, Cyprus and East Africa.

General description: This coniferous tree is highly contorted and valuable only as a veneer. The burr grows underground as a root burr, formed by stooling and the repeated destruction of coppice growth which causes increased growth below ground. It is dug out rather than felled. The colour is a rich golden-brown to orange-red; the grain interlocked, contorted, hard and full of knots, resulting in a beautiful mottled or bird's eye figure, producing very striking and highly-prized burr veneers. It is fine textured, resinous and aromatic. Requires slow kilning and care in drying. Weighs 650–700 kg/m³ (40–43 lb/ft³).

Working properties: Needs suitable preparation and flatting as it is inclined to be brittle. Glues easily and polishes extremely well.

Uses: Decorative veneering for caskets, fine cabinetmaking, small boxes, etc., panelling and marquetry.

TULIPWOOD, BRAZILIAN (H)

Dalbergia frutescens, Britton
var. *D. tomentosa*, Standl.
D. variabilis, S.
Family: *Leguminosae*

Commercial names: pinkwood (USA); bois de rose (France).
Other names: pau rosa, pau de fuso, jacaranda rosa (Brazil).
Distribution: Tropical South America, particularly Brazil.
General description: The heartwood is a beautiful pink-yellow with a pronounced striped figure in varying shades of salmon pink, and rose red to violet. It has a fragrant scent. The grain is straight but more often irregular; the texture is moderately fine. Weight about 960 kg/m³ (60 lb/ft³); specific gravity .96. A hard, heavy, compact hardwood, fissile and splintery.
Mechanical properties: For the purposes this wood is used its strength properties are of secondary importance. The timber is usually sold in small logs or billets. It is a decorative timber and fairly wasteful in conversion.
Seasoning: The timber dries easily, although there is a little risk of checking or twisting. It tends to split after being sawn. There is small movement in service.
Working properties: Tulipwood is extremely hard to work, with severe blunting of cutting edges. A reduction in the cutting angle to 20° when planing the irregular grain on quartered material is essential. The timber is capable of a very high natural finish and can be planed and sanded smoothly. Pre-boring for nailing is necessary; it glues well, and takes an excellent polish.
Durability: The timber is non-durable, but resists insect and fungal attacks. Highly resistant to preservative treatment.
Uses: Turnery, brush backs, fancy woodware, cabinets, caskets, jewellery boxes, marquetry and inlay work, inlaid bandings, marimba keys, and small decorative items. Selected billets are sliced for decorative veneers for inlay work and marquetry, or sawcut for antique repairs.
Note: Not to be confused with tuliptree (*Liriodendron tulipifera*, L.)

UTILE (H)
Entandrophragma utile, (Dawe & Sprague) Sprague
Family: *Meliaceae*

Commercial names: assié (Cameroon); sipo (Ivory Coast).
Other names: Tshimaje rosso (Zaire); mebrou zuiri (Ivory Coast); kosi-kosi (Gabon); afau-konkonti (Ghana).
Distribution: West and East Africa.
General description: The heartwood matures from a pink-brown when fresh cut to deep red-brown. The grain is interlocked to rather irregular, producing a wide irregular striped figure on quartered surfaces. Weight varies from 550–750 kg/m³ (34–47 lb/ft³), but averages 660 kg/m³ (41 lb/ft³); specific gravity .66. Texture, uniformly moderate.
Mechanical properties: This heavy density wood has only medium bending strength, and a high crushing strength with low stiffness and resistance to shock loads. It has a very poor steam bending classification as it buckles severely.
Seasoning: The wood dries fairly rapidly with a tendency for twisting to occur. If allowed to dry moderately slowly the degrade is not severe. Original shakes tend to extend. There is medium movement in service.
Working properties: Utile works well with hand or machine tools with only a moderate blunting effect on cutting edges; a reduced cutting angle will prevent tearing the interlocked grain on quartered material. Nailing is satisfactory, it glues and stains well, and when filled can be brought to a good finish.
Durability: The wood is durable; the sapwood liable to attack by powder post beetle, and the heartwood is moderately resistant to termites in West Africa. It is extremely resistant to preservative treatment and resistant to decay.
Uses: Furniture and cabinetmaking, counter tops, high-class exterior and interior joinery, flooring, boat building and planking, musical instruments, sports goods, and general construction work. Selected material used for plywood manufacture and sliced for decorative veneers.

VINHATICO (H)

Plathymenia reticulata, Benth.
(principally)
Family: *Leguminosae*

Other names: vinhatico castanho, vinhatico algodas, vinhatico amarello, vinhatico espinho, angiko (Brazil); tatare, jaruma (Argentina); Brazilian mahogany, yellow mahogany, gold wood, yellow wood (USA).

Distribution: Principally Brazil, also Argentina and Columbia.

General description: The heartwood is a lustrous, yellow-orange brown with variegated streaks or stripes of lighter or darker shades. The grain is straight to roey, with a medium to slightly coarse texture. Weight 600 kg/m^3 (37 lb/ft^3); specific gravity .60.

Mechanical properties: This is a tough and strong wood in relation to its weight, with medium bending strength, low stiffness and resistance to shock loads, and high crushing strength. It has a moderate steam bending classification.

Seasoning: Dries readily and well with no tendency to twist or check. It is a stable wood with small movement in service.

Working properties: Vinhatico works well with hand or machine tools and produces a clean finish. Holds nailed or screwed joints well; glues, stains and polishes, when filled, to a high finish.

Durability: The timber is moderately durable and fairly resistant to insect and fungal decay. Moderately resistant to preservative treatment, but the sapwood is permeable.

Uses: It is in great demand for furniture and cabinetmaking, superior joinery and turnery; also used for shoe heels, domestic flooring, shopfitting, shipbuilding, and the denser specimens for vehicle bodywork. The timber peels and slices easily and is used for plywood and decorative veneers for cabinets, panelling and marquetry.

Note: The name Vinhatico is applied to several genera which have similar coloured wood in weight range 560–640 kg/m^3 (35–40 lb/ft^3).

'VIRGINIAN PENCIL CEDAR' (S)

Juniperus virginiana, L.
J. silicicola, (Small) Bailey
Family: *Cupressaceae*

Other names: eastern red cedar (USA); pencil cedar (UK).
Distribution: USA and Canada.
General description: The heartwood is a uniform reddish-brown colour with an aromatic 'cedar' scent. A thin dark line of latewood marks the boundary of each growth ring. The wood is soft, straight grained, with a fine, even texture and grain. Weight is 530 kg/m^3 (33 lb/ft^3); specific gravity .53.
Mechanical properties: Medium bending and crushing strength, with very low stiffness and resistance to shock loads. Poor steam bending classification.
Seasoning: The wood should be allowed to dry slowly to avoid fine surface checking and end splitting. There is small movement in service.
Working properties: It works readily with hand and machine tools and has little blunting effect on cutting edges. Selected straight grained material works very easily, but the more decorative stock of knotty cedar has disturbed grain around the knots which tends to tear in planing or moulding. Cutters must be kept very sharp to obtain a good finish. It is liable to split when nailed, but glues, stains and produces a fine finish with the usual treatments.
Durability: The wood is durable and resists insect attack.
Uses: The standard material for making lead pencils, and whittles excellently, (the chips and shavings are recovered and distilled for essential oils). The fragrant, aromatic wood is used for cigar boxes, linen and blanket chests, ship building, coffins, and interior trim. Selected logs are sliced for highly decorative panelling and furniture veneers.
Note: Not a true cedar.

VIROLA, LIGHT (H)

Virola spp., including:
V. koschnyi, Warb., *V. sebifera*, Aubl.,
V. surinamensis, Warb., *V. melinonii*, (R. Ben) A.C. Smith
Family: *Myristicaceae*

Other names: banak, baboen (UK); palo de sangre (Belize); sangre (Guatemala); fruita colorado (Costa Rica); bogabani (Panama); tapsava (USA); St Jean rouge, muscadier a grive (French Guiana); moonba, hoogland baboen (Surinam); baboen ordalli, dalli (Guyana); ucuuba (Brazil).

Distribution: Central and tropical South America.

General description: The heartwood colour varies from pinkish, golden brown on exposure to deep reddish-brown on maturity. The grain is straight, medium to coarse texture and low lustre. Weight range 430–580 kg/m^3 (26–36 lb/ft^3), average 530 kg/m^3 (33 lb/ft^3); s.g. .53.

Mechanical properties: The wood is of medium density, low bending strength, medium crushing strength, low stiffness and very low resistance to shock loads. Steam bending classification is poor.

Seasoning: Virola requires care in drying. Material over 50 mm thick tends to retain moisture despite rapid surface drying, and due to a high shrinkage ratio causes excessive distortion, deep checking and splitting. Thinner sizes dry more successfully. Medium movement in service.

Working properties: The timber works easily and well with only slight blunting effect on tools. Nails and screws well; glues, stains and finishes satisfactorily.

Durability: Perishable and liable to fungal attack requiring anti-stain treatment. Logs subject to pinhole borer attack and rapid conversion is required to prevent serious degrade. Sapwood liable to attack by powder post and common furniture beetle, and susceptible to termites. Heartwood is permeable to preservative treatment.

Uses: General utility and interior work, light-weight joinery, mouldings, boxmaking, cigar boxes, coffins, matches and matchboxes. When treated, used below water level for foundation boarding, concrete shuttering, slack cooperage. Plywood manufacture and corestock, and sliced into veneers for decorative work.

Note: Related spp. includes *V. bicuhyba*, Warb., **heavy virola**, weight 670 kg/m^3 (41 lb/ft^3).

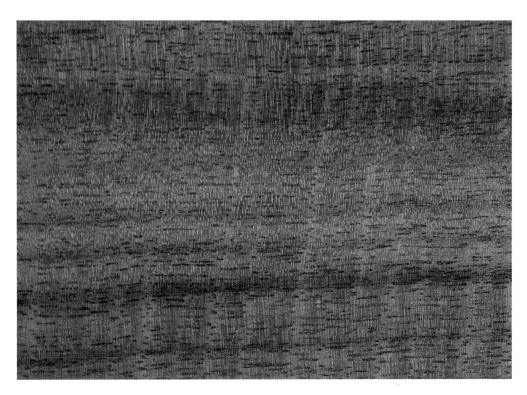

WALNUT, AMERICAN (H)

Juglans nigra, Linn.
Family: *Juglandaceae*

Commercial names: black American walnut, Virginia walnut (UK); walnut (USA); black walnut (UK and USA).

Other names: canaletto, black hickory nut, Canadian walnut, walnut tree.

Distribution: Eastern USA and Ontario, Canada.

General description: The heartwood is a rich dark brown to purplish-black, mostly straight grained, but with wavy or curly grain occasionally present. The texture is rather coarse. Weight averages 640 kg/m^3 (40 lb/ft^3); specific gravity .64.

Mechanical properties: This is a tough, hard timber of medium density, with moderate bending and crushing strengths, and low stiffness. It has a good steam bending classification.

Seasoning: Dries rather slowly with a tendency to honeycomb and requires care to avoid checking and degradation. There is small movement in service.

Working properties: Works with hand or machine tools without difficulty with moderate blunting effect on cutting edges. Holds nails or screws well, glues satisfactorily, and polishes to a high finish.

Durability: Very durable. Sapwood liable to attack by powder post beetle. The heartwood is resistant to preservative treatment and biodegradation.

Uses: In the USA it is the standard timber for rifle butts and gunstocks. It is extensively used for high-quality furniture, cabinetmaking and interior joinery, boatbuilding, musical instruments, clockcases, turnery and carving. A major timber in plywood manufacture and sliced for panelling, cabinet veneers and decorative veneers for all kinds in the form of stumpwood, crotches, burrs, burls, etc.

WALNUT, EUROPEAN (H)

Juglans regia, L.
Family, *Juglandaceae*

Commercial names: Named after the country of origin, e.g. English, French, Italian, Circassian, Persian walnut etc.

Distribution: Europe, including the UK, Asia Minor and South West Asia.

General description: The colour of the heartwood varies according to origin. Usually grey-brown with infiltrations of darker colouring irregularly distributed as streaks of smokey-brown. The grain is straight to wavy, with a rather coarse texture. The figured wood sometimes forms a well defined central core. Weight averages 640 kg/m^3 (40 lb/ft^3); specific gravity .64.

Mechanical properties: Walnut has medium bending strength and resistance to shock loads, high crushing strength and low stiffness, and a very good steam bending classification.

Seasoning: The material seasons well but slowly and drying should not be forced as there is a tendency for honeycomb checks to develop in thicker material. Medium movement in service.

Working properties: This timber works easily and well with both hand and machine tools and finishes cleanly, with only a moderate blunting effect on cutting edges. Nailing and screwing is good; gluing is satisfactory and the material polishes to a high finish.

Durability: Moderately durable. The sapwood is liable to attack by powder post and common furniture beetle, and the logs are susceptible to longhorn and Buprestid beetle attack. The heartwood is resistant to preservative treatment, but the sapwood is permeable.

Uses: This excellent timber is used in the solid and veneer form for high-class furniture, cabinetmaking, bank and office fitting, rifle butts and gunstocks, turnery and carving, doors, sports goods, and fascias and cappings in cars. It is cut into veneer in several forms to provide flat cut and striped veneers for plywood faces, and stumpwood, crotches and burr veneers are used according to type for panelling, cabinets or marquetry.

Note 1: Related spp. includes *J. sieboldiana*, Maxim, **Japanese** or **Japanese claro walnut**.

Note 2: The best Italian walnut was considered to be Ancona walnut and this name was given to any highly figured, variegated, darkish walnut.

WALNUT, SOUTH AMERICAN (H)

Juglans neotropica, Diels.
also *J. columbiensis*, Dode,
J. autralis, Gris.
Family: *Juglandaceae*

Commercial names: Peruvian walnut (UK & USA).

Distribution: Peru, Columbia, Ecuador, Venezuela, Argentina and Mexico.

General description: The quartered wood displays a beautiful dark brown colour with a blackish striped figure. The grain is straight to wavy, and the texture is rather coarse. Weighs 650 kg/m³ (40 lb/ft³); specific gravity .65.

Mechanical properties: The bending strength and resistance to shock loads is medium, with high crushing strength and low stiffness. The steam bending classification is very good. It is compact, elastic wood with excellent strength properties.

Seasoning: The timber dries well, but care should be taken to see that it dries out slowly to avoid twisting. There is medium movement in service.

Working properties: This wood works easily with both hand and machine tools and joints hold perfectly. Nails and screws take easily and although there is a moderate blunting effect on cutting edges the wood finishes cleanly, and planed and sanded surfaces have a silken lustre. Can polished to a very good finish.

Durability: Moderately durable. The sapwood is liable to attack by powder post beetle and the common furniture beetle. The material is resistant to preservative treatment and biodegradation. The sapwood is permeable.

Uses: High-class furniture and cabinetmaking, musical instruments, rifle butts and gunstocks, shop, office and bank fittings, turnery and carving, sports goods. It is sliced for plywood faces and quartered for beautiful, figure-striped veneers for panelling, cabinets and marquetry.

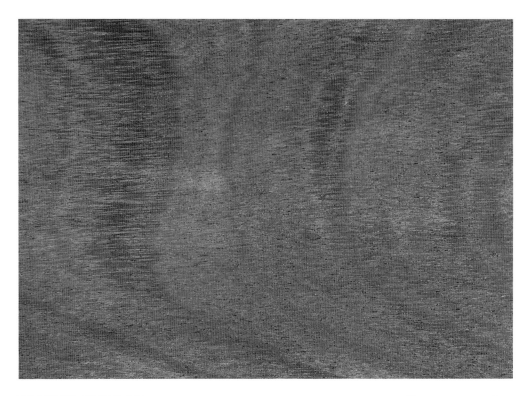

WATER GUM (H)

Eugenia spp., also
Syzygium buettnerianium,
Family: *Myrtaceae*

Numerous species are grouped and collectively sold as PNG Water Gum, principally: *E. cerina*, *E. flosculifera*, *E. glauca*, *E. Griffithii*, *E. longiflora*.

Other names: kelat (Malaysia, Papua New Guinea); satinash (Australia).

Distribution: Malaysia, Papua New Guinea, the Solomon and Santa Cruz Islands.

General description: The heartwood colour varies from grey-brown to reddish-brown to chocolate-brown with a purple cast. The grain varies from straight, interlocked, wavy or irregular. The texture is medium to fine. It has no lustre. The weight of the contributing species also varies between 640 and 960 kg/m^3 (40–60 lb/ft^3), averaging 770 kg/m^3 (48 lb/ft^3); s.g. .77.

Mechanical properties: The wood has medium bending and crushing strengths with low stiffness and resistance to shock loads, and a moderate steam bending classification.

Seasoning: Requires care in drying and may be prone to end splitting and face checking when kiln dried from green. Partial air drying will improve the results and the weighting down of stacks will virtually eliminate cupping and twisting. There is medium movement in service.

Working properties: The wood works fairly easily with hand or machine tools with a moderate blunting effect on cutting edges. Interlocked and irregular grain tends to pick up. Pre-bore for nailing; takes glue, stain and polish, and may be brought to a high finish.

Durability: Moderately durable. The heartwood is extremely resistant to preservative treatment, but the sapwood is permeable.

Uses: Furniture and cabinet work, ship and boat building, general construction and joinery, light flooring, tool handles, turnery, sporting goods, hardboard and blockboard manufacture. Treated wood used for piles, railway sleepers, etc. Selected logs for decorative veneers.

Note: Closely related spp. include *Tristania laurina*, also producing water gum, but also known as **kanuka**, "**hickory**", **river box** and **tea tree**.

WENGE (H)

Millettia laurentii, De Wild.
Family: *Leguminosae*

Other names: dikela, mibotu, bokonge, tshikalakala (Zaire); awong (Cameroon); nson-so (Gabon); palissandre du congo (Congo).

Distribution: Mainly Zaire, also Cameroon Republic and Gabon.

General description: The clearly defined heartwood is dark brown, with very close, fine, almost black veins. The closely spaced whitish bands of parenchyma give the wood a most attractive appearance. It is fairly straight grained with a coarse texture. Weight 880 kg/m^3 (55 lb/ft^3); specific gravity .88.

Mechanical properties: This heavy density wood has a high bending strength and high resistance to shock loads, with medium crushing strength and low stiffness. It has a low steam bending classification.

Seasoning: The timber seasons slowly and requires care to minimise surface checking tendencies. There is small movement in service.

Working properties: The material works fairly well with machine tools and with a moderate blunting effect on cutting edges. The presence of resin cells in the wood sometimes interferes with gluing and polishing. Nailing is difficult and requires pre-boring. When filled, it can be brought to a satisfactory finish.

Durability: Durable and resistant to termites. It is extremely resistant to preservative treatment.

Uses: The high natural resistance to abrasion makes this timber very suitable for flooring strips or blocks. Also used for interior and exterior joinery and general construction work. It is an excellent turnery wood. Wenge is unsuitable for plywood manufacture because of its weight but it is sliced for panelling and decorative veneers for cabinets, marquetry, etc.

Note: Related spp. include *M. stuhlmannii*, Taub., **panga panga**.

WHITEWOOD (FIR/SPRUCE) (S)

Abies alba, Mill, **silver fir** (UK)
Picea abies (L) Karst, **Norway spruce** (UK)
(Whitewood comprises the above two
spp. when imported)
Family: *Pinaceae*

Other names: European silver pine (UK); white deal and 'white' (UK); Baltic, Finnish, etc. whitewood (according to port of shipment) see also related spp. for fir and spruce names.

Distribution: Widely distribu ed throughout Europe, with the exception of Denmark and the Netherlands, but including the UK and western Russia.

General description: The timber varies from almost white to pale yellowish-brown with a natural lustre. The growth rings viewed on the plain sawn surfaces are less prominent than those of Scots pine. Resinous but not obtrusive. Straight grained and with a fine texture. Weight 470 kg/m³ (29 lb/ft³); specific gravity .47.

Mechanical properties: Spruce has low stiffness and resistance to shock loads, medium bending and crushing strengths. It has a very poor steam bending classification.

Seasoning: Dries rapidly and well with little tendency for splitting or checking, although knots may split and loosen. There is some risk of distortion in young growth timber with pronounced spiral grain. Medium movement in service.

Working properties: With sharp cutters, spruce works easily with hand or machine tools with little dulling effect on the cutters, and gives a good clean finish. It takes nails satisfactorily, glues well, takes stain, paint and varnish for a smooth finish.

Durability: Damage by longhorn and pinhole borer beetles, and by wood-wasps. Sapwood susceptible to attack by the common furniture beetle. The wood is non-durable and resistant to preservative treatment.

Uses: Larger timber is used for interior construction, interior joinery and carpentry, boxes and crates. Smaller trees used in the round for scaffold or flag poles, masts, pitprops, etc. Spruce from the UK is seldom used for high-class joinery, and suitable only for building work, carcassing, carpentry and domestic flooring. Spruce from central and eastern Europe produces musical "tone" woods for soundboards of pianos and bellies of violins and guitars and for the soundboards of key instruments, due to its unsurpassed resonance qualities. Rotary cut for plywood manufacture (in conjunction with *Pinus sylvestris*) and sliced for face veneers. Thinnings sold as Christmas trees.

Note 1: Related fir spp. *A. alba*, Mill, **silver fir** (UK); *A. amabilis* (Dougl) Forbes, **amabilis fir** (Canada/USA), and **white fir** and **Pacific silver fir** (USA); *A. balsamea*, (L) Mill, **Balsam fir** (USA/Canada); *A. grandis* (Dougl) Lindt., **grand fir**, **lowland fir** and **Western balsam fir** (USA/Canada); *A. lasiocarpa*, (Hook) Nutt., **alpine fir** (USA/Canada); *A. procera*, Rehder, **Noble fir** (UK/USA).

Related spruce spp. *P. engelmannii*, Engelm., **Engelmann spruce** (Canada/USA), and **mountain spruce** or **rocky mountain spruce**; *P. glauca*, (Moench) Voss, **Western white spruce** and **Eastern Canadian spruce**, also known as **white spruce** (Canada/USA) and **Quebec spruce** (UK) and as distinguished by port of shipment. See also **sitka spruce**.

Note 2: Shipments of spruce lumber often include **balsam fir** and **amabilis fir** (*abies spp.*), they are also mixed with **Western hemlock** (*tsuga spp.*).

'WESTERN RED CEDAR' (S)

Thuja plicata, D. Don
Family: *Cupressaceae*

Other names: British Columbia red cedar (UK); giant arborvitae (USA); red cedar (Canada).

Distribution: Canada, USA and introduced into the UK and New Zealand.

General description: Straight grained, rather coarse textured, with a prominent growth ring figure and non-resinous. The heartwood shows considerable colour variation when fresh, from a dark chocolate-brown to a salmon pink colour, perhaps variegated, maturing down to a reddish-brown and, in time, to silver-grey – this weathered appearance sometimes sought-after by architects. Weighs 370 kg/m^3 (23 lb/ft^3); specific gravity .37.

Mechanical properties: The material has low bending and crushing strength, with very low stiffness and resistance to shock loads. Steam bending classification is very poor.

Seasoning: Thin stock dries readily with little degrade, but thicker sizes tend to hold moisture at the centre and care is needed to avoid internal honeycombing and collapse. This is especially true of UK timber. There is small movement in service.

Working properties: The wood works easily with hand and machine tools, with little blunting effect on cutters. Nailing properties are good (hot-dipped galvanised or copper nails should be used). It screws well and takes stain and polish satisfactorily. Its acidic properties cause corrosion of metals and black stain in the timber.

Durability: The material is durable. Standing trees liable to attack by the Western Cedar borer and seasoned timber liable to attack by common furniture beetle. Resistant to preservative treatment.

Uses: Glass house and shed construction, shingles, interior finishing, exterior boarding and cladding, beehive construction, poles, posts and fences.

Note 1: Other spp. include *T. occidentalis*, L., **white cedar** (USA).

Note 2: Not a true cedar.

WHITEWOOD, AMERICAN (H)

Liriodendron tulipifera, L.
Family: *Magnoliaceae*

Commercial names: poplar, canary wood, canary whitewood, yellow poplar, hickory poplar, tulip poplar, saddletree, popple, tulipwood (USA); tulip tree (USA, Canada and UK); canary whitewood (UK).

Distribution: Eastern USA and Canada and introduced into Europe.

General description: In second growth trees the sapwood is very wide, whitish in colour and streaked. It is sharply defined from the heartwood which varies from pale yellowish-brown to pale olive-brown streaked with olive green, dark grey or pinkish-brown, and when mineral stained, streaks of steel blue. Weight 510 kg/m³ (31 lb/ft³); specific gravity .51. Uniform, straight grain; regular, fine texture.

Mechanical properties: This medium density wood has low bending and resistance to shock loads, low stiffness and medium crushing strength. It also has a medium steam bending classification.

Seasoning: The material kiln dries easily and well with no risk of checking or warping, and air dries with little degrade. There is small movement in service.

Working properties: It is easy to work with both hand and machine tools and can be planed to a very smooth finish. Nailed, screwed and glued joints hold perfectly, and it can be stained, polished or painted and holds hard enamels.

Durability: Non-durable, the sapwood is prone to attacks by the common furniture beetle. It is moderately resistant to preservation treatment and the sapwood is permeable.

Uses: Pattern making, carving, cabinetmaking, interior fittings, interior joinery, light construction work, interior trim for boats, toys, doors. It is also used for plywood and corestock. When treated with preservatives it is used for external joinery and work not in contact with the ground. Selected logs are sliced for very decorative veneers suitable for panelling, cabinets and marquetry.

Note: Not to be confused with the softwood known as **whitewood**, *Picea abies* and *Abies alba*.

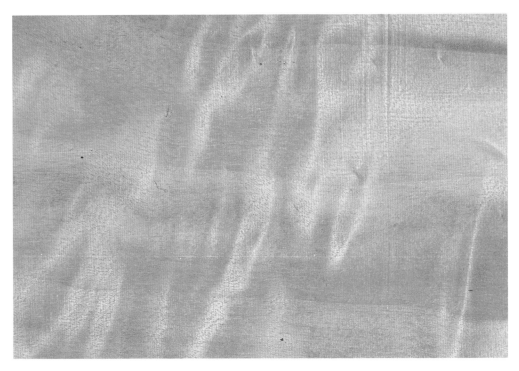

WILLOW (H)
(1) *Salix alba*, L. (2) *S. fragilis*, L. (3) *S. alba* var. *coerlea (cultivar calva*, G. Mayer) (4) *S. nigra*, Marsh

Family: *Salicaceae*

Commercial names: (1–2) white willow or common willow (2) crack willow (3) cricket bat willow or close-bark willow (4) black willow.

Other names: saule (France); wilg (Netherlands); weide (Germany).

Distribution: (1–2) UK, Europe, W. Asia and North Africa. (3) UK, Europe and N. Asia. (4) USA and Canada.

General description: Willow is light, resilient, flexible and difficult to fracture. The heartwood is a white-pinkish colour. The white sapwood varies in width according to growth conditions. Growth rings appear on longitudinal surfaces as faint zones. It is typically straight grained, and with a fine, even texture. Weight: 340–450 kg/m^3 (21–28 lb/ft^3); average s.g. .34 to .45

Mechanical properties: Low strengths in bending, crushing and in resistance to shock loads. It also has very low stiffness. The steam bending classification is poor.

Seasoning: Dries fairly rapidly but often retains pockets of moisture. The moisture content should be checked for uniformity. Degrade is minimal, and there is small movement in service.

Working properties: Willow works easily with both hand and machine tools but very sharp cutting edges should be maintained to avoid woolliness. Crack willow tends to split badly during conversion. The wood nails and screws well, glues excellently and can be brought to a high finish.

Durability: Perishable and liable to insect attack. The heartwood is resistant to preservative treatment and the sapwood is permeable.

Uses: The best butts of (3) are cleft for cricket bat blades. All other wood is used for artificial limbs, toys, sieves, trugs, wickerwork, baskets, punnets, bottoms for carts and barrows, boxes and crates, and slack cooperage. It is also employed as plywood corestock, and sliced for decorative veneers for panelling, interiors and marquetry, etc., producing the extremely attractive moiré figure.

'YELLOW CEDAR' (S)

Chamaecyparis nootkatensis, (D.Don) Spach.,
syn. *Cupressus nootkatensis*, D.Don.
Family: *Cupressaceae*

Other names: Alaska yellow-cedar, nootka false cypress (USA), yellow cypress, Pacific coast yellow cedar (Canada).

Distribution: The Pacific coast of Canada and from Alaska to Oregon in the USA.

General description: The heartwood is a pale yellow colour, and has a fine, even texture, and is straight grained. It has no appreciable odour when dry. Weight about 500 kg/m³ (31 lb/ft³). Specific gravity .50.

Mechanical properties: The wood has medium bending and crushing strengths, with low stiffness and resistance to shock loads. It has a very poor steam bending classification, with severe rupturing and buckling likely to occur.

Seasoning: Should be allowed to dry slowly to avoid end splitting. It will dry without much degrade except for a tendency for thick stock to show surface checking. There is small movement in service.

Working properties: The wood works well with hand or machine tools with only a very slight dulling effect on cutting edges. If wavy grain is present there is a tendency to pick up in planing when a reduced cutting angle is recommended. It glues, nails, screws, stains and takes paint and varnish very well, and can be brought to an excellent finish.

Durability: The timber is durable, and resistant to preservative treatment.

Uses: High-class joinery, boat building, drawing boards, cabinet work, external joinery, shingles, posts, poles and marine piling. It is resistant to acids, and ideal for battery separators. Selected logs are sliced for decorative veneers suitable for architectural panelling.

Note: Not a true cedar.

YEW (S)

Taxus baccata, L.
Family: *Taxaceae*

Commercial names: common yew, European yew, yewtree.

Distribution: Scandinavia, Europe, UK, W. Russia, Asia Minor, N. Africa, Burma and the Himalayas.

General description: The heartwood colour is golden orange-brown streaked with dark purple, mauve and brown in patches with veins, tiny knots and clusters of in-growing bark. The grain is straight, but sometimes curly and irregular. The texture is medium. Weight is about 670 kg/m³ (42 lb/ft³); specific gravity .67.

Mechanical properties: The bending and crushing strengths are medium, with low stiffness and resistance to shock loads. Yew has a good steam bending classification, with straight grained air dried material for preference.

Seasoning: Yew dries rapidly and well with little degrade, although care is necessary to avoid shakes developing and existing shakes extending. Distortion is negligible. There is small movement in service.

Working properties: Moderately difficult to work, but straight grained material works readily and can be planed to a good smooth finish; irregular, curly or cross grained material tends to tear out. Nailing may need pre-boring, and the oily nature of the wood demands some care in gluing. It can be polished to a beautiful finish.

Durability: The wood is durable, but not immune from common furniture beetle attack. It is resistant to preservative treatment and biodegradation.

Uses: For centuries this was the wood used for bowstaves by the bowmen of England. It is excellent for turnery, some carving, furniture making, interior and exterior joinery, fences, gate posts, chairs, doors, tables, and rustic furniture. In veneer form it requires careful preparation, patching, flattening and handling, due to its buckled, fragile nature. It is an exceptionally decorative veneer used for every kind of application, including panelling, cabinetwork and marquetry.

ZEBRANO (H)

Microberlinia brazzavillensis, A. Chév
M. bisulcata A. Chév
syn. *Brachystegia fleuryana*, A. Chév.
Family: *Leguminosae*

Commercial names: zingana (France, Gabon); zebrawood (UK, USA); allene, ele, amouk (Cameroon).

Distribution: West Africa, chiefly Gabon and Cameroon Republic.

General description: The heartwood is a light golden-yellow with narrow veining or streaks of dark brown to almost black, giving the quartered surfaces a zebra-stripe appearance. The grain is interlocked or wavy and produces alternating hard and soft grained material which makes the timber difficult to work. Zebrano has a coarse texture and a lustrous surface. Weight 740 kg/m³ (46 lb/ft³); specific gravity .74.

Mechanical properties: This hard, heavy, stable timber is mainly used for decorative purposes due to its nature, where strength and mechanical properties are unimportant.

Seasoning: The material is difficult to dry and requires care in order to avoid surface checking, splitting and distortion. There is small movement in service.

Working properties: Although the wood works fairly readily with hand or machine tools, it is very difficult to get a good finish from machines due to the alternative nature of the grain. A belt sander will provide a smooth finish. Gluing is satisfactory with care, and it finishes well once filled.

Durability: Non-durable. Liable to attack by insects, and resistant to preservative treatment.

Uses: The main use for zebrano is as sliced decorative veneers for small cabinetwork, flush doors, cross bandings or inlay bandings, fancy goods, marquetry and panelling. Bundles of this veneer tend to buckle unless kept under weights. Also used by turners and carvers for decorative work.

Selected Wood Grains

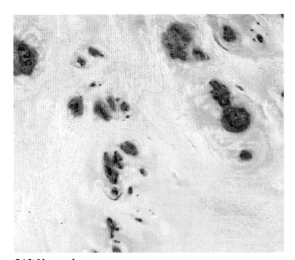

Willow butt

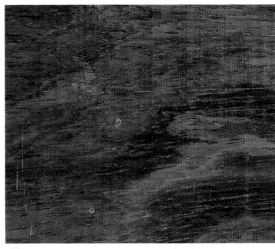

Kevasingo

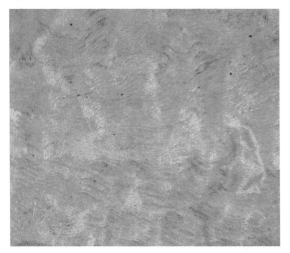

Satinwood

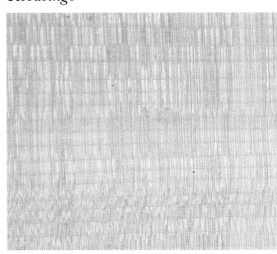

Sycamore, lace figure

Pommelle

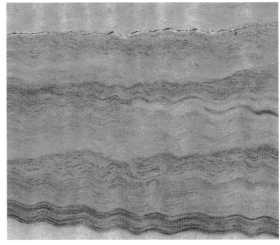

Olive ash

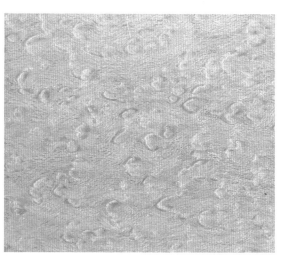

Bird's eye maple

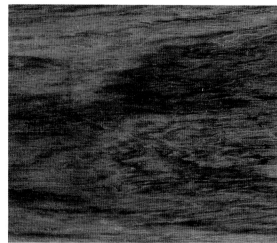

Andean rosewood

Wormy sugar maple

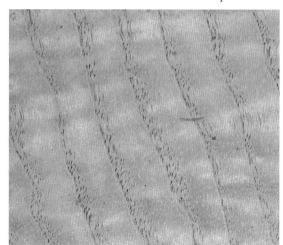

Mottled European ash

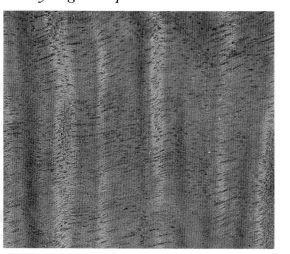

Quilted maple

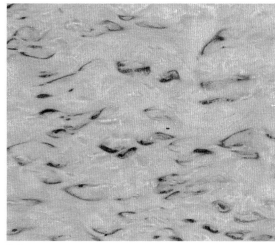

Masur birch

Burrs/Burls

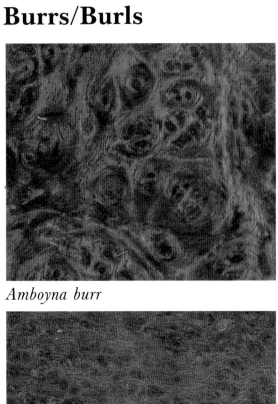

Amboyna burr

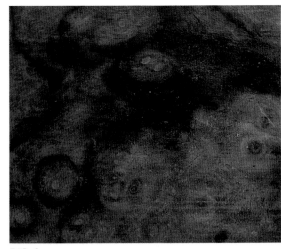

Walnut

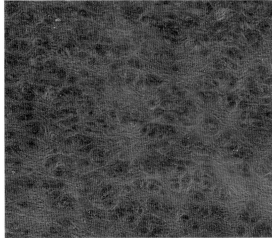

Plane, European

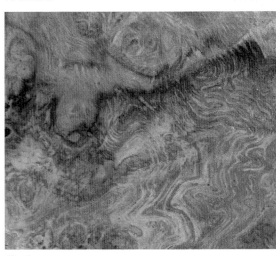

Oak

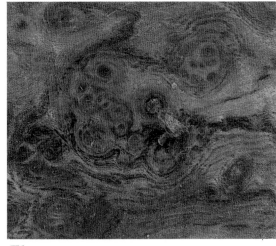

Elm

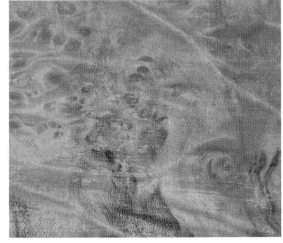

Maple

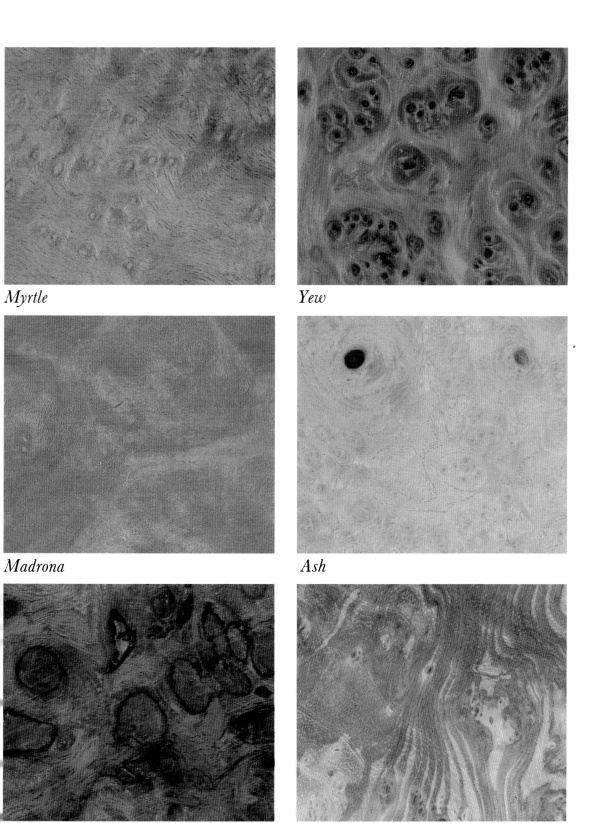

Myrtle

Yew

Madrona

Ash

Maidu

Olive ash (stumpwood)

Table of Uses

Right-side note: Also for Heat, sound and vibration insulation; bouyancy; protective packaging; modelmaking

Use	Abura	Afara	"African walnut"	Afrormosia	Afzelia	Agba	Akossika	Albizia	Alder, Common	Alder, Red	Alone	Amboyna	Andiroba	Aningeria	Antiaris	Apple	Arariba	Ash, American	Ash, European	Ash, Japanese	Aspen, Canadian	Aus. Ash, white	Aus. Birch, white	Australian cedar	Australian silky oak	Avodiré	Ayan	Balau	*Balsa
Wharves, decking, sleepers pitprops, above water jetties etc.					*	*			*	*	*			*															V
Vehicle and coach building, bodywork etc.	*		*		*		*					*							*	*	*	*	*			*			*
Turnery woods	*	*				*	*		*	*		*	*					*	*	*	*	*			*				
Tool handles and implements					*	*												*		*	*	*							
Structural timbers		L		L	*	L	L	*					L		L			L	L	L		L	L			*			*
Sports equipment, gunstocks etc.			G				*					*							*	*	*								
Solid doors	*	*		*	*	*						*	*					*							*				
Shop, bank and office fittings	*	*	*	*	*	*							*						*	*	*						*	*	
Ship and boat building, superstructures etc.				*	*	*						*	*					*	*	*	*				*				*
Marine timbers (Non-Teredo waters)				*	*	*			*																				
Marine timbers (Teredo infested waters)				*	*				*																				
Musical instruments.													*													*			
Laminated articles chip baskets, punnets etc.										*	*			*					*	*	*	*							
Joinery – exterior			*	*	*	*			*				*					*							*				
Joinery – interior	*	*	*	*	*	*	*	*				*	*	*	*	*		*	*	*	*	*	*	*	*	*	*	*	*
Food and laundry containers																						*							
Flooring timbers	*		*	*	*	*	*	*				*	*					*					*			*		*	*
Fancy woods for inlays brushbacks, trinkets etc.										*	*		*			*	*									*	*	*	
Coffins and caskets (cases, crates, boxes etc.)	*	*		*								*	*									*		*	*				
Cooperage and vat making	V			V														*				*							
Carving and sculpture	P					*			*	*		*				*													
Cabinets and furniture (fitments, framing etc.)	*	*	*	*	*	*						*	*	*	*	*		*	*	*		*	*	*		*	*	*	*

Basswood	★	★	★	★			★	★		★	★								★	★		
Beech, American	★		★			★	★	★		★	★	T		★			★	L	★	★	★	★
Beech, European	★		★			★	★	★		★	★	T		★			★	L	★	★	★	★
Beech, Japanese	★		★			★	★	★		★	★	T		★			★	L	★	★	★	★
Beli						★		★						★					★			
Berlinia	★							★									★	★			★	
Birch, European	★				★	★		★		★								L		★		
Birch, Japanese	★				★	★		★		★							★	L		★		
Birch, paper				★						★									★	★		
Birch, yellow	★		★			★		★		★	★					★				★		
Blackbean	★	★			★			★							★		★	★	★	★		
Blackbutt						★			★					★				★	★		★	★
*Blackwood, African	★	★			★						★						★		★	★		
Blackwood, Austr.	★		★		★			★	★					★	★		G		★	★	★	
Bombanga	★							★														
Box, white topped						★			★									★	★	★		★
Boxwood, European	★	★			★						★						★		★	★		
Brazilwood	★				★	★		★	★		★						G	★		★		★
Bubinga	★				★			★	★										★	★		
Butternut	★	★		★	★			★						★								
Calantas	★	★		★				★			★			★			★	L				
Cedar	★	P		★			★	★	★					★		★		L				★
Cedar of Lebanon	★							★	★							★						
Celery top pine	★							★						★					★		★	
Cerejeira						★		★	★					★							★	
Cherry, American	★	★			★			★		★	★			★						★		
Cherry, European	★	★			★			★		★	★			★						★		
Cherry, Japanese	★	★			★			★		★	★			★						★		
Chestnut, American	★			★				★	★						★							★
Chestnut, Horse	★	★		★			★	★									★			★		
Chestnut, Horse, Jap.	★	★		★			★	★							★		★			★		
Chestnut, Sweet	★		V	C				★	★									L		★		
Coachwood	★					★		★			★						G			★		
Cocobolo		★			★														★	★		
Copaiba	★					★		★	★					★								
Cordia, Light American	★					★		★	★					★	★	★		L			★	
Cordia, West African	★							★			★								L			
Courbaril	★					★		★	★				★	★			★	★	★	★		★
*Cypress	★		V	★		★		★	★					★		★		★	★		★	
*Dahoma						★		★	★				★					★			★	
Danta						★		★	★					★	★		★	L	★	★	★	★
*Degame	★	★						★									★		★	★		

Use \ Wood	Douglas Fir	E. African Camphorwood	Ebony, African	Ebony, Macassar	*Ekki	Elm, American white	Elm, English/Dutch	Elm, Japanese	Elm, Rock	Elm, Smooth leaved	Esia	Etimoe	Fir, Japanese	Freijo	Fustic	Gaboon	Gedu Nohor	Gonçalo Alves	*Greenheart	Guarea	Gum, American red	Gum, Red River	Guanacaste	Hackberry	Hemlock, Japanese	Hemlock, Western	Hickory	Holly	Hoop Pine
Wharves, decking, sleepers pitprops, above water jetties etc.	*					*	*	*	*	*	*							*	*						*	*			
Vehicle and coach building, bodywork etc.		*				*	*	*	*	*	*							*			*				*	*	*	*	
Turnery woods			*	*		*	*	*	*	*	*		*					*	*	*							*	*	*
Tool handles and implements			*	*		*	*	*	*	*	*	*															*		
Structural timbers	*			V		*	*	*	*	*	*	*	L		*		*		V	*		*		L	L	*			L
Sports equipment, gunstocks etc.			* G	*				*							*			*		*	*			*			*		
Solid doors	*		*														*			*					*	*			
Shop, bank and office fittings																	*			*									
Ship and boat building, superstructures etc.	*					*	*	*	*	*	*		*	*		*		*	*		*				*	*			
Marine timbers (Non-Teredo waters)	*					*			*				*						*	*	*								
Marine timbers (Teredo infested waters)	*					*			*		*								*		*								
Musical instruments.			*	*																				*	*				
Laminated articles chip baskets, punnets etc.	*																	*			*	*					*		
Joinery – exterior	*	*			*					*		*	*		*	*		*	*					T	T				
Joinery – interior	*	*			*	*	*	*	*	*	*	*	*		*			*	*	*		*	*	*			*		
Food and laundry containers				*															*										
Flooring timbers	*	*			*	*	*	*	*	*	*	*			*			*	*	*		*			*	*			
Fancy woods for inlays brushbacks, trinkets etc.			*	*														*							*				
Coffins and caskets (cases, crates, boxes etc.)	*			C	C	C	C	C			*			* C				*			*	*					*		
Cooperage and vat making	V			S	S	S	S	S					*						S										
Carving and sculpture		*			*	*	*												*						* P				
Cabinets and furniture (fitments, framing etc.)	*	*	*	*		*	*	*	*	*	*		*	*		*	*	*	*		*	*	*	*	*	*			

Hornbean, European					★	★					★						★		★	★	★	
Huon Pine	★							★	★					★				L				
Idigbo	★					★		★	★			★			★	★						
Imbuia	★					★		★	★								G					
Indian Almond	★							★							★							
Indian Laurel	★				★			★			★		★	★	★				★	★	★	★
Ipé	★					★		★	★					★				★	★	★	★	★
Iroko	★	★				★		★	★			★	★	★	★	★		★	★	★	★	★
Ivorywood, Red	★	★			★	★		★			★									★	★	★
Izombe	★	P		★		★		★	★							★		★		★		
Jacaranda Pardo	★	★			★	★		★	★		★							★	★	★		
Jarrah	★		V			★						★		★				★	★			★
Jelutong	★	P						★										L				
Jequitiba	★							★	★					★				★				
Kaataon, Bangkal	★	★		★														L		★		
Kahikatea	★			★		★		★		★				★				★		★		
Kaki	★				★	★		★									★			★		
Kapur	★					★			★				★					V			★	★
Karri	★					★				★			★	★		★		★	★		★	★
Katsura	★	★																				
Kauvula	★					★		★												★		
*Kempas																		V				★
*Keruing						★		★	★				★					★			★	★
Keyaki	★	★						★	★					★				L		★		
Kingwood	★				★															★		
Kiri	★				★					★	★						★					
Koa	★										★			★	★		G					
Kokko	★	★	★					★					★					L				
Kwila	★					★		★	★					★	★			★	★			★
Lampati	★			★				★														
Larch, European	★					★		★		★		★	★	★				L	★			★
Larch, Japanese	★					★		★		★		★	★	★				L	★			★
Lati						★		★										★				
Lauan, white	★					★		★	T	★				★	★		★	★			★	
*Lignum vitae			V										★	★			★		★			
Lime		★		★				★			★									★		
Louro Preto	★							★	★					★				★		★		
Macacauba	★					★		★			★			★				★				★
Madrona	★				★															★		
Magnolia	★			★	★	★		★												★	★	
Mahogany, African	★	P		★	★	★		★	★		★			★	★	★	G	L		★	★	
Mahogany, S. American	★	★		★	★	★		★	★	★	★			★	★	★	G	★		★	★	

Use	Makore	Mangeo	Mansonia	Maple, European	Maple, Japanese	Maple, Rock	Maple, Soft	'Maracaibo Boxwood'	Marblewood Andaman	Mengkulang	Meranti, Dark Red	Meranti, Light Red	Meranti, White	Meranti, Yellow	Merbau	Mersawa/Krabak	Mesquite	Moabi	Muhimbi	*Muhuhu	Muninga	Mutenye	Myrtle	Nargusta	'New Guinea Walnut'
Wharves, decking, sleepers pitprops, above water jetties etc.	*	*	*							*					*		*		*	*					
Vehicle and coach building, bodywork etc.	*	*	*								*	*	*	*	*	*	*		*						
Turnery woods	*	*	*	*	*	*	*	*		*							*		*	*	*	*	*		*
Tool handles and implements		*				*		*		*					*							*			
Structural timbers	*	*	*							L	L	L	*	L	L	*	*	*	*	*	*				L
Sports equipment, gunstocks etc.	G			*	*	*	*				*	*	*	*	*										
Solid doors	*					*					*	*		*	*										
Shop, bank and office fittings	*		*								*		*												*
Ship and boat building, superstructures etc.	*	*									*		*	*		*			*			*			
Marine timbers (Non-Teredo waters)																		*							
Marine timbers (Teredo infested waters)	*																		*	*					
Musical instruments.				*	*	*	*	*		*			*	*		*					*				
Laminated articles chip baskets, punnets etc.				*	*	*	*				*	*	*	*	*		*								
Joinery – exterior	*	*	*							T	T	T	T	*		*	*		*	*			*		*
Joinery – interior	*	*	*	*	*	*	*			*	*	*	*	*	*	*	*			*	*	*	*		*
Food and laundry containers						*	*																		
Flooring timbers	*	*		*	*	*				*	*	*	*	*	*	*	*	*	*	*	*	*			*
Fancy woods for inlays brushbacks, trinkets etc.				*	*	*	*	*		*												*			
Coffins and caskets (cases, crates, boxes etc.)											*		*												
Cooperage and vat making	*																								
Carving and sculpture								*	*		*				*			*							
Cabinets and furniture (fitments, framing etc.)	*	*	*	*	*	*	*			*	*	*	*	*	*		*	*		*	*	*	*		*

Wood	1	2	3	4	5	6	7	8	9	10	11	12	13	14	15	16	17	18	19	20	21	22	23	24	25	26	27	28	29	30	31	32	33	34	35	36	37	38
Niangon														G																						*		*
Niove			P	S	C	*	*					T																										
Nyatoh				*	C	*	*																															
Oak, American, Red	*	*	*	*	*	*	*	*	*	*	*																											*
Oak, American, White	*	*	*	*	*	*	L	G	*	*	*	*																										*
Oak, European	*	*	*	*	*	*	L		*	*	*																									*	*	*
Oak, Japanese	*	*	*				L	*	*																													
Obeche	*	*		*																																		
Ogea	*	*					*																															
Okwen	*		*			*		*																														
Olive, E. African	*	*	*	*																																		*
Omu	*		*					G							*																							
Opepe	*		*		V		*	*	*	*		*	*				*			*	*																	
Ovangkol	*							*																														
Padauk, African	*	*	*				*								*			*																				*
Padauk, Andaman	*		*			*	*																															
Padauk, Burma	*						*	*					*																									
Paldao	*	*													*																							
Panga Panga	*						*					*																										
Parana Pine	*		*			*	*	*										*			*		*															
Pau marfim	*						L		*	*																												
Pear	*						*	*																														
Pecan	*						*	*																														
Peroba, rosa							*																															
Peroba, white	*		*				*	*																														
Persimmon	*	*		*			*																															
*Pitch pine, American			*			*	L	*	*	*	*	*	*				*			*	*																	
Pine, Japanese Red	*		*			*	*	*			*	*					*			*																		
Pine, Ponderosa	*		*				*																															
Pine, Radiata	*	P				*	L				*																											
Pine, Siberian yellow	*	*	*			*	L																															
Pine, Western White	*	*				*	L				*																											
Pine, Yellow	*						L																															
Planetree	*								*																										*			
Podo	*																																		*			
Poplar	*						L	*	*				*	*				*	*																			
Port Orford Cedar	*				V		L																												*			
Prima Vera	*		*	V	V			*																														
Pterygota	*			*		*																																
Purpleheart	*						*	G				*																							*		*	
Quandong, White	*								*																										*			*
"Queensland Maple"	*							G	*	*	*																								*		*	*

Use	"Queensland Walnut"	Ramin	Rata	Red Beech, N.Z.	Red Tulip Oak	Rengas	Rewarewa	Rimu	Robinia	Rosewood, Brazilian	Rosewood, Honduras	Rosewood, Indian	Sapele	Sassafras	Satiné	Satinwood, Ceylon	Sen	Sepetir	Sequoia	Scots pine (Redwood)	Silver, ash	Silver beech	Siris, yellow	Snakewood	Sophora	S. American cedar	*"Southern White Cedar"	Spruce, Japanese	Spruce, Sitka	Sterculia brown	Stinkwood	Sucupira	Sugi
Wharves, decking, sleepers pitprops, above water jetties etc.		*	*	*		*	*														*	*						*				*	
Vehicle and coach building, bodywork etc.		*		*			*										*				*	*	*					*				*	
Turnery woods	*		*		*					*	*	*			*	*	*				*	*	*								*	*	
Tool handles and implements	*									*							*				*	*									*	*	
Structural timbers	L	*		L	L			L							*	L	*	L	*	L	L	L			L	L	L	L	*	L	*		L
Sports equipment, gunstocks etc.			*		*	G	G						*		*	*	*		*				*					*		*			
Solid doors							*				*								*			*	*										
Shop, bank and office fittings	*	*			*					*	*	*	*			*																	
Ship and boat building, superstructures etc.		*	*	*		*						*				*	*		*	*	*	*	*			*		*	*	*		*	
Marine timbers (Non-Teredo waters)															*				*														
Marine timbers (Teredo infested waters)																			*														
Musical instruments.										*	*	*	*		*	*	*	*	*			*			*			*	*				
Laminated articles chip baskets, punnets etc.	*																*												*	*			
Joinery – exterior		*				*	*			*	*		*			*	*T				*	*	*								*	*	*
Joinery – interior	*	*	*	*	*	*	*	*	*				*	*		*	*	*	*	*	*	*	*			*	*	*	*	*			*
Food and laundry containers																	*	*															
Flooring timbers	*		*	*	*	*		*	*							*	*	*	*		*		*								*	*	*
Fancy woods for inlays brushbacks, trinkets etc.				*	*					*	*	*	*		*	*			*				*									*	
Coffins and caskets (cases, crates, boxes etc.)		*											*				*	*	*							*		*	*	*			
Cooperage and vat making									S						V											*							
Carving and sculpture		*								*					*		*																
Cabinets and furniture (fitments, framing etc.)	*	*	*	*	*	*				*	*	*	*		*	*	*		*	*	*	*				*	*			*	*	*	

Niangon	*					*		*	*					*	*							
Niove						*		*	*					*			G	*				
Nyatoh	*	P						*	T	*						*		L				
Oak, American, Red	*		S			*		*		*				*				L		*	*	
Oak, American, White	*	*	*	C		*		*	*					*	*	*			*	*	*	*
Oak, European	*	*	*	C		*		*	*			*		*	*	*		L	*	*	*	*
Oak, Japanese	*	*	*	C		*		*						*	*	*		*	*	*	*	*
Obeche	*							*			*						*					
Ogea	*			*				*														
Okwen						*		*		*									*			*
Olive, E. African	*				*	*		*							*				*	*	*	
Omu	*					*		*						*	*							
Opepe	*					*		*	*			*		*	*			*		*	*	*
Ovangkol	*				*	*		*							*					*		
Padauk, African	*	*			*	*		*						*	*		*	*	*	*		
Padauk, Andaman	*				*	*		*	*		*	*		*	*		G	*	*	*	*	
Padauk, Burma					*	*		*						*	*		*	*			*	
Paldao	*					*		*			*				*					*		
Panga Panga						*		*	*									*				
Parana Pine	*							*		*								L		*	*	*
Pau marfim	*					*		*						*						*		
Pear	*	*			*						*									*		
Pecan	*																*		*	*	*	
Peroba, rosa	*				*	*		*	*									*		*		
Peroba, white			V		*	*		*	*					*				*			*	*
Persimmon		*		*										*			*	*		*		
*Pitch pine, American				*		*		*						*		*			*		*	
Pine, Japanese Red								*						*		*		L				*
Pine, Ponderosa	*	*		*		*		*								*		L		*		*
Pine, Radiata				*				*										L				
Pine, Siberian yellow		P						*								*		L				*
Pine, Western White	*	*				*		*		*				*		*		L				
Pine, Yellow	*	*				*		*			*			*		*		L				
Planetree	*				*			*						*		*		L		*	*	
Podo	*							*		*							*					
Poplar				*		*		*		*								L			*	
Port Orford Cedar	*								*		*	*	*	*				L				
Prima Vera	*							*												*		
Pterygota	*			*				*		*												
Purpleheart	*		V		*	*		*	*				*	*	*		*	*	*	*		*
Quandong, White	*		*					*												*		
"Queensland Maple"	*	*						*						*	*	*	G			*	*	*

	"Queensland Walnut"	Ramin	Rata	Red Beech, N.Z.	Red Tulip Oak	Rengas	Rewarewa	Rimu	Robinia	Rosewood, Brazilian	Rosewood, Honduras	Rosewood, Indian	Sapele	Sassafras	Satiné	Satinwood, Ceylon	Sen	Sepetir	Sequoia	Scots pine (Redwood)	Silver, ash	Silver beech	Siris, yellow	Snakewood	Sophora	S. American cedar	*"Southern White Cedar"	Spruce, Japanese	Spruce, Sitka	Sterculia brown	Stinkwood	Sucupira	Sugi
Wharves, decking, sleepers pitprops, above water jetties etc.			*	*	*		*	*												*		*					*					*	
Vehicle and coach building, bodywork etc.			*		*				*								*			*	*	*					*				*		
Turnery woods		*		*			*			*	*	*			*	*	*				*	*		*							*	*	
Tool handles and implements		*								*										*		*		*	*					*	*		
Structural timbers	L		*				L	L					L			*	L	*	L	*	*	L	L		L	L	L	L	*	L	L	*	L
Sports equipment, gunstocks etc.			*		*					G	G		*				*	*			*			*				*			*		
Solid doors										*			*							*						*	*						
Shop, bank and office fittings	*	*				*				*	*	*	*			*																	
Ship and boat building, superstructures etc.			*	*	*		*		*			*	*	*			*		*	*	*	*	*			*	*	*	*			*	
Marine timbers (Non-Teredo waters)																*				*													
Marine timbers (Teredo infested waters)																				*													
Musical instruments.										*	*	*	*				*	*	*	*	*			*		*		*	*				
Laminated articles chip baskets, punnets etc.		*																		*								*		*			
Joinery – exterior			*				*	*		*	*		*			*			*	T					*	*	*					*	*
Joinery – interior	*	*		*	*	*	*	*	*	*	*		*	*		*	*	*	*	*	*	*	*		*	*	*	*	*	*	*		*
Food and laundry containers																					*	*											
Flooring timbers	*			*	*		*	*		*		*								*	*	*	*			*	*			*	*	*	
Fancy woods for inlays brushbacks, trinkets etc.						*	*			*	*	*	*		*	*			*					*								*	
Coffins and caskets (cases, crates, boxes etc.)				*										*					*	*		*				*		*	*	*			
Cooperage and vat making														S					V										*				
Carving and sculpture		*								*							*				*												
Cabinets and furniture (fitments, framing etc.)	*	*		*	*	*	*	*		*	*	*	*	*	*	*	*	*		*	*	*			*	*	*				*	*	*

Sycamore
'Tasmanian myrtle'
'Tasmanian oak'
Tatajuba
Taun
Tawa
Tchitola
Teak
Thuya
Tulipwood
Utile
Vinhatico
Virginian
   pencil cedar
Virola light
Walnut, American
Walnut, European
Walnut S. American
Water gum
Wenge
Western red cedar
Whitewood (Spruce)
Whitewood, American
Willow
"Yellow cedar"
Yew
Zebrano

Codes used above:
P. Pattern making
V. Vat making
S. Slack cooperage
C. Coffins, caskets
T. Treated with
   preservatives
G. Gunstocks
L. Light construction
V. Very Heavy
   construction

* Indicates this species is not usually sliced for decorative veneering.

Sources of Further Information

British Research Establishment
(Department of the Environment),
Forest Products Research Laboratory,
Princes Risborough, Aylesbury, Bucks.

British Standards Institute,
2, Park Street, London W1A 2BS.

Timber Research and Development
Association,
Stocking Lane, Hughenden Valley,
High Wycombe, Bucks. HP14 4ND.

Fine Hardwoods/American Walnut
Association,
5603 West Raymond Street, Suite O,
Indianapolis, Indiana 46241, USA.

Food and Agriculture Organization of the
United Nations,
Via delle Terme di Caracalla 00100,
Rome, Italy. (Information Division: Photo
Library, etc)

University of Oxford, Department of
Foresty,
Forestry Library, Commonwealth Forestry
Institute,
South Parks Road, Oxford OX1 3RB

International Wood Collectors Society,
World of Wood Bulletin,
E.B. (Gene) Himelick, 601 Burkwood
Court E.,
Urbana, Illinois 61801, USA.

National Lumber Grades Authority,
1460–1055 West Hastings Street,
Vancouver, BC., Canada V6E 2G8.

UK Representative,
Council of Forest Industries of British
Columbia,
Tileman House, 131–133 Upper
Richmond Road,
Putney, London SW15 2TR.

Southern Forest Products Association,
PO Box 52468, New Orleans, Louisiana,
70152, USA.

Western Wood Products Association,
1500 Yeon Building, Portland, Oregon 97204,
USA.

UK Representative, SFPA–WWPA,
4th Floor, 69 Wigmore Street, London
W1H 9LG.

U.S. Department of Agriculture,
Washington DC, USA.

World Wood (International Forest Products
Magazine)
Suite 530, 2700 Cumberland Parkway N.W.,
Atlanta, Georgia 30339, USA.

Bibliography

GENERAL

BRITISH STANDARDS INSTITUTION
Nomenclature of Commercial Timbers, including sources of supply B.S. 881 & 589, London, 1974

BUILDING RESEARCH ESTABLISHMENT (Princes Risborough Laboratory)
Handbook of Hardwoods, 3rd Edition. H.M.S.O. 1981
Handbook of Softwoods, 3rd Edition. H.M.S.O. 1983

BROWN H.P., PANSHIN A.J., AND FORSAITH C.C.
Textbook of Wood Technology, McGraw Hill, New York, 1949

CONSTANTINE, Albert Jr.
Know Your Woods. Chas. Scribner's Sons Inc., New York 1959

CORKHILL, Thomas
A Glossary of Wood. Stobart & Son Ltd., London, 1979
(Published by Stein and Day, New York, 1982, as The Complete Dictionary of Wood)

DALLIMORE, W., and JACKSON, A.B.,
A Handbook of the Coniferae. Edward Arnold & Co., London 1948

EDLIN, Herbert L.
What Wood is That? A Manual of Wood identification with 40 actual wood samples. Stobart & Son Ltd., London, 1977

HOWARD, Alexander L.
Timbers of the World, their characteristics and uses.
Macmillan & Co Ltd., London, 1951

LINCOLN, W.A.
Complete Manual of Wood Veneering (includes a list of 250 veneering timbers). Stobart & Son Ltd., London, 1984 and Chas. Scribner's Sons Inc., New York, 1985

LITTLE, E.L.
Native and Naturalized trees of the United States.
Dept. of Agriculture Handbook No. 41. Washington, USA.

RENDLE, B.J.
World Timbers. Vol. 1. Europe and Africa
Vol. 2. North and South America, Central America and West Indies
Vol. 3. Asia, Australia and New Zealand. Ernest Benn Ltd., London, 1969–1970

TITMUSS, F.H.
Commercial Timbers of the World. 3rd Edition
The Technical Press, Oxford, 1965

UNITED STATES FOREST SERVICE
Wood Handbook. Forest Products Laboratory
US Dept Agriculture No. 72. Washington, 1955

YALE UNIVERSITY, SCHOOL OF FORESTRY
Tropical Woods. 16 vols. New Haven, Yale University, 1925–1959

AFRICAN TIMBERS

TIMBER RESEARCH & DEVELOPMENT ASSOCIATION
Timbers of Africa. Red Booklet No. 1. TRADA, 1978

BOLZA, Eleanor and KEATING, W.G.
African Timbers: properties, uses and characteristics of 700 species. Melbourne Division of Building Research, CSIRO, 1972

BRYCE, J.M.
The Commercial Timbers of Tanzania. Moshi, Forest Division 1967

GHANA TIMBER MARKETING BOARD. Takoradi.
Ghana Hardwoods, 1969

KRYN, Jeanette M., and FORBES, E.W.
Woods of Liberia. U.S. Forestry Laboratory 2159. Madison FPL, 1959

ORGANISATION FOR EUROPEAN ECONOMIC CO-OPERATION
African Tropical Timber: Nomenclature and description
OECD, Paris, 1951

OKIGBO, L.
Nigerian Woods. 2nd Edition. F.M.O.I., Lagos, 1964

STONE, Herbert and COX, H.A.
Timbers of Nigeria. Crown Agents for School of Forestry, Cambridge University, London 1922

WIMBUSH, S.H.
Catalogue of Kenya Timbers. Nairobi Govt. Printer, 1950

AUSTRALASIAN TIMBERS

TIMBER RESEARCH AND DEVELOPMENT ASSOCIATION
Timbers of Australasia, Red Booklet No. 8. TRADA, 1978

AUDAS, J.W.
Native Trees of Australia. Whitcombe & Tombs Pty., Melbourne, 1952

BLAKELY, W.F.
A key to the Eucalyptus. 3rd Edition. Canberra Forestry and Timber Bureau, 1965

BOAS, I.H.
Commercial Timbers of Australia. Government Printer, Melbourne, 1947

BOLZA, E.
Properties and uses of 175 timber species from Papua New Guinea and West Irian, Australia. CSIRO, Australia, 1975

BOLZA, E. and KLOOT, N.H.
Mechanical properties of 174 Australian Timbers. CSIRO, Australia, 1963

BOOTLE, K.R.
Wood in Australia: types, properties and uses.
McGraw Hill, Sydney, 1980

BRITISH SOLOMON ISLANDS PROTECTORATE. Forestry Dept. Solomon Islands Timbers. Honiara Forestry Dept., 1970

ENTRICAN, A.R. and others.
The Physical and Mechanical Properties of the Principal Indigenous Woods of New Zealand. New Zealand Forest Service, Wellington, N.Z., 1951

FIJI
Fiji Timbers and their Uses. Dept. of Forestry, Suva Dept. of Forestry, 1966

KEATING, W.G. and BOLZA, E.
Characteristics, Properties and Uses of Timbers, S.E. Asia, Northern Australia and the Pacific, Vol 1. 1982

PLEYDELL, G.J.
Timbers of the British Solomon Islands.
United Africa Co (Timber) Ltd., for Levers Pacific Timbers Ltd., London 1970

REID, J.S.
Building Timbers in New Zealand. N.Z. Forest Research Inst., Wellington, 1950

SWAIN, E.H.F.
The Timbers and Forest Products of Queensland.
Queensland Forest Service, Brisbane, 1928

CENTRAL AMERICA AND THE CARIBBEAN

TIMBER RESEARCH AND DEVELOPMENT ASSOCIATION
Timbers of Central America and the Caribbean. Red Booklet No. 9. TRADA, 1979

FRASER, H.
Principal Timber Trees of the Windward Islands.
Conservator of Forests, Kingston, Jamaica, 1957

LONGWOOD, F.R.
Puerto Rican Woods. Agriculture Handbook 205. US Dept. of Agriculture, 1961

LONGWOOD, F.R.
Present and Potential Commercial Timbers of the Caribbean, West Indies, the Guianas and British Honduras. US Dept. of Agriculture, Washington, USA, 1962 (1971)

RECORD, S.J. AND HESS, R.W.
Timbers of the New World. New Haven, Yale University Press, and London, Oxford University Press, 1943

U.S. DEPT OF AGRICULTURE, WASHINGTON D.C.
Present and Commerical Timbers of the Caribbean.
Agriculture Handbook No. 207, 1971

EUROPEAN TIMBERS

TIMBER RESEARCH AND DEVELOPMENT ASSOCIATION
Timbers of Europe. Red Booklet No. 6. TRADA, 1978

HOWARD, Alexander L.
Trees in Britain and their Timbers. Country Life Ltd.,
London 1947

HOWARD, Alexander L.
Timbers of the World. 3rd Edition. Macmillan & Co Ltd., London, 1948

RENDLE, B.J.
World Timbers Vol 1, Europe and Africa. Ernest Benn Ltd., London, 1969

NORTH AMERICAN TIMBERS

TIMBER RESEARCH AND DEVELOPMENT ASSOCIATION
Timbers of North America. Red Booklet No. 7 TRADA, 1978

BROWN, H.P. and PANSHIN, A.J.
Commercial Timbers of the United States. McGraw-Hill, New York and London, 1940

HARRAR, E.S.
Hough's Encyclopaedia of America Woods. 17 Vols. (text and plates) Robert Speller & Sons, New York (text not completed at time of going to press)

KRIBS, David A.
Commercial Foreign Woods on the American Market.
Dover Publications Inc., New York, 1968

LITTLE, E.L.
Native and Naturalized Trees of the United States.
Dept. of Agriculture Handbook No 41. Washington, USA

RECORD, Samuel J.
Identification of the Timbers of Temperate North America. John Wiley & Sons Inc., New York; Chapman & Hall Ltd., London, 1934

McELHANNEY and Associates
Canadian Woods: their properties and uses. Forest Products Laboratories of Ottawa, 1935

PHILIPPINES AND JAPANESE TIMBERS

TIMBER RESEARCH AND DEVELOPMENT ASSOCIATION
Timbers of the Philippines and Japan. Red Booklet No. 5. TRADA, 1978

HOWARD, Alexander L.
A Manual of Timbers of the World. 3rd Edition. Macmillan & Co Ltd., London 1948

JANE, F.W.
The Structure of Wood, revised by K. Wilson and D.J.B. White. Adam & Charles Black. 2nd Edition. London, 1970

MENIADO, José A. and others
Timbers of the Philippines Vol. 1. Govt. Printing Office for Forest Products, Research and Industries Development Commission. Manilla, 1974

PHILIPPINES FOREST PRODUCTS RESEARCH AND DEVELOPMENT INSTITUTE
Philippine Timber Series No. 1 to 14, Laguna, Philippines

REYES, Luiz J.
Philippine Woods. Bureau of Forestry Technical Bulletin No. 7, Manilla, 1938

SOUTH AMERICAN TIMBERS

TIMBER RESEARCH AND DEVELOPMENT ASSOCIATION
Timbers of South America. Red Booklet No. 2. TRADA, 1978

BRAZILIAN TRADE CENTRE
Brazilian Timber. Brazilian Trade Centre, London, 1971

RECORD S.J. and HESS R.W.
Timbers of the New World. Yale University Press USA.
Oxford University Press, London, 1943

WILLIAMS, Llewelyn
Woods of North Eastern Peru. Chicago Field Museum of Natural History (Botanical series, Vol. XV) 1936

UNIVERSIDADE DO SAO PAULO, INSTITUTO DE PESQUISAS TECHNOLOGICAS
Fichas de caracteristicas das madeiras Brasileiras.
Sao Paulo University (In Portuguese) 1971

SOUTH EAST ASIAN TIMBERS

TIMBER RESEARCH AND DEVELOPMENT ASSOCIATION
Timbers of South East Asia. Red Booklet No. 4. TRADA, 1978

BURGESS, P.F.
Timbers of Sabah. Sabah Forest Records 6. Sandakan Forest Dept., 1966

DESCH, H.E.
Manual of Malayan Timbers. Malayan Forest Records 15. Vol. 1. Kuala Lumpur. Federal Malay States Govt. 1941
Vol. 2. Singapore, Malaya Publ. House Ltd., 1954

DESCH, H.E.
Dipterocarp Timbers of the Malay Peninsula. Malayan Forest Records 14. Kuala Lumpur. Fed. Malay States Govt., 1941

JANSSONIUS, H.H.
Key to Javanese Woods. E.J. Brill, Leiden, 1952

KEITH, H.G.
The Timbers of North Borneo. North Borneo Forest Records 3. Sandakan Forest Dept., 1947

KLOOT, N.H. and BOLZA, E.
Properties of Timbers imported into Australia. Forest Products Technological Paper No. 12. CSIRO, Melbourne, 1961

LEE, Yew Hon and CHU, Yue Pen
Commercial Timbers of Peninsular Malaysia. Dept. of Forestry, Malaysian Timber Industry Board, Kuala Lumpur, 1975

MEMON, P.K.B.
Structure and Identification of Malayan Woods
Forest Research Institute, Record No. 25. Kuala Lumpur, 1967

SOUTHERN ASIAN TIMBERS

TIMBER RESEARCH AND DEVELOPMENT ASSOCIATION
Timbers of Southern Asia. Red Booklet No. 3. TRADA, 1978

GAMBLE, J.S.
Manual of Indian Timbers. Sampson, Low, Marston & Co., London, 1922

KLOOT, N.H. and BOLZA, E.
Properties of Timbers imported into Australia. Div. of Forest Products Technological Paper No. 12., CSIRO, Melbourne, 1961

LUSHINGTON, A.W.
Nature and Use of Madras Timbers. SPCK Press., Madras, 1919

PEARSON, R.S. AND BROWN, H.P.
Commercial Timbers of India. 2 Vols. Govt. of India Central Publications Branch, 1932

RAO, K. Ramesh and PURKAYASTHA, S.K.
Indian Woods: their identification, properties and uses. Vol. III. Leguminosae to Combretaceae. Forest Research Institute, Dehra Dun, 1972

RAO, K. Ramesh and JUNEJA, K.B.S.
A Handbook for Field Identification of fifty important timbers of India, Forest Research Institute, Delhi, 1971

TROTTER, H.
The Common Commercial Timbers of India and their Uses. (Rev. Edition) Govt. of India Press, Calcutta, 1941

Index of Standard Names

Index of Vernacular, Trade and Other Names

Index of Botanical Names

Index of Botanical Family Names